Matteo Giardiello

When (Left) Populism Makes it to Government

Matteo Giardiello

When (Left) Populism Makes it to Government

The Case of Podemos

DE GRUYTER

ISBN (Hardcover) 978-3-11-159151-3
ISBN (Paperback) 978-3-11-159159-9
e-ISBN (PDF) 978-3-11-159153-7
e-ISBN (EPUB) 978-3-11-159157-5

Library of Congress Control Number: 2025933995

Bibliografische Information der Deutschen Nationalbibliothek
Die Deutsche Nationalbibliothek verzeichnet diese Publikation in der Deutschen
Nationalbibliografie; detaillierte bibliografische Daten sind im Internet über
http://dnb.dnb.de abrufbar.

© 2026 Walter de Gruyter GmbH, Berlin/Boston, Genthiner Straße 13, 10785 Berlin
Cover image: "Evolving symbols" by Salvatore Caruso

www.degruyterbrill.com
Fragen zur allgemeinen Produktsicherheit:
productsafety@degruyterbrill.com

To all those who believe that 'Sí, se puede!'

List of Abbreviations

15M	*Movimiento 15 de Mayo* (15 May Social Movement/Indignados Movement)
AI	Artificial Intelligence
CIS	*Centro de Investigaciones Sociológicas* (Center for Sociological Research)
CS	*Cordon sanitaire*
Cs	*Ciudadanos* (Citizens)
EHB	*Euskal Herria Bildu* (Basque Country Gather)
ERC	*Esquerra Republicana de Catalunya* (Republican Left of Catalonia)
EU	European Union
FI	*La France Insoumise* (Rebellious France)
FPÖ	*Freiheitliche Partei Österreichs* (Freedom Party of Austria)
GAL	Green-Alternative-Libertarian and
IU	*Izquierda Unida* (United Left)
LGBTQI+	lesbian, gay, bisexual, transgender, queer, intersex and additional identities
LN	*Lega Nord* (Northern League)
M5S	*Movimento 5 Stelle* (Five Star Movement)
MEP	Member of the European Parliament
NFP	*Nouveau Front Populaire* (New Popular Front)
NUPES	*Nouvelle Union Populaire Écologique et Sociale* (New Ecological and Social People's Union)
PASOK	Πανελλήνιο Σοσιαλιστικό Κίνημα (Panhellenic Socialist Movement)
PD	*Partito Democratico* (Democratic Party)
PP	*Partido Popular* (People's Party)
PSOE	*Partido Socialista Obrero Español* (Spanish Socialist Workers' Party)
RN	*Rassemblement National* (National Rally)
SYRIZA	Συνασπισμός Ριζοσπαστικής Αριστεράς (Coalition of the Radical Left)
TAN	Traditional-Authoritarian-Nationalist
TC	Tainted coalition
UP	*Unidas Podemos* (United We Can)

https://doi.org/10.1515/9783111591537-001

List of Figures

https://doi.org/10.1515/9783111591537-002

List of Tables

https://doi.org/10.1515/9783111591537-003

Contents

Introduction

A growing number of populist movements and parties are no longer on the margins of European political systems; indeed, in many cases, these political actors are fully integrated within their respective national contexts. The economic, social, and political crisis of 2008 has revived the debate about the crisis of democracy and the ability of representative institutions to effectively support the demands and needs of "popular sovereignty" (Crouch 2004; Mouffe 2013; Tormey 2015). Particularly in the context of the European Union, the debate on democratic representation has been punctuated by the *querelle* on populist forces that, in the post-2008 economic and social crisis electoral rounds, burst onto the European political scene. An entry, or rather a return to the political scene, has changed the European political "cartography" to such an extent that the 21st century has been defined as "the century of populism" (Rosanvallon, 2020).

The management of the crisis and the "famous" *austerity* policies have produced one of the greatest moments of distrust of European institutions in the entire history of integration (European Parliament, Eurobarometer, 2007–2019). This, combined with other factors that will be analyzed in the following pages, has led to what has been called a "populist moment" (Mouffe, 2005), especially in the countries of Southern Europe (Portugal, Italy, Greece, and Spain, not coincidentally called PIGS), which have been most affected by the economic and social effects of the crisis. A moment characterized by a specific conjuncture marked by a high politicization of the population, the development of mass social movements, and the sudden birth and growth of new political subjectivities, now included in the representative-electoral scenario.

The macro-conditions for the rise of populism in Southern Europe are best understood as a combination of long-term and short-term crises. In addition to the worsening material conditions of the working and middle classes, the perceived convergence of political *elites* around austerity policies has opened a wide breach between a large part of the citizenry and its representatives, thus accentuating what has been called the "post-democratic" nature of contemporary politics (Mouffe, 2005) and the crisis of the traditional party system.

The term "populism" now pervades mainstream political news as a protagonist of television programs, public debates, and newspaper articles, assuming almost always a merely negative connotation. As political scientist Benjamin Arditi (2007) has also pointed out, there is a lot of "verbal smoke" around the concept of populism, both at the scholarly and media level. Academic and scholarly research on the phenomenon of populism has expanded exponentially in recent years, becoming a real field of study within Political Science, however, largely privileging

https://doi.org/10.1515/9783111591537-004

the analysis of the discussed phenomenon of so-called "right-wing populisms" (Katsambekis, Kioupkiolis, 2019). For this reason, it is particularly interesting to fit within the strand of analysis that, in recent times, has undertaken the study of the other side of populism, the "leftist" side. In fact, in response to the political and social changes of the 2008 economic crisis, the so-called "leftist populist" forces have gained support and media attention in the U.S. and European contexts, transcending the boundaries that, *mutatis mutandis*, had seen them preeminent especially in the Latin American context. In particular, the 2014 European elections, in which political parties such as SYRIZA in Greece and Podemos in Spain achieved hitherto unpredictable results, should be mentioned here.

This phenomenon has therefore also gained greater prominence within media and scholarly analysis, although it does not yet hold a space commensurate with the importance that some of these forces have occupied and occupy in their respective countries. Consider, for example, Jean-Luc Mélenchon, who, starting in 2012, first with the *Front de Gauche* and then with *La France Insoumise*, achieved increasing successes in a state, such as France, the beating heart of European politics, becoming in 2024 one of the leaders of *Nouveau Front Populaire*, which in that year's legislative elections became the coalition with the most seats (180) in the French National Assembly, surpassing even those of *Ensemble* (159), President Emmanuel Macron's coalition.

Therefore, this research is part of the studies and insights that Political Science has devoted to the topic in question, with the aim of contributing to the scholarly debate through the analysis of a specific phase of leftist populist action, namely the "institutional moment", that is, participation in a government coalition. In fact, analyses of left-wing populist forces have mainly focused on a few relevant aspects, such as, to name but a few, the modes of participation, the practices implemented, the digital tools used for internal organization and external communication, the causes of the sudden electoral success that led them to enter the European political scene, and the relations with social movements. The same attention, however, has not been paid to the "institutional moment", partly because of the recent temporality of this phenomenon. For this very reason, this book aims to investigate the ways in which leftist populist forces face the challenge of institutionalization in the European Union scenario and aims to highlight the changes that occur within a populist political force when it achieves important positions of national government.

Thus, the research fits within the analytical *framework* of the relationship between populist forces and government (Albertazzi, McDonnell, 2015; Kaltwasser, Taggart, 2016; Dieckhoff, Jaffrelot, Massicard, 2022), which will be analyzed extensively in Chapter 2. Taking power or participating in governing coalitions poses significant challenges for populist forces and so-called traditional parties, becoming a breaking point for these actors and the political-institutional context in which they operate. While the literature has been primarily focused on the latter, i.e., the consequences that arise on the "outside" of populist subjects in government (especially right-wing populism), this study intends to examine the challenges and changes occurring within these political forces.

What happens to an outsider force, like a left-wing populist force, when it comes to government? This is the main question this book seeks to answer. More specifically, the analysis is approached from two main perspectives: the internal organizational structure and its communicative discourse with the outside world.

In this regard, a leftist populist force is particularly compelling as a subject of study because it introduces alternative and innovative forms of organization and communication compared to the traditional party system. These organizational forms emerge in response to social demands for participation and representation of new *cleavages* (Lipset, Rokkan, 1967: 1–64) that European liberal democracies have ignored or weakly incorporated. Examining how these new organizational forms adapt to the functions of government, and how the "new" integrates into the traditional structure, is of fundamental interest to understanding not only the changing party system but also the evolution of European democracies.

Indeed, it is intriguing to explore how forces born from a crisis of representation confront and ultimately become active players within that system. Put differently, how do parties and forces that once identified as anti-system become part of the system? Reflecting on these political actors provides further insight into the changing nature of progressive and leftist forces within the European context. The crisis of social-democratic forces, in particular, has spurred the emergence of new political actors and organizational models, such as movement parties (Kitschelt, 2006), which have been able to address new divisions, social mistrust, and dissatisfaction that traditional political organizations have failed to represent (Damiani, 2016; Damiani, 2020; Ricolfi, 2017; Sassoon, 2020). Supporting this theory, Della Porta, Kouki, and Mosca provide critical insights in their seminal volume *Movements Parties Against Austerity:*

> Movement parties emerged in fact as established parties were most dramatically losing citizens' trust and the relations of cooperation of center-left parties with social movements have been reduced as left-wing parties moved to the center, while movements increasingly addressed social issues. Similar to the Latin American cases, in Europe the movement parties seem therefore to have emerged and succeeded when center-left parties were perceived as compromising with austerity policies. As we are going to see, during the economic crisis the PASOK in Greece, the Democratic party in Italy, and the PSOE in Spain all turned toward neoliberal policies based on structural reforms and privatization programs which translate into cutting social spending, increasing the retirement age, reforming the labor market, reducing the public sector, and so on. (Della Porta et al., 2017: 10–11)

Thus, focusing on leftist populist forces offers a means of analyzing the key political actors that have emerged in the countries most affected by distrust and the delegitimization crisis of European institutions. Understanding the role of these actors, now central within their respective institutional contexts, contributes to the analysis of the evolution of the European political system in the coming years, mapping future trajectories and transformations. Moreover, it provides a practical framework for understanding the tangible effects of the representation crisis in the European Union and supports the development of effective tools for addressing it.

Podemos as a Paradigmatic Case Study

The so-called "anti-austerity" political forces (Della Porta et al., 2018), which emerged in the European Union after the economic and social crisis of 2008 and grew out of the crisis of distrust and political delegitimization of both European institutions and traditional political systems, are the subject of this research. The lens through which they will be analyzed is the phenomenon of populism, particularly the interpretation of left-wing populism. The evolution of the endogenous characteristics of left-wing populist forces in the transition from opposition to national government will be the focal point of analysis.

As will be highlighted in subsequent chapters, it can be argued that left-wing populism has proven to be an effective political strategy, enabling significant institutional achievements in contexts of economic crisis and the decline of traditional political systems. It has become apparent, even to casual observers, that populist forces are no longer "alien creatures" within the European political and institutional framework. Instead, they have become integrated actors nearly fifteen years after the major crisis of Western economic, social, and political models. This is a fact that cannot be overlooked by those seeking to envision the development of the European institutional system. In some contexts—particularly those defined by peripheral relationships within Europe or where austerity policies have had the most profound impact—left-wing populism has served as a reference point and response to new cleavages and demands that traditional political entities have failed to assimilate. This has been particularly evident in Southern European countries, where social movement practices have taken root and articulated new democratic demands. In Spain and Greece, for instance, leftist populist strategies have allowed emerging political forces to channel the practical, communicative, and ideological concerns raised by social movements, thereby becoming indispensable players in the formation of national governing coalitions.

While populist strategies have demonstrated impressive consensus-building capabilities in the short term, this research assumes that they have not achieved the same effectiveness in the medium to long term. This has compelled these political actors to adapt and evolve away from the original characteristics that initially secured their success. Once in government, leftist populist political actors undergo significant changes to their foundational characteristics. As some of the cited literature confirms (Albertazzi, McDonnell, 2015; Fittipaldi, 2021), the populist subject in government is not necessarily doomed to fail or face severe electoral backlash. If such outcomes occur, they are often due to challenges unrelated to their populist nature. Instead, "the problems they faced were inevitably the same as those encountered by any party that finds itself governing (especially in a coalition government) for the first time" (Albertazzi, McDonnell, 2015: 172).

However, these political forces must necessarily adapt to ensure the maintenance of consensus and their survival in the medium to long term. This process involves bureaucratization and institutionalization, creating tensions between the horizontal organizational structure characteristic of leftist populist origins and the need for greater centralization and direction. Additionally, they are compelled to transition from a broad, *catch-all* approach typical of their formative phase to one more clearly situated on the left-right political spectrum.

These considerations were the driving force behind this research, prompting to test such a theoretical evolutionary framework through the analysis and observation of a paradigmatic case study. For this purpose, the analysis of a specific case—Podemos—and its socio-institutional context within Spain will be used to construct a theoretical paradigm that synthesizes and explains the evolution of the processes outlined.

Podemos represents an "outside the box" political force that has influenced both national and supranational levels. It is particularly useful for analysis for several reasons. First and foremost, Podemos' formative period makes it *unique* within the European political context. It is an innovative entity in both organization and practice, arising from a convergence of crises and disrupting Spain's traditional two-party system.

Moreover, the distinctiveness of its model has enabled it to achieve electoral results previously unimaginable for an outsider force, establishing itself as a decisive player within the European party and institutional framework. Its media influence and experimental approaches to digital communication make it one of the most innovative political forces in the realm of so-called digital populism. Political scientists Mazzolini and Borriello, who similarly analyze Podemos in *The Normalization of Left Populism? The Paradigmatic Case of Podemos* (2021), describe the Spanish political force as "a paradigmatic case":

Among the few existing cases of left populism across Europe, Podemos appears as a paradigmatic case. The claim rests on the belief that Podemos highlights in an exemplary way some of the general characteristics defining left populism in Europe [...]. Its insistence on the praxis-theory nexus, its rapid and out-of-ordinary electoral ascent, its negation of the old leftist symbolism and its capacity to embody 'newness' have been prototypical. As put by Heidegger, a paradigm can be discerned because it shines [...] – and, arguably, at the beginning Podemos shone, being one the most talked about political phenomena in Europe." (Mazzolini, Borriello, 2021)

For these reasons, Podemos is an ideal case study for examining a broader political phenomenon, such as leftist populisms in government.

The goal of this book is to create a paradigm capable of analyzing the characteristics and transformations of leftist populist subjects in government. In this regard, both the organizational and communicative dimensions will be examined. According to Mazzolini and Borriello (2021), Podemos serves as an example, or rather a *proxy*, for analyzing the "short duration" of the electoral strategy of left-wing populism: while it initially achieves strong results by rapidly and forcefully entering the political space following crises and mass social movements (alongside Podemos, other forces such as *La France Insoumise* and SYRIZA are also mentioned), maintaining the same level of visibility and mobilization beyond the electoral discourse has been more challenging. As we will see, on the road to executive power, Podemos has lost 2 million votes since 2015, faced significant internal tensions, and moved away from its initial "populist moment" while attempting to realign its internal structure and positioning. From this perspective, Mazzolini and Borriello argue that the movement has lost its sense of novelty, undergoing a normalization process typical of all leftist populist actors. This process is evident through four main features: partial institutionalization of party structures and loss of connection with social movements; the mitigation of Manichean rhetoric and redefinition of electoral ambitions; a loss of electoral consensus; and a shift to the more traditional left-right axis. As will be shown, these characteristics have emerged to some extent.

However, rather than "normalization", some authors (Campolongo and Caruso, 2021) have referred to "mutation", a concept that is considered more applicable to Podemos, as well as other forces affiliated with left-wing populism. Podemos is a fluid movement party, or, as one of its deputies, Manuel Monereo, has described it, "a mutant gene" that changes according to the situations, tactics, and actions of other parties. Therefore, it can be argued that Podemos, particularly in its early phase, used a populist discourse as a communicative tool, especially applying Ernesto Laclau's theory expressed in *The Populist Reason* (Laclau, 2005). Since 2017, it has adjusted its tactics, aligning more with the left-right axis and losing the "transversality" that had originally defined it. From this perspective, Podemos' changes (whether successful or not) are understood in light of its fluid nature and its use of populist tools as "a communicative technology that allows it to target broader segments of the population than those reached by the traditional radical left" (Campolongo and Caruso, 2021: 243). According to this interpretation, Podemos is not seen as a populist force per se, but rather as a movement that pursues popular policies through the instruments of populism:

> A popular policy is one whose main objective is the redistribution of power and resources for the benefit of popular social sectors. [...] Populist rhetoric is functional to the possibility of implementing popular policies, that is, of acquiring the consensus necessary to become a decisive formation in the constitution of governments, and possibly a hegemonic formation. Gramscianly, hegemony cannot be constructed from positions alien to common sense. (Campolongo and Caruso, 2021: 242)

For these reasons, in this book, Podemos is used as an exemplary case study to analyze the evolution of leftist populist parties in government. This "implicit form of comparison" (Mazzolini, Borriello, 2021) has been termed by American political scientist Richard Rose as an "extroverted case study" (Rose, 1991: 454), a research strategy that seeks to generalize some of the findings to a broader range of political phenomena, while still allowing for an in-depth examination of a specific context.

Elements of the analysis

What we are interested in understanding here is how a radical populist subject changes internally when it comes to government. We believe that the two best perspectives to measure its evolution are its internal organization, political discourse, and communication with the outside world.

From an organizational perspective, we analyze how Podemos, once in government, has faced institutionalization pressures that have altered its original organizational nature. The academic literature suggests that movement parties, the organizational form typical of early populist left anti-austerity forces (Kitschelt, 2006; Della Porta et al., 2018), face significant pressure to structure or, as Bolognese political scientist Panebianco puts it, to become more institutionalized when they enter government. Movement parties are seen as a transitional phenomenon: they transform when elected politicians act for opportunistic purposes or in response to changing voter preferences, or to gain relevance for other issues within the electoral arena. This transition results in the loss of many of the initial organizational characteristics:

> Perversely, the more a movement party achieves in terms of procedural gains and/or substantive policy change, the more it may change its voters' preferences or salient interests such that the party experiences growing pressure to abandon its existing profile of organization and policy appeal." (Kitschelt, 2006: 11)

However, this area of inquiry has not yet been sufficiently explored within the literature on populisms in power. Albertazzi and McDonnell, among the leading theorists of this phenomenon, in their *Populists in Power* (2015), identify the organizational question as the primary focus for future research, particularly regarding the issue of structuring political subjects:

> In fact, as we explain below, several of our suggestions for future research focus on the need to better understand populist party organization. [...] The study of this area should also explore [...] the extent to which populist parties that rely on a party model similar to 'mass party' are more likely to survive a change of leadership, or not. (Albertazzi, McDonnell, 2015: 177–178)

Subsequent research has continued in this direction. One of the most comprehensive texts is *Understanding Populist Party Organization* (2016) by political scientists Reinhard Heinisch and Oscar Mazzoleni. Their work focuses on analyzing the "most successful" right-wing populist parties in Western Europe, outlining the main organizational characteristics, which are key to understanding the evolution and success of populist forces, although they do not address the issue of government. The authors argue that "the tendency [of the seven cases of populism analyzed] toward centralization can be considered the main feature we observed. Moreover, the concentration of power in a leadership is frequently accompanied by formal or informal mechanisms designed to limit democracy within the party" (Heinisch, Mazzoleni, 2016: 227). The question of internal democracy in populist party organizations has garnered particular interest from scholars in recent years. A recent article by Böhmelt, Ezrow, and Lehrer, titled *Populism and Intra-party Democracy* (2022), addresses this issue through an interesting quantitative analysis, reaching conclusions similar to those of Heinisch and Mazzoleni. At the same time, however, the authors note that these findings can be valuable when analyzing populisms in government:

> our result that populism is associated with less democratic party organizations highlights possible extensions to understanding how these parties influence government formation and termination, and for considering how they respond to public opinion. (Böhmelt, Ezrow, Lehrer, 2022: 1151)

However, this book's perspective will not focus on the level of internal democracy within populist forces or the different modes of participation[1] but will concentrate on the types of organizational patterns that left-wing populist forces in government adopt. In this sense, Heinisch and Mazzoleni argue that although right-wing populist parties are outsider formations that challenge the status quo and appeal through their anti-system discourse and style, "this perception hides the fact that, if we compare these parties in Europe, they conform to some extent to conventional forms of party organization. However, importantly, they also challenge party organizational models in important ways" (Heinisch, Mazzoleni, 2016: 238). As the two authors argue, populist forces tend to move toward an "organizational normality", toward institutionalization, but they also introduce strong elements of discontinuity and innovation, evolving the model. It is in this direction that this research intends to move.

Second, it is important to combine this dimension with the discursive and communicative dimension directed toward the outside world, which is highly characteristic of the very nature of populist forces. Hence, from a discursive point of view, we analyze how Podemos in government has moved away from its original cross-discourse ('low vs. high' axis) toward greater identification with the left-right axis. The analysis of the evolution of political communication in ruling populist forces has particularly developed in recent years. Some scholars (Akkerman, 2016; Bernhard, 2020; Krause, Wagner, 2019) have theorized that ruling populists change their discourse according to the so-called "inclusion-moderation thesis", originally used to explain the moderation effects on parties of religious origin. Akkerman, for example, explains that this thesis "argues that participation in democratic institutions and procedures will change the radical nature and ideology of political parties" (Akkerman et al., 2016: 3). This is due to two factors: first, it is believed that populist parties in power are inclined to soften their discourses and demands to appeal to a broader electorate that will allow them to remain in power. Second, participation in government office is often associated with a moderating effect when the respective parties participate in coalition governments (Akkerman et al., 2016; Bernhard, 2020). In this sense, discussion and compromises with coalition partners are necessary for survival in government.

Political scientist Jakob Schwörer tests these theories in his interesting research, *Less Populist in Power? Online Communication of Populist Parties in Coalition Governments*, noting that "we are faced with a growing number of studies

---

1 Of which, however, the main features will be addressed, participation being an integral part of the model of organization and democracy proposed by leftist populisms.

dealing with the outcomes and consequences of populist participation in government, but with very little empirical evidence on the validity of the inclusion-moderation thesis for populist communication" (Schwörer, 2021: 472). His research shows a countertrend to the theories mentioned, as Schwörer does not find a clear tendency for populist parties to tone down their populist rhetoric once they enter a governing coalition. Electoral losses and public opinion, often associated with a change in communication, do not explain communicative changes either. In this regard, the author argues that the quality and quantity of populist messages depend on developments in the political and institutional contexts of individual countries. That is, "the discourses of populist parties should not be expected to be tamed by offering them participation in a coalition government" (Schwörer, 2021: 486).

The change in populist communication in government, therefore, seems to be an important element to analyze. In light of the above, it is argued here that it is incorrect to speak of moderation in the language of populist forces. The goal is to show that the change is not a decrease in the degree of radicality, but rather a change in characteristics: from a more transversal communication, in which the "high-low" axis was the dominant rhetoric of opposition to power, to a communication that is more responsive to the issues and ideological characteristics of the political force. This is not only a change in content but also a change in 'the people,' and therefore the target electorate, making greater use of the differences arising from positioning on the left-right axis. This fits with the research currently being conducted on these issues, using Podemos as a case study, as it has interesting characteristics and lines of evolution, identifying digital communication as one of its main strategic assets. For example, the analysis by Campolongo, Raniolo, and Tarditi (2021) in *Podemos' Online Communication in the Time of Government* sets out the following hypothesis:

> Our second hypothesis is therefore that Podemos representatives have focused their communication on issues related to government activity, promoting the party no longer as a protest actor, but rather as a responsive governmental force and, at the same time, capable of accountability. (Campolongo, Raniolo, Tarditi, 2021)

Demonstrating the validity of the evolutionary scheme proposed leads to a necessary rethinking about the nature of Podemos' mutation. While part of the literature, as we have mentioned, such as Mazzolini and Borriello (2021), has referred to the "normalization" of the phenomenon—that is, the end of Podemos' propulsive and innovative drive—it is intended to show that Podemos is a "mutant gene" that has implemented an evolution of its genetic model to adapt to the new institutional context, without being "absorbed" into the forms of traditional parties.

The evolution of Podemos is therefore not a "normalization", but rather a paradigm shift from its original "populist moment" to a different party model necessitated by its entry into government. Podemos is an evolving organization that has made the "populist moment" an essential tool for its electoral and media success. Indeed, there could be a variation, if not an interruption, in the use of populism as the main tool of a political force's discourse due to changes in the socio-institutional context in which it operates. Exogenous and endogenous causes have led Podemos to reposition itself on the left-right axis and, once in government, to undergo a discursive, communicative, and organizational change that is still progressing toward a more institutionalized organizational form, but not "normalized" into classical party structures. Podemos now shows a higher level of institutionalization than in its earlier stages, moving from the nature of a movement party with weak boundaries and low levels of bureaucracy, to a fully established political party. At the same time, however, it exhibits a party form that is not comparable to that of traditional parties, as it retains within itself certain inheritances —both in structure and forms of participation—typical of the horizontal thrust of its origins. It is therefore speculated that the current organizational form of Podemos can be described as a "hybrid party". From this point of view, the research follows in the footsteps of the analysis highlighted by Daniela Chironi and Raffaella Fittipaldi in *Social Movements and New Forms of Political Organization: Podemos as a Hybrid Party* (2017), where they define the "hybrid" nature of Podemos:

> In sum, our analysis suggests that movement mobilization played a large role in shaping Podemos' foundational choices. The result is a 'hybrid' party that, in order to flourish in times of crisis of representation, has found a balance between the horizontalism of social movements and the efficiency of a party that aims to manage a share of state power. Overall, its genesis, as well as its evolution and organizational features, confirm our evaluation on the crucial nature of this case study. We believe indeed that other new parties, born under conditions of protest and crisis, may have followed similar paths of emergence and organizational development. (Chironi, Fittipaldi, 2021)

The Paradigm

For these reasons, we propose a useful analytical framework to summarize and assess the evolution of a left-wing populist party and determine its actual direction of development. The proposed framework is summarized in Fig. 1. The different stages of Podemos' evolution will be evaluated by crossing two dimensions: the discursive dimension, represented on the x-axis, and the organizational dimension, represented on the y-axis.

Fig. 1: Paradigm of the evolution of left-wing populisms in government. Dimensions of the analysis. Source: author's elaboration.

Regarding the "discourse" variable (x), a range of characteristics was identified, from "transversal discourse", which is assigned a value of -5, to "leftist discourse", which is assigned a value of +5. Regarding the "organization" variable (y), a range of characteristics was identified, from "weakly institutionalized organization", assigned a value of -5, to "strongly institutionalized organization", assigned a value of +5.

The qualitative indicators are defined as follows:

Transversal Discourse (x = -5): A political force that uses a transversal discourse builds its communication and strategy around the "high-low" cleavage, identifying 'the people,' and thus its target subject, as those who are not represented by the elite—i.e., those who hold political, economic, and media power. Thus, the construction of "the people" does not occur according to socioeconomic, ethnic, or national criteria:

> It is argued that in general the 'left' expresses the interests of specific socioeconomic sectors and neglects the demands that, according to the populist strategy, should be included in the construction of the collective will. I believe that this is a more than substantive objection. In truth, when conceived from a sociological perspective as representing the interests of specif-

ic social groups, the notion of the left is inadequate to qualify a 'we', a 'people' resulting from the articulation of heterogeneous democratic claims. The construction of a 'people' in a transversal manner, with the aim of creating a popular majority independent of previous political affiliations, is in fact what distinguishes the populist political frontier from the traditional right and left. (Mouffe, 2018)

Leftist Discourse (x = +5): A political force using a radical left-wing discourse builds its communication and strategy around the "capital-labor" cleavage, identifying the people—and thus its subject of reference—as the working class, those who suffer exploitation and injustice socially and economically, those who are discriminated against on the basis of class, gender, and race. The construction of "the people" thus takes place according to socioeconomic criteria. According to the view proposed by Cas Mudde and Luke March (March, Mudde, 2005), and adopted by Charalambous and Ioannou:

> the radical left today is said to either reject consumerism and neoliberalism or even fundamentally oppose capitalist profit; it advocates major redistribution and the establishment of alternative (political and economic) power structures; it identifies economic inequality as the basis of existing arrangements and espouses its elimination through the establishment of collective economic and social rights; it is more anti-capitalist and less anti-democratic but does articulate a critique of capitalist and representative democracy; it embraces international solidarity and asserts that national and regional socio-political issues have global structural causes. (Charalambous, Ioannou, 2019: 7)

Weakly Institutionalized Organization (y = -5): An organizational structure that the Italian political scientist Panebianco calls "weakly institutionalized" has a low degree of bureaucracy and systematicity, with little interdependence between different parts of the organization. In this sense, the political party is more open to its surroundings, "less autonomous", and more inclined to reflect grassroots demands:

> A weakly institutionalized party is one within which the margins of autonomy of competing actors are wider, the ties of organizational sub-units to different sectors of the environment ensure competing groups' autonomous control over external resources. An organization with weak institutionalization is one that can experience abrupt transformations. (Panebianco, 1982: 118).

Such an organization leaves relative freedom of organization and action to its territorial manifestations, which can be influenced or, in the worst case, determined by external actors. It is close to the organizational modes characteristic of social movements. A low-institutionalization organization is based on a "system of solidarity", focusing on the pursuit of shared goals rather than balancing special interests necessary for the organization's survival. As a result, it is dominated by a clear and obvious ideology. The concept of a "system of solidarity" is part of the theory developed by sociologist Alessandro Pizzorno (Pizzorno, 1966) to describe political participation. For Pizzorno, a system of solidarity is "a system of action with a view to solidarity among actors", creating a community of equals in which participants' ends coincide. In this type of organization, participation is also of the "social movement" type, where the prevailing incentives are collective or, rather, identity-based. Collective participation as a decision-making and driving force creates an organization with an essentially bottom-up dynamic.

Strongly Institutionalized Organization ($y = +5$): An organizational structure with "strong institutionalization" has a high degree of bureaucracy and systematization, with close interdependence between different parts of the organization. In this sense, it is a highly autonomous party with respect to the external context, with clear organizational boundaries:

> A party that has experienced a strong process of institutionalization is an organization that drastically limits the internal actors' room for maneuver. The organization imposes itself on the actors, channeling their strategies along narrow and obligatory paths. A party with strong institutionalization is a party in which changes are slow, circumscribed, and laborious; it is an organization that can break down through excessive rigidity rather than experience deep and sudden changes. (Panebianco, 1982: 118)

An organization, therefore, with a clear hierarchy and division of tasks, in which a top-down logic prevails. This type of organization is based on participation with a "system of interests", "a system of action in view of the actor's interests" (Pizzorno, 1966). The participation system can thus be called "professional", and the incentives are either material (i. e., tangible rewards, such as monetary compensation, patronage, or support services) or status advancement (also referred to as power incentives).

The qualitative analysis of Podemos was conducted by comparing and discussing existing literature on the issues addressed and performing a comparative analysis of the two distinct periods in the political entity's life: the pre-government and governmental periods. This analysis aimed to identify both points of continuity and points of discontinuity.

The analysis of the evolution of political consensus for Podemos, along with the polling data for the main political forces in the Spanish context, was carried out by pooling data provided monthly by the *Centro de Investigaciones Sociológicas* (CIS)'s *Estimación de Voto* and the electoral histories provided by the *Junta Electoral Central del Congreso de los Diputados*.

Organizational analysis was carried out by comparing various congressional documents and Podemos' official organizational documents. The contents of these documents were also analyzed using Nvivo software.

Discourse analysis was performed using the same software, which allowed for careful collection and identification of the most frequently used terms. These were then grouped according to a chronological criterion and summarized graphically through a word cloud. The software also allowed for the reconstruction of profile publication statistics. The personal Twitter profiles of Pablo Iglesias (@PabloIglesias), Irene Montero (@IreneMontero), and Ione Belarra (@IoneBelarra) were analyzed, as they are central to political communication during both the electoral and post-election governmental moments and because these individuals have held institutional positions at the national level. The organization's official profile (@podemos) was also analyzed using the same method. Additionally, FanpageKarma (https://www.fanpagekarma.com) was used to analyze the same profiles on the Facebook platform.

The analysis of all the areas described was also conducted through ten semi-structured interviews, which took place between May and November 2022 and in April 2024. These interviews were conducted with leading members of the Spanish party and government, as well as with experts and scholars on the issues under analysis. Tab.1 summarizes the details of the nine semi-structured interviews.

Interviews Details	Date	Name	Role
Interview 1	17/11/2022	Pablo Iglesias	Founder of Podemos, former Vice-President of the Spanish Government Council, founder of *La Base*
Interview 2	27/10/2022	Lilith Verstrynge	Former Secretary of State for the 2030 Agenda and former Secretary of Organization of Podemos
Interview 3	18/07/2022	Chantal Mouffe	Philosopher
Interview 4	05/07/2022	Manu Levin	Philologist, former head of communication of the deputy prime minister and discourse secretary of Podemos, currently a journalist for *La Base*
Interview 5	20/06/2022	Pablo P. Ganfornina	Activist of the Andalusian 15M movement, head of the *Anticapitalistas* Party of Sevilla
Interview 6	19/06/2022	Ángela Rodríguez Martínez	Former Secretary of State for Equality and against Gender Violence, former Secretary of Feminisms and LGTBIQA+ of Podemos
Interview 7	13/06/2022	Juan Antonio Delgado	Former Podemos MP, current Member of the Andalusian Parliament

Continued

Interviews Details	Date	Name	Role
Interview 8	13/05/2022	**Juan Carlos Monedero**	UCM Political Science Professor, Founder of Podemos
Interview 9	13/05/2022	**Jorge Verstrynge**	Former *Alianza Popular* secretary, populism theorist, active since the first Podemos
Interview 10	12/04/2024	**Clara Serra**	Former deputy of Podemos in the Madrid Assembly and later of *Más Madrid*.

Tab. 1.: Details of semi-structured interviews conducted. Source: author's elaboration.

The structure of the book

Starting from the research questions and considerations just presented, the analysis is structured as follows: the first part forms the theoretical core of the book, providing an "orientation map" within the *mare magnum* of literature on the widely discussed—and in some cases, misused—phenomenon of "populism." Chapter 1, *Defining Populisms*, will examine two theoretical approaches that have gained significant traction within the field: the ideational approach, developed primarily by Cas Mudde, and the so-called discursive approach, whose main exponents are Ernesto Laclau and Chantal Mouffe.

Chapter 2, *Placing Podemos in Context: A Populist Party in Power*, situates the case of Podemos within the Spanish political landscape, with particular attention to its entry into government. Drawing on the comparative literature on populist and radical left-wing parties, the initial conjectures are examined. The first section of the chapter reviews key analytical insights from existing literature on populism in government. Subsequently, the analysis shifts to the Spanish political and institutional framework in which Podemos's trajectory unfolds. The party's history is traced, emphasizing both continuities and divergence from similar political phenomena in Europe. Leveraging insights from studies on parties such as SYRIZA (left-wing populism) in Greece and *Movimento 5 Stelle* (hybrid populism) and *Lega* (right-wing populism) in Italy, Podemos's case is contextualized within a comparative theoretical framework.

Chapter 3, *Podemos's Electoral Trajectory*, is an in-depth analysis of Podemos' electoral support, tracing its evolution from its inception to the latest available data. This chapter compares Podemos' electoral performance across various levels: European, national, and within autonomous communities, which are pivotal electoral battlegrounds in the Spanish context. Podemos' electoral success is juxtaposed with that of other Spanish political entities, notably Vox, the primary opposition force exhibiting distinct characteristics of right-wing populism. Additionally, a segment titled the "Political Barometer" explores potential future scenarios. This chapter situates Podemos within the Spanish electoral landscape, documenting its successes and challenges following its participation in government.

The following chapters form the core of the research. Chapter 4, *Evolution of Organizational Structure*, aims to assess whether Podemos, upon entering government, experiences pressures toward institutionalization that alter its original organizational dynamics. Specifically, the focus lies on the evolution of party structures at the national level, exploring the dynamics and tensions between the party in power and its grassroots base, particularly regarding demands for grassroots participation. The analysis will show that the transformation shifted Podemos from a loosely structured movement with minimal bureaucracy to a fully-fledged political entity. Nonetheless, Podemos retains certain characteristics inherited from its origins, presenting a party model that diverges from traditional party structures and emphasizes horizontal modes of participation. Thus, I posit that Podemos's current organizational form can best be described as that of a "hybrid party."

Chapter 5, *Transitioning from Challenger to Governing Party: The Evolution of Discourse*, delves into an examination of the "external face" of Podemos, focusing on its communication strategies and public discourse. Both points of departure and continuity between Podemos's role as an opposition or challenger party and its status as a governing entity are highlighted. It becomes clear that this transformation has been profound, fundamentally reshaping the party's essence. The shift in populist communication, once governmental responsibilities are assumed, emerges as a critical aspect of analysis. It is contended here that characterizing the language of populist forces as moderate once they enter government is misleading. The transformation involves not just a reduction in populist rhetoric, but also an internal shift from a broad populist communication style to a more class-based one, typical of leftist parties. This entails not only a change in content but also a shift in the target electorate and a clearer positioning along the left-right spectrum. Therefore, this case challenges the notion of party de-radicalization upon entering government; rather, it demonstrates how rapidly the party becomes immersed in the traditional ideological conflicts it initially aimed to disrupt.

The *Conclusions* summarize the key findings of my analyses and discuss their implications for comparative theory. We illustrate how Podemos, while in government, has undergone a significant paradigm shift from its original populist "moment", evolving both organizationally and discursively. This ongoing evolution has altered the fundamental nature of Podemos, yet it remains distinct from traditional political parties. On the one hand, there is a trend toward an institutionalized party structure that nevertheless transcends conventional party frameworks by successfully integrating top-down executive actions with participatory elements and grassroots engagement. On the other hand, Podemos positions itself as a left-wing entity striving to innovate traditional left-leaning discourse, symbolism, and vocabulary while maintaining clear ties to its ideological roots. The party's initial populist stance has swiftly given way to more experimental, though ideologically grounded, organizational and communicative approaches.

Chapter 1 – Defining Populisms

1.1 A *mare magnum* of definitions

Populism is a phenomenon for which the scholarly literature has yet to find a consensus definition, even though it is now so pervasive in public and media debate that some authors have even referred to it as an "overused" term (Caiani, Della Porta, 2011). The same introductory statement of this paragraph can be found in many treatises on populism in almost identical form. Following the advice of Greek political scientists Katsambekis and Kioupkiolis in their *The Populist Radical Left in Europe* (Katsambekis, Kioupkiolis, 2020), the intention here is to propose a more optimistic approach to this *magnum sea* of definitions, starting from what can be considered the core of the phenomenon of populism. This core brings together all the attempts developed in recent years that help us understand its main characteristics. To date, the most essential definition of populism is surely that of Margaret Canovan, who suggests that:

> Populism in modern democratic societies is best seen as an appeal to 'the people' against both the established structure of power and the dominant ideas and values of the society. (Canovan, 1999: 3)

This definition contains characteristics on which all the literature agrees. The first is that populism emphasizes the central position of 'the people'. This is what Jagers and Walgrave (2007) call "the thin definition of populism", the foundational element of the phenomenon and its necessary condition. We cannot generally say what 'the people' is, since its boundaries, characteristics, and values vary depending on the type and degree of populism, as will be explored later.

The construction of 'the people' involves creating a closed group with certain interests, values, and identities, which can be defined, for example, in ethnic or racial, religious, geographical, or economic terms. 'The people' is the central figure of democracy, often considered the repository of truth—that is, the expression of a general will, the true needs, and fair principles that ensure the sociopolitical and economic well-being of the majority. The general will of the people is often embodied by a strong and charismatic leader, whose presence obviously influences the organizational structure of populist political entities.

However, constructing an 'us' requires constructing a 'them' as the threat and enemy of 'us'. This Manichean construction of society is the second key characteristic without which a populist discourse cannot exist. The 'them' is not merely opposed to 'us' but represents a fundamental threat to the very existence of the peo-

https://doi.org/10.1515/9783111591537-005

ple and the fulfillment of their interests and needs. Opposing and fighting this 'them' is the main driving force of populist action, the energy prompting the formation of a cohesive 'us'. This boundary reinforces the definition and identity of 'the people'. Again, the variations of 'them' can be multiple: it can be 'above', referring to a political and/or economic *establishment* detached from the people's needs; it can be 'downward', referring to those deemed inferior, parasitic, or dangerous, a threat to the people's integrity, as in cases where 'them' is constructed along ethnic lines. The ways in which 'them' is constructed have repercussions on different spheres of the political entity, starting with public discourse and organization.

As Cas Mudde and Cristòbal Rovira Kaltwasser (2007)—two of the leading theorists of the phenomenon—rightly point out, populism cannot be associated only with party political actors but also with organized social movements. Therefore, the presence of strong leadership cannot be considered an inescapable characteristic of every populist movement, although even these authors see it as a key feature. Populist leaders can take many forms but share certain traits: they represent the vox populi through a demagogic discourse and communicative style, using direct and emotional language that breaks with institutional communication norms and draws on both positive and negative sentiments. Populism constructs an understanding of reality through its own rhetorical simplification and may employ a detailed theoretical framework to support each of its rhetorical elements.

A necessary sociopolitical precondition for the effective development of a populist strategy is a moment of crisis, which facilitates this Manichean division of reality and heightens the urgency of action and change. However, even on this point, there is no consensus within the literature. The staunchest advocates of the necessary link between 'crises' and 'populism' are the Argentine philosopher Ernesto Laclau and the theorists of the Essex School who follow his discursive approach to populism—an approach that will be explored in more detail in the following paragraphs. In one of his most renowned works, *On Populist Reason*, Laclau identifies 'crisis' as one of the indispensable elements for the development of populism:

> This is because, as we have seen, populism never emerges from an absolute outside and advances in such a way that the previous state of affairs dissolves around it, but proceeds by articulating fragmented and dislocated demands around a new core. So some degree of crisis in the old structure is a necessary precondition of populism for, as we have seen, popular identities require equivalential chains of unfulfilled demands. (Laclau, 2005:177)

Laclau refers to the "crisis of the old structure", identifying within it "the crisis of representation [that] underlies every populist and anti-institutional outburst" (Laclau, 2005:137). In contemporary literature on Latin American populism, crises are also seen as causes and opportunities for the emergence, development, and success of populist actors. These scholars analyze populism not as a discursive practice but as a mode of organization or strategy. For example, Kenneth Roberts (1995: 113) argues that populism "emerges most strongly in contexts of crisis or profound social transformation, when pre-existing patterns of authority or institutional referents lose their ability to structure the political behavior and identities of popular sectors". This later led him to consider, for example, Hugo Chávez's success in Venezuela as closely connected to and encouraged by a "crisis in Venezuelan democracy" (Roberts, 2012: 138).

A second orientation can be described as 'agnostic' toward the relationship between populism and crisis: some authors, especially those associated with the ideational approach, such as Cas Mudde and Cristòbal Rovira Kaltwasser, do not see a direct connection between the two phenomena. Rather, they believe that the link between crisis and populism is essentially weak. In this regard, for example, Cas Mudde (2007) acknowledges that the concept of crisis should not be dismissed, since the empirical literature shows a significant correlation between variables we might associate with crisis—such as economic instability, political distrust, or specific crises involving migration and social issues—and the electoral success of European radical right populists. However, "the main problem with this literature is the relationship between these variables and the general concept of crisis" (2007: 205). In other words, these variables do not automatically equate to systemic crises or anything easily relatable to the concept of crisis. Moreover, Mudde believes that almost all modern political epochs have been in crisis: if crises are a defining feature of contemporary European politics, it becomes difficult to assert a strict relationship and argue that populism is an extraordinary phenomenon occurring only periodically in times of crisis.

The third group of authors rejects the link between crisis and populism *in toto*. Historian Alan Knight, in his celebrated studies on Latin America, argues that crisis is "a vague, promiscuously used, and poorly theorized concept that defies measurement and lacks explanatory power" and that the link between populism and crisis "is at best a trend or rough correlation" (1998: 227).

Political scientist Benjamin Arditi (Arditi, 2007) is equally critical of identifying a direct link between populism and crisis, arguing that "the reference to 'crisis' also narrows the scope of the populist experience to moments when politics fails to respond to participatory, distributive or other demands. [...] The emphasis on the exception does not allow us to differentiate populist politics in opposition from populism in government". In fact, the author believes that overemphasizing crisis leads us to focus only on exceptional moments rather than on the specific characteristics populist actors may display when they hold positions of power without an "external" crisis triggering their electoral *appeal.*

Benjamin Moffitt is the author who innovates this field of research on the re-lationship between crisis and populism by shifting the perspective. He argues that the debate has focused only on viewing crisis as something external—a sum of systemic failures that may or may not foster populism's rise. Instead, he believes that crisis can be seen as a subjective creation of populists, or rather, as the sum of more or less failed events made performative through the mediation of populist actors. For Moffitt, crisis performance is integral to populism and justifies mobi-lization against those responsible for the crisis or those who failed to manage it. In short, for populism to exist, it must enact and perform a sense of crisis:

> Instead, it has argued that crisis should also be seen as an internal feature of populism, given that crises are never 'neutral' events, but are actively mediated and performed by populist actors who attempt to 'spectacularize' failure to propagate a sense of crisis. Having outlined the mechanisms of this performance, it has shown that this performance allows populists a method for dividing 'the people' against a dangerous other, for presenting themselves as the sovereign voice of 'the people' and for radically simplifying political procedures and institu-tions. It must be stressed that the performance of crisis should not be viewed just as a par-ticular political strategy among others that populists can choose to deploy if they feel it would politically advantageous – rather, the performance of crisis should be seen as an essential core feature of populism itself. (Moffitt, 2015: 210–211)

As will be explored in the following sections, the decline of traditional political affiliations has created another avenue for populist actors to articulate new de-mands and reformulate political identities. However, this does not mean that it is significantly easier today to establish newly created affiliations through populist strategies. New political agents do not operate in a field completely stripped of previous political ties: the crisis is present, but the void is only partial. Although weakened, traditional *cleavages* (with their corresponding institutions and affili-ations) remain and impose limits on the operations of populist actors or those using populist tools. Paradoxically, the erosion of democracy and the traditional party system is both too incomplete and too advanced for populist actors. On one hand, their progress is hampered by the relative resilience of traditional cleavages, which narrows the available political space. On the other hand, once they have successfully entered the political scene, they find it difficult to stabilize due to extreme political volatility and the lack of solid intra- and extra-party struc-tures. This explains the dilemmas faced by left-wing populisms.

Furthermore, since social networks have become a new global environment, populist forces have turned the digital realm into one of their main battlegrounds and communication tools. In particular, the figure of the leader—the digital prince described by Calise and Musella (2019)—has found in social media a fundamental field of social and political legitimacy, to the point that some authors have referred to digital populism (Dal Lago, 2017) or *platform leadership*, "an unprecedented form of political leadership derived from the intersection between the processes of personalization and the flat-forming of politics" (Nunziata, 2021).

As will be analyzed in the following chapters, Podemos can be considered one of the most innovative forces within the European digital populist landscape, in terms of social communication and digital tools for participation and internal democracy. In general, populist forces are increasingly focusing on the use of microtargeting, big data analytics software, and the development of direct digital participation tools for supporters, leading to the concept of "digital parties" (Gerbaudo, 2020) that aim to move beyond forms of representative democracy and build direct citizen participation.

It is useful to outline the general characteristics of digital populist communication[1], since this topic will be a focal point of one of the hypotheses of this research[2]. In digital populist communication, the leader takes on an even more central role, creating a direct, unmediated relationship with the audience, which feels personally involved and capable of commenting on, evaluating, and sharing the disseminated message. The leader thus builds a direct emotional connection, often through simple and swift language that can be polarizing, basic, provocative, and ambiguous (Dal Lago, 2017). The leader's interpersonal relationship with the user base is strengthened through the heavy use of images and videos—tools that serve as agenda-setting devices, dramatize politics, aid in emotional appeals, build the external image of the leader or an individual candidate, foster stronger identification, and connect to social symbols (Kirk, Schill, 2021).

Especially regarding right-wing and hybrid populisms, provocative language is further intensified by strong aggression and constant references to the concepts of 'normality' and 'common sense'. Far-right forces portray society as a homogeneous community that must combat the enemy, and they present the leader as the repository of truth, often resulting in fierce anti-intellectualist rhetoric. Identification and closeness with the leader and the political force are reinforced by frequent calls-to-action, direct appeals for audience participation, and storytelling through common, everyday events that encourage even sentimental identification.

---

1 Characteristics that were explored in more detail in another analysis in which the phenomenon of digital populism was observed during one of the biggest "external" crises that the system-world has experienced in recent history, namely Covid-19. May we refer to Giardiello, 2021, *Digital Populisms in the Time of Covid-19*, Journal of Digital Politics, Il Mulino.
2 See in this regard Chapter IV.

1.2 Defining populisms

Here, the theoretical orientation on the phenomenon of populisms is mainly based on the definitions of Cas Mudde and Ernesto Laclau and follows the perspective suggested by the previously mentioned volume by Katsambekis and Kioupkiolis. Indeed, although these two definitions are often, and rightly so, considered to be at opposite ends of the spectrum, they both provide valuable elements that, when combined, can be useful for analyzing different types of populism.

We intend to present their main characteristics here, without claiming to be exhaustive. Other authors, while starting from the same analytical core, have defined populism in other terms, such as a mere political rhetoric (Betz, 1994), a mode of organization (Taggart, 2004), a strategy, or a particular communicative style (Jagers and Walgrave, 2007; Tarchi, 2002). Populism, as a "different way of doing politics" (Katsambekis, Kioupkiolis, 2020), shapes the political subjects that adopt its main characteristics. According to the conception expressed here, a political force is not considered ontologically populist, but rather uses this political strategy, which can manifest as a discursive practice (Laclau, 2005) or as a thin-centered ideology (Mudde, Kaltwasser, 2007). This practice characterizes its discourse, organization, communication, and, when it attains governmental positions, even its policies. A political subject may be born as a populist force, but as will be shown, this does not define its nature for its entire existence.

1.2.1 Cas Mudde and the ideational approach

> More concretely, we define populism as a thin-centered ideology that considers society to be ultimately separated into two homogeneous and antagonistic camps, 'the pure people' versus 'the corrupt elite', and which argues that politics should be an expression of the *volonté générale* (general will) of the people. (Mudde, Kaltwasser, 2007: 5–6)

This definition of populism is one of the most widely accepted in the scholarly community. One of its merits is certainly that Dutch political scientist Cas Mudde introduced Giovanni Sartori's logic of a 'minimum definition' into populism studies, enabling the use of this definition as the basis for numerous quantitative and qualitative investigations of populist political forces. One of Mudde's main aims, like that of all such approaches, is to find the lowest common denominator—the core central features—of the phenomenon's empirical manifestations in different geographical and temporal contexts.

Analyzing the definition in detail, the main feature is the articulation of this phenomenon around a 'people', defined in various ways, expressing a *volonté générale* that stands in opposition to that of an elite. According to the author, the essence of the populist divide lies in a moral struggle between the virtuous people and 'the other', a corrupt enemy. If this moral dimension is not prominent in the discursive structuring of a social movement or political party, it cannot be considered populist, merely anti-establishment. For this reason, the populist 'us' and 'them' is constructed with predetermined characteristics.

The three elements that summarize the manifestations of all types of populism are: the people, the *elite*, and the general will. In their *Populism. A Short Introduction* (2017), the most widely used basic handbook for studying populism, Mudde and Kaltwasser outline the main properties of these elements.

Starting with 'the people', the authors consider this concept a vague construction that allows for great flexibility. However, it is most often employed in one or several combinations of three main meanings: 'the sovereign people', 'the common people', and 'the nation people'. Each of these meanings is linked to a secondary characteristic defining its boundaries and peculiarities in relation to 'the other', namely the *elite*. 'The sovereign people' is associated with the modern democratic idea that defines 'the people' not only as the source of political power but also as those who should govern. Political power and the right to rule are seen as being taken from those who rightfully hold them, in the 'rulers vs. ruled' dichotomy leading to theories and demands for alternative forms of democracy. In other words, the notion of 'the people as sovereign' is, as the authors state, "a theme common to different populist traditions, functioning as a reminder that the ultimate source of political power in a democracy derives from a collective body, which, if disregarded, can lead to mobilization and revolt" (Mudde, Kaltwasser, 2017:10).

The meaning of 'common people' refers to socioeconomic status and thus to the concept of class. It criticizes the dominant hegemony that regards ordinary citizens' judgments, tastes, and values as inferior or worthless. This anti-elitist perspective is common among various populist types, employing an "inclusive" identity around common socioeconomic and sociocultural characteristics and a "divisive" identity against a small group, bureaucracy, power structure, organization, or institution that despises them.

The third and final meaning is the notion of the people as a nation. Here, "the people" refers to the national community, defined in civic or ethnic terms. As will be analyzed, this is the main feature of so-called exclusionary populisms, or right-wing populisms, which identify national boundaries as the dividing line between 'us' and 'them'. This implies that all "natives" of a particular country are included and together form a community with a shared identity reinforced by founding myths and national rituals. "However, defining the boundaries of the nation is far from simple. Equating 'the people' with the population of an existing state has proven to be a complicated task, especially since different ethnic groups exist on the same territory" (Mudde, Kaltwasser, 2017:10).

Regarding the second element, Mudde and Kaltwasser identify 'they' as the construction of an elite, following a high-low logic. "The crucial aspect" in constructing the elite is its morality and thus the distinction between the "pure" people and the "corrupt" elite. This represents the initial, almost instinctive sense of populist division in society. Applying the categories described earlier, an elite can be defined based on power and thus include all those who hold political, media, economic, cultural, etc., power. As already pointed out, in this logic, the elite is seen as holding power illegitimately. This perspective can also appear when populist forces are in government: "real power" is not in the hands of democratically elected authorities but lies with unseen forces that, through economic, media, and political means, continue to hold illegitimate power over the people's will.

In contrast, the link between the nature of the elite and socioeconomic status is typical of leftist populisms. The elite is defined in class terms— 'the rich', 'the privileged', 'the exploiters', 'the multinationals', etc. Power is expressed as economic power, often considered more important than political power. Indeed, as the authors note, "linking the economic power of elites is particularly useful for populist power because it helps them 'explain' their lack of political success; for example, they are sabotaged by the elite, who may have lost political power but continue to have economic power" (Mudde, Kaltwasser, 2017:13). This view of populism is not necessarily "anti-capitalist", but right-wing populisms can also adopt it, connecting elites holding political power and those wielding economic power, both conspiring against the will of the people, often with an ethnic dimension.

The final connection links the concept of elites to nationalism, in which "the distinction between people and elites is both moral and ethnic. Here the elite is not only seen as an agent of an alien power, but is itself considered alien" (Mudde, Kaltwasser, 2017:14). In this case, we can refer to ethno-populism. All these features make the elite a polysemic concept that can be flexibly used, overlapping and employing different conceptions simultaneously.

The third and last key concept of populist ideology is 'the general will'. For Mudde and Kaltwasser, the concept is closely related to philosopher Jean-Jacques Rousseau's distinction between the general will (*volonté générale*) and the will of all (*volonté de tous*). The former refers to the people's ability to unite as a community to legislate for the common good; the latter describes a mere aggregation of particular interests at a given time. Finding—or rather, creating—the general will is the objective of populist forces and leaders who, through their charisma, must shape a cohesive community that seeks it. By embracing the concept of the general will, populist forces can incorporate a different vision of democracy into their discourse, following Rousseau's critique of representative democracy:

> Hence, it can be argued that an elective affinity exists between populism and direct democracy, as well as other institutional mechanisms that are helpful to cultivate a direct relationship between the populist leader and his/her constituencies. To put it another way, one of the practical consequences of populism is the strategic promotion of institutions that enable the construction of the presumed general will. [...] From this angle, populism can be seen as a democratizing force, since it defends the principle of popular sovereignty with the aim of empowering groups that do not feel represented by the political establishment. (Mudde, Kaltwasser, 2017:17–18)

At the same time, populism can also have "a dark side": the almost monistic view of the people's general will, filtered and directed by the leader's discourse, may lead to support for authoritarian tendencies and attacks on those who threaten the homogeneity of the general will. This observation allows us to address another important feature of the two authors' theorizing. Determining what can be considered populist necessarily involves defining what cannot be considered populist. Mudde and Kaltwasser believe there are at least two direct opposites of populism: elitism and pluralism. For elitists, the 'people' are seen as dangerous, dishonest, and vulgar, culturally and intellectually inferior to the *elite*. For this reason, elitists reject democracy or advocate a limited form of it. Pluralists, on the other hand, view diversity as a strength rather than a weakness: society consists of various social groups with different ideas and interests that must be satisfied through compromise and consensus. Thus, the main idea is that power must be distributed so that no single group can impose its will on others.

In addition to these general features, the key contribution of the ideational approach is using the concept of a 'thin-centered ideology' to describe populism. British political scientist Michael Freeden (2003) first coined this term. While 'complete ideologies' are bodies of ideas, values, and principles that describe what society is like and imagine what it should be, thin ideologies "do not have much to offer". In other words, applying it to this case, one cannot identify a specific idea of societal transformation called 'populist', as can be done for ideologies such as socialism, liberalism, or communism.

A thin-centered ideology like populism needs to be "attached" to a "complete ideology" that determines its direction and boundaries, generating a variety of possible "subtypes" of populism. For this reason, it is now common in academic research to speak of "populisms". According to the authors, the ideational approach has four advantages. First, it explains why populism is such a "malleable" phenomenon, encompassing a wide range of facets since it can be connected to large "complete ideologies" or "thick ideologies", as well as smaller, subtler ideologies. Second, this definition allows the concept to be applied to a broader set of political actors: not only classical political parties but also individual leaders, social movements, and what can be termed movement parties. Given the improved ability to study different aspects of populism, the third advantage is the chance to better address the long, complex debate on the relationship between populisms and democracy. For the authors, "the relationship is complex, as populism is both friend and foe of (liberal) democracy, depending on the stage of the democratization process" (Mudde, Kaltwasser, 2017:20). Finally, the fourth advantage of defining populism as an ideology is that it allows consideration of both the demand and supply sides of populist politics. While the supply side has long been more studied, examining the demand side provides "a more complete understanding of the causes of populist episodes and the costs and benefits of democratic responses to populism" (Mudde, Kaltwasser, 2017:20).

1.2.2 Ernesto Laclau, Chantal Mouffe and the discursive approach

> Populism is, quite simply, a way of constructing the political.
> (Laclau, 2005: XI)

Ernesto Laclau's theorization of populism, developed with the participation of French political scientist Chantal Mouffe, is certainly one of the most articulate. At the same time, it has been particularly influential not only in academic circles but also in shaping the theory and practice of some of the most successful leftist populist movements, including Podemos itself.

For the Argentine political scientist, populism is the logic proper "of the political": therefore, it makes no sense to define whether a political force or movement is populist or not, but rather to analyze the degree of populism within it. This view stems from a post-Marxist reading of society fully realized in "On Populist Reason" (2005).

The first fundamental distinction he proposes is between "field of discursivity" and "discourse" proper (Laclau, Mouffe, 1985). Laclau seeks to break away from the traditional Marxist division of the social field—considered excessively economistic—into "base" and "superstructure" and aims to reduce everything to the discursive field. Nothing exists outside of discursive practices, he argues; every social practice is linguistically or discursively "constructed", always semantized (Tarizzo, 2008). For Laclau, discourse is understood as "a complex of elements in which relations play a constitutive role" (Laclau, 2005). Yet, if the entire social field is a "field of discursivity", this does not mean there is only one "discourse". For the Argentine author, society as a single entity does not exist; it is always the object of hegemonic contention, producing fractures and exclusions.

If the discursive field is the social, discourse is the political, which aims at an operation that will always be contested—and therefore impossible—but necessary: constructing a society that is nothing more than a set of heterogeneous demands. These "social questions" are the minimal units for building "popular identities" and can be articulated in two distinct ways. When they remain individual questions, they are articulated through "the logic of difference" and are thus called "democratic": they are depoliticized and resolved by institutions. When institutions, or those who lead them, become unable or unwilling to address these questions, dissatisfaction arises, producing a crisis of democratic hegemony.

For Mouffe and Laclau, a "populist moment" occurs when, because of political, social, or economic transformations, existing institutions fail to maintain the confidence of the historical bloc—the social base that sustains the dominant hegemony. At that point, the possibility emerges of constructing a new collective actor —the people—capable of articulating a new social order. This was the case during the crisis of liberal hegemony following the European crisis of 2008. Therefore, according to the authors, populism is:

> a discursive strategy for the construction of a political frontier, operating through the division of society into two camps and calling for the mobilization of 'the derelicts', those who are underprivileged, against 'those in power'. Populism is not an ideology and cannot be traced to a specific programmatic content. Nor is it a political regime. It is a way of doing politics that can take different forms depending on time and place and is compatible with different institutional frameworks. (Mouffe, 2018:5)

A force is populist when it can build a discursive strategy capable of uniting individual demands through the logic of "equivalence"—chains of equivalences that create a "popular demand". In this way, a new "we" can be formed along an antagonistic frontier with "them". However, it is necessary that a difference, without ceasing to be a particular difference, becomes the representation of a totality, a "we."

> This operation of taking up, by a particularity, of an incommensurable universal signification is what I have called hegemony. And, given that this embodied totality or universality is, as we have seen, an impossible object, the hegemonic identity becomes something of the order of an empty signifier, its own particularity embodying an unachievable fullness. (Laclau, 2005, p. 70–71)

This leads to a process of positive popular identification with an empty signifier (e.g., "the people") that becomes hegemonic. In this regard, it is evident that one important consequence of this theory is the assumption of vagueness and indeterminacy in articulated social heterogeneity. Laclausian left-wing populism is thus transversal, losing any anchoring to the concept of "class" that characterizes left-wing movements and political forces (which in most cases refer to Marxist theory), where the capital-labor divide frames their identity (the so-called class consciousness) and their "we."

On these points, I interviewed Chantal Mouffe during her participation in *the Cursos de Verano de San Lorenzo de El Escorial* organized by the Universidad Complutense de Madrid on July 18 and 19, 2022:

> Author (A): Do you believe that it is still appropriate to talk about 'transversality' for the construction of a hegemonic strategy of a leftist populism?
> Chantal Mouffe (CM): Yes, for me it is fundamental. This is what I call the populist element. I would define leftist populism through the fundamental operation of creating equivalence. An 'us' and a 'them'. Step one. The second step involves a rupture, setting a frontier. For example, even in Marxism there is a frontier: capital-labor; proletariat-bourgeoisie. The difference with populism is that populism is transversal in the sense that the 'we' is constructed not only through capital-labor, but to the whole system of exploitation. (Mouffe, 2022, Interview 3)

Consequently, if a transversal strategy is still necessary, I wondered whether we remain in a populist moment today, compared to what Mouffe wrote in 2018 in her *For a Left Populism:*

> CM: This strategy *[that of leftist populism]* still works. However, the conjuncture is different than when I wrote this book. We are not in a populist moment where there is an effervescence, however, the strategy is still valid because I don't see any other plausible winning strategy for the left. Certainly not the traditional one. Right now, the conjuncture is basically the urgency of the climate issue, so you must articulate it. [...] I used to name this urgency, but I didn't give it a fundamental importance. Now there is an urgency. What I propose is to say that a green democratic revolution is a way to articulate the whole chain of equivalence for an ecological transition project. (Mouffe, 2022, Interview 3)

Today, for Chantal Mouffe, the hegemonic signifier around which the "people" of European leftist populism must be built is what she calls the "green democratic revolution".

1.3 Leftist Populisms

Going beyond the theoretical definition and examining empirical cases, different types of populism can be identified to the extent that it is now common practice to speak of "populisms". Indeed, some scholars (Caiani, Graziani, 2019; Zulianello, 2020) agree on distinguishing between right-wing populism, left-wing populism, and *valence populism* (or hybrid populism). These differences concern the entire framework of values, content, and aims pursued, arising from a different conception of "us" and consequently redefining the field of "them." To simplify, *right-wing populisms* identify "the people" through ethnic and national boundaries, while *left-wing populisms* use a "socioeconomic" lens, i. e., class-based criteria. *Valence* populisms are hybrid forms, drawing on both repertoires without clearly aligning with the right or the left of the party system.

More recently, comparative studies have moved beyond the traditional right-left axis and proposed a differentiation between inclusive populism and exclusionary populism (Mudde, Kaltwasser, 2017). This distinction is based on three main dimensions—the material, the political, and the symbolic. Within these dimensions, populisms differ in terms of the envisaged level of inclusiveness (e. g., favoring mass welfare programs versus adopting chauvinist welfare, proposing inclusive migration policies versus advocating border closures and combating illegal immigration, or emphasizing the dignity of indigenous peoples versus enacting symbolic exclusion). These differences again affect the definition of the boundary between "us" and "them". We can say that the inclusive-exclusionary distinction encompasses the right-left one: inclusive populism is associated in most cases with left-wing populism, while exclusionary populisms, since the 1980s, are associated with right-wing organizations (Caiani, Graziani, 2019).

In her insightful quantitative study *Measuring populism worldwide* (2020), Pippa Norris measures global political forces. A first level of classification is based on whether they use populist rhetoric—a rhetoric that typically questions the legitimacy of established political institutions and insists that the will of "the people" should prevail. The opposite of a populist rhetoric is "liberal pluralism", which rejects these ideas, upholding that elected leaders should rule, constrained by minority rights, bargaining and compromise, and checks and balances on executive power. This distinction is "colored" by a second level of classification intersecting the position on economic issues (the right-left axis) with the position on social values (the liberal-conservative values axis), or in other words, the GAL (*green, alternative, libertarian*) – TAN (*traditionalist, authoritarian, nationalist*) axis. It is precisely the intersection of these axes that generates the variety of populisms:

> Party and leadership competition is therefore understood as multidimensional, with cleavages over populism or pluralism, state versus markets in the economic sphere, and authoritarianism versus libertarianism in the moral and social sphere. (Norris, 2020: 700)

More specifically, focusing on the typology under study, the emergence and development of left-wing populist forces within the post-crisis European scenario must be understood in light of the broader radical transformation of the traditional party system and the gradual defeat of socialist and social-democratic forces in many European countries.

The crisis of the traditional party system is a phenomenon now acknowledged in academic literature. Since the 1980s, there has been a gradual "unfreezing" of traditional social cleavages—particularly the capital-labor divide, which underpins the left-right axis—along with the emergence of new cleavages and the birth of different political actors and organizational models. As pointed out in the interesting work *Cleavage theory meets Europe's crises: Lipset, Rokkan and the transnational cleavage* by Libstet Hooghe and Gary Marks (2018), traditional parties have shown very limited flexibility in adapting to the new cleavages that arose during the economic and social crisis. This rigidity provided space and opportunities for the rise of new political forces capable of responding to these emerging divisions:

> Cleavage theory implies that party system change is discontinuous. It is characterized by periods of relative stability as political parties jostle to gain support and by periods of abrupt change when new political parties rise up in response to a critical juncture. The evidence presented here suggests that the crises of the past decade may be such a critical juncture for Europe. In a Downsian model of issue competition, one would expect existing political parties to respond to voter preferences by supplying appropriate policies. However, as cleavage theory predicts, the positional flexibility of political parties is heavily constrained. Change has come not because mainstream parties have shifted in response to voter preferences, but because voters have turned to parties with distinctive profiles on the new cleavage. (Hooghe, Marks, 2018)

The gradual dissolution of the "mass party" led to the emergence of new party models[3] and, at the same time, a transition from "total" to "limited and partial" participation in political life, reflecting the gradual weakening of collective identities. These transformations were accompanied by a radical critique of the "party-form" itself and the triumph of the "establishment/anti-establishment" (or "us/them", "people/caste") dichotomy characteristic of the populist appeal. According to the three-tiered theory developed by Katz and Mair, this progressive distancing from the grassroots has led to the decline of the "party in society" and the consequent strengthening of the "party in institutions" (Katz, Mair, 1995: 5–28).

This decline has clearly not spared Europe's main social democratic forces; indeed, they have suffered some of the greatest losses. Historian Donald Sassoon

---

[3] Such as, for example, as the "catch-all party" (Kirchheimer, 1966), the "professional-electoral party" (Panebianco, 1988), the cartel party (Katz and Mair, 1995), the "neoliberal populist party" (Della Porta et al., 2017).

analyzes this phenomenon in *Morbid Symptoms: An Anatomy of a World in Crisis* (Sassoon, 2020): according to him, social democratic forces lost their constituents' trust because they openly alienated their base by pursuing austerity policies, welfare and social rights cuts, and embracing a "pro-market" stance. As a result, social democrats increasingly appeared hostile to the fundamental needs of those who had once been their key stakeholders:

> So, traditional social democracy, the kind of social democracy that had prevailed and had been in government at times for long periods, was largely defeated not only in Europe but almost everywhere. None of this should be surprising. Most democratic parties embraced a policy of austerity, allowed wages to stagnate, inequality to grow, and privatized public services to an extent unimaginable thirty years ago. This had a twofold negative effect: it made the neoliberals think that they were right to say that the private sector could run these services better, and when it became clear that services had not particularly improved, the social democrats could not even say 'we told you so'. They allowed inequality to increase and dared not tax the wealthy beneficiaries. (Sassoon, 2020)

Against this backdrop, some parties have developed in recent years that display innovative features in their organization, political practice, and communication: the so-called "movement parties". As Della Porta, Fernández, Kouki, and Mosca have recently argued:

> Literature on political parties described, in fact, a double trend with initially an opening to civil society, with the development of the ideological mass party, but then a continuous approaching of the parties to state institutions and distancing from society. It is in this evolving context that movement parties emerge, as innovators but also in part adapting to existing institutional structures. (Della Porta et al, 2017:12–13)

In a movement party, the two opposing organizational ideal types—the political party and the social movement—coexist within the same organization, as if the line between these two categories has become increasingly blurred, allowing these two worlds to contaminate each other. According to political scientist Kitschelt:

> Movement parties are coalitions of political activists who emanate from social movements and try to apply the organization and strategic practice of social movements in the arena of party competition. (Kitschelt, 2006:280)

Among the main movement parties, we can mention Podemos in Spain, *La France Insoumise* in France, SYRIZA in Greece, *Bloco de Esquerda* in Portugal, and *Mo-*

mentum[4] in Britain. The *Movimento 5 Stelle*, although it has an organizational structure similar to a "movement party", has been considered by several authors a case apart, since it operates outside the traditional "right-left" axis and employs a type of *populism* termed *valence populism*[5].

---

4 Movement that coordinated Jeremy Corbyn's election campaign within Labour.
5 To distinguish it from "right-wing populism" and "left-wing populism", to which the above-mentioned forces belong. See: (Zulianello, 2020).

Chapter 2 – Placing Podemos in Context: A Populist party in power

2.1 A complicated debate

> There has been a dominant strain in the populism literature that argues that populist parties are destined for success in opposition and failure in government. (Mudde, 2013:15)

If the debate about the nature of populisms, as illustrated, has expanded tremendously in recent years, the same cannot be said about the phenomenon of populisms in government. Attention to the relationship between populism and power in contemporary European democratic systems has emerged only recently. Between the late 1990s and early 2000s, prominent scholars often dismissed populist forces as peripheral to power or as a phenomenon unlikely to influence institutional structures. To cite a few examples, in one of her most famous articles on populism, Margaret Canovan (1999: 12) argues that if a populist force were to enter government, "its inability to deliver on its promises would be exposed". Similarly, in their volume *Democracies and the Populist Challenge*, political scientists Yves Mény and Yves Surel contend that "populist parties are by their very nature neither enduring nor sustainable governing parties. Their fate is either to be integrated into the *mainstream*, only to disappear, or to remain permanently in opposition" (2002: 18). This negative view is also found in the work of Herbert Kitschelt and Anthony J. McGann, who, in *The Radical Right in Western Europe*, state:

> simple political dichotomies dividing the world into friend and foe may help populist parties to rally support as long as they are in opposition ... It is questionable, however, whether the negative electoral coalition brought together by populist parties will stick together once these parties have to act on policy problems as governing parties. (Kitschelt, McGann, 1995: 201)

In essence, these analyses share the notion that populism tends to be episodic. They see populist forces as a momentary phenomenon triggered by crises that create strong but fleeting support for parties of "rupture", a consensus that is ultimately short-lived and bound to be absorbed again by traditional forces. Coexisting with this notion is the idea that populist forces are ontologically incapable of governing. Once in power, they would allegedly face insurmountable issues arising from their lack of experience in policy-making, shortage of qualified personnel, and pressure to moderate their radical agenda and presentation (Heinisch, 2003: 101).

https://doi.org/10.1515/9783111591537-006

In recent years, however, a new strand of scholarship has emerged to challenge the early 21st-century claims about the transience and episodic nature of populist parties. One of the key texts in this regard is *Populists in Power* by Daniele Albertazzi and Duncan McDonnell, which Cas Mudde described[1] as "the first truly empirical systematic study on the subject, shattering many old comforting 'truths' and raising uncomfortable new questions". Published in 2015, the book investigates the relationship between populism and power through the empirical analysis of three European right-wing populist forces: *Lega Nord* and *Popolo delle Libertà* in Italy, and *Schweizerische Volkspartei* in Switzerland. The authors aim to show that:

> Our findings run contrary to much of the received wisdom. Populist parties are neither inevitably episodic nor are they destined to fail in government. As regards their being episodic, while some populist parties may be flash parties or personal parties, others have established structures and grassroots organizations that have remained in place for decades and are built to last beyond the current leadership. Moreover, when in government, populists have shown that they can introduce key policies in line with their core ideologies and election promises. Crucially, they have also shown that they can survive the experience of government, despite the inevitable compromises and disappointments this brings, without losing the support of either the voters or those within their parties. (Albertazzi, McDonnell, 2015: 3)

The development of populist forces on the European political scene, especially in Western Europe, is relatively recent. Early phenomena began emerging in the 1970s, for example, *Anders Lange's Party* in Norway (precursor of the *Fremskrittspartiet*, Norwegian Progress Party) or *Mogens Glistrup's Progress Party* in Denmark (forerunner of the *Dansk Folkeparti*, Danish People's Party). From 1972 onward, there was the well-known *Front National* in France and, from the 1980s, several regionalist parties such as the *Lega Lombarda* in Italy, which would later give birth to the *Lega Nord* (LN). It is not irrelevant that all these early appearances can be traced back to exclusionary, regionalist/nationalist versions of populism affiliated with right-wing populism. As Albertazzi and McDonnell note, some of these forces, such as the LN (merged into the *Lega per Salvini Premier* as of 2019) and the *Front National* (*Rassemblement National* in 2018), continue to hold significant positions in their respective national contexts, disproving the "episodic hypothesis".

At the mainstream level, the rise of populist forces has permeated debates on democratic representation in the EU. These forces gained prominence in Europe following electoral rounds in the aftermath of the 2008 economic and social crisis.

---

1 In preface to Albertazzi, McDonnell, 2015.

Thus, "populism" entered the public narrative, becoming a widespread term beyond academic analysis. In this context, populism has frequently been portrayed
negatively as a "widespread threat", a "ghost roaming Europe", and "disturbing
and oppressive" (Diamanti, 2014). The results of the 2014 European elections
showed increased support for mainly right-wing populist and Eurosceptic forces
throughout the continent, leading in many major EU countries to significant upheavals in the traditional political-electoral balance:

> If sociological researches have long been talking about the end of 'permissive consent' to Eu-
> rope in many public opinions, the scenario that opens up with the results obtained by the
> array of anti-European parties is of a definitive strengthening of what is called, more recent-
> ly, 'constringent dissent' [...] meaning an increasingly critical, and in this case ideologically
> determined, politicization of the integration process, which will most likely place the Euro-
> pean Union in a dilemma in terms of policies. (Caiani, 2014)

2.2 The effects on populisms in government

Populisms not only are not irrelevant in the European party system, but they are
also capable of governing and have become key actors in government, very often
indispensable if not inevitable partners for the so-called traditional parties. The
shift from outsider to insider, from the periphery to the center of the political system, obviously brings difficulties and dilemmas—the same ones that, as mentioned, have led some scholars to dismiss outright the possibility of effective populist governance.

Albertazzi and McDonnell (2015) in this regard outline *the main challenges*
and *uncertainties* facing populist subjects before entering government. First, the
two authors point out that the main dilemma for most[2] populist forces entering
government involves weighing costs and benefits: is it better to maintain purity
and consistency toward their electorate by remaining in external opposition, at
the risk of becoming irrelevant, or to serve as the voice of the outsiders by joining
a governing coalition with other actors, risking the loss of coherence, credibility,
and radicality? Second, once in government, other dilemmas arise, particularly organizational ones, which all political forces—even non-populist ones (McDonnell,
Newell, 2011: 450)—face when they first participate in power:

---

2 As the authors rightly point out, one cannot generalize here because there are also populist
parties (among those analyzed, Albertazzi and McDonnell identify Forza Italia, for example) that
are specifically created as government parties, or otherwise aim at government.

> In particular, it requires (a) the leadership finding sufficiently competent people to take up
> ministerial roles and (b) the party in office learning quickly how to communicate and justify
> its actions to the party on the ground especially when faced with the inevitable compromises
> of coalition government. (Albertazzi, McDonnell, 2015:8)

Afterwards Albertazzi and McDonnell describe the main effects of populisms *in government*, dismantling "the myth that populists are something incompatible with government" through observing and analyzing the cited case studies. First, their analysis of electoral flows shows a broad range of possible electoral outcomes at every level. The possibility of a decline in electoral support is only one of many potential scenarios for populist forces, and being part of a government is only one possible cause of lost support. The issue of the electoral consequences of populist participation in government is much debated. Here we refer to considerations put forth in a recent contribution by Pedro Riera and Marco Pastor (2022), which do not align with those just mentioned. In their study, *Cordons sanitaires or tainted coalitions. The electoral consequences of populist participation in government*, the two Spanish political scientists analyze coalition strategies as a key determinant of populists' success or failure in power. Once populist parties have become part of the institutional system of "advanced democracies", according to these authors, traditional parties face the following dilemma:

> Either to create a cordon sanitaire (CS) by agreeing not to ally with populists, or to invite
> them into government by forming a tainted coalition (TC). The creation of a CS can prevent
> populists from entering government in the short-term, but it also risks galvanizing their sup-
> port in subsequent elections. In contrast, the formation of a TC may stifle the subsequent
> electoral success of populists in exchange for giving them some institutional power in the
> short run. (Riera, Pastor, 2022)

As reported in the article, there is no consensus among scholars regarding the use of CS or TC tactics. While some analyses find no evidence that building a cordon sanitaire around populist forces can halt their progress (Akkerman, Rooduijn, 2015), others argue that inviting them into a governing coalition can grant legitimacy and high visibility (Levitsky, Ziblatt, 2018), and contribute to the polarization of the political arena, pushing voters toward more extreme ideological positions (Bischof, Wagner, 2019). The results of Riera and Pastor's analysis show that inviting populist forces into a governing coalition as junior partners is far more effective than creating a cordon sanitaire. This is because if traditional forces can reach a parliamentary agreement and maintain control of the cabinet, this strategy more effectively curbs populist growth, especially among radical forces. In fact, their analysis indicates that participation in government, particularly in a majority government, imposes greater costs on populist partners. Such forces "lose four percentage points more in subsequent elections after entering coalition governments as junior partners than non-populist parties, suggesting that populists suffer higher costs of government" (Riera, Pastor, 2022).

The second issue addressed in Albertazzi and McDonnell's volume concerns the effectiveness of implemented policies. Part of the literature, including mainly Peter Mair (2009), identifies a behavioral dichotomy: on the one hand, traditional parties govern responsibly, being willing to compromise, make tough decisions, and accept external pressures from domestic, supranational, and global bodies; on the other hand, populist parties, as Cas Mudde also believes (Mudde, 2004), seek to be 'responsive' to popular demands:

> On the rare occasions when they [i.e. populists] do govern, they sometimes have severe problems in squaring their original emphasis on representation and their original role as voice of the people with the constraints imposed by governing and by compromising with coalition partners. Moreover, though not the same as the anti-system parties identified by Sartori […], they share with those parties a tendency toward 'semi-responsible' or 'irresponsible' opposition as well as toward a 'politics of outbidding'. (Mair, 2009: 17)

Albertazzi and McDonnell consider this dichotomy simplistic, stemming from myths and beliefs about populists generated not only by academic literature but also by the media and the common sense prevailing in European public opinion. They believe populists can effectively combine accountability with reactive approaches. They can act as sophisticated political operators who, "keeping one foot in and one foot out of government", behave responsibly in various ways without abandoning their radicalism or the priority actions identified by their base. Riera and Pastor (2022) similarly argue that populisms in government retain greater appeal if they combine a combative and a moderate approach, although the key to greater success lies in radicalism and an anti-establishment spirit.

The third issue concerns the quality of the party's staff and representatives in office. Some of the literature suggests that populist forces are inherently unable to govern due to the poor institutional qualities and skills of their representatives. This would directly affect the structure of government and the types of policies these forces must manage, leading them to occupy weaker ministries than other coalition partners (Mudde, 2007: 280). In this regard, for example, political scientist Reinard Heinisch, commenting on the Austrian FPÖ (*Freiheitliche Partei Österreichs*) coalition's institutional failure in the early 2000s, argued:

> Populist parties may be severely hampered also by their complete orientation toward the leader, their lack of institutional development and, given the limited talent pool, their lack of qualified personnel. (Heinisch, 2003:101)

Albertazzi and McDonnell counter that such statements depend solely on evaluating the first governmental experiences of populist parties that emerged in the late 1990s. Instead, their analyzed cases show that populist parties can hold important government positions without difficulty in finding high-level representatives capable of managing the issues they care about most (for instance, immigration or federalism for the Northern League, with regard to which—especially in its latest governmental experiences—the party has been a key player in the Italian institutional system). The final issue involves the assessment that members of populist political forces make after participating in government. Through semi-structured interviews submitted to members and representatives of the populist forces studied, Albertazzi and McDonnell conclude that "it is not inevitable [as most of the literature believes] that populist leaders will fail to 'take' their members with them when they are in power" (Albertazzi, McDonnell, 2015: 175).

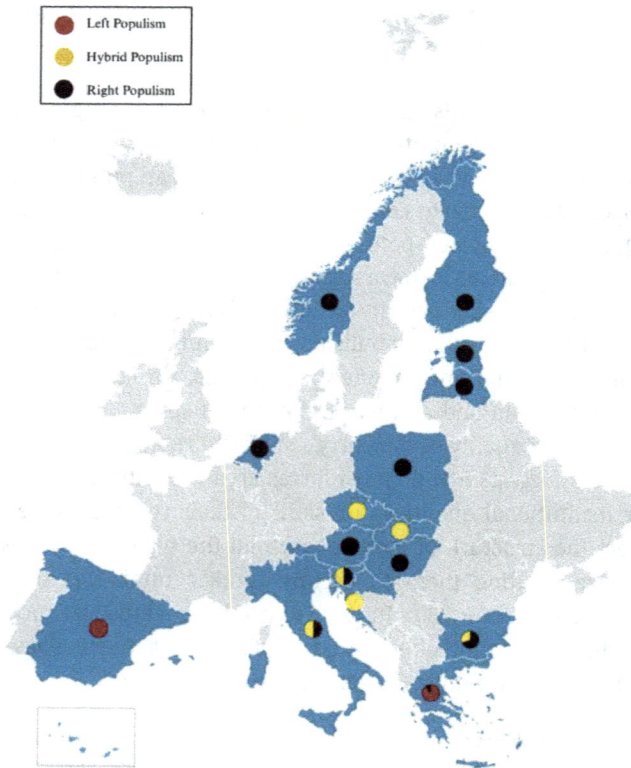

Fig. 2: Populisms in government in the European Union. Source: author's elaboration.

When we examine this phenomenon firsthand, it becomes clear that political forces that have used populist strategies are now fully integrated into the European political and institutional system. Once seen as outsider actors who "threatened" democratic order, they have since become key players in the political landscape of many countries, in some cases successfully attracting and shifting substantial segments of the electorate. Populism is far from a fleeting episode in contemporary European political history, as Fig. 2 illustrates. The map highlights all EU countries that have had populist forces in their national governments—either governing alone or as part of coalitions, whether as majority or junior partners. Additionally, it categorizes the different types of populism that have been in power in each country. In cases where multiple forms of populism coexisted, the map visually represents the relative weight of each type within the governing coalitions.

As can be seen, the countries that have had populist governments form a kind of "belt" around the central states of the EU, starting from the south (Spain, Italy, Greece), passing through some countries in the Balkan peninsula (Croatia, Romania, Slovenia), then Austria, and reaching the Eastern European states (Hungary, Poland, Czech Republic, Slovakia, Estonia, Lithuania), Northern Europe (Norway and Finland) and finally Netherlands. This geopolitical location is no coincidence: many of these countries have been the most affected by the various crises that have occurred in the EU (economic and social crises, migrant crisis, etc.), which have given rise to Eurosceptic sentiments and particular distrust toward European institutions. Consequently, as Swen Hutter and Edgar Grande describe in their *Politicizing Europe in the national electoral arena*, European issues have become highly politicized in recent decades, even within the national electoral arena. Moreover, these are the same countries in which the political responses of traditional parties have also been delegitimized, in many cases causing real crises for liberal and social democratic forces. Most government positions have been occupied by right-wing populist forces, especially in Scandinavia and Eastern Europe. Eastern European countries have a notable presence of hybrid populist forces, particularly in places like the Czech Republic, Slovakia, and the Balkans.

Italy is the only state in Southern Europe that has not yet had a left-wing populist force in government, instead presenting right-wing populist forces (*Lega, Fratelli D'Italia*, and *Forza Italia* are partners in the current Giorgia Meloni-led government) as well as the peculiarity of the *Movimento 5 Stelle*, a hybrid populist force that has governed both with La Lega and with Italy's largest social-democratic force, the *Partito Democratico* (PD).

Spain and Greece are the only two countries in Europe that have formed governments with leftist populist forces (in Greece SYRIZA was a majority partner), and this is also no coincidence: both were among the countries hardest hit by the 2008 social and economic crisis and the subsequent austerity policies that led to the mobilization of the largest mass anti-austerity social movements in Europe.

As Hooghe and Marks (2018) point out, this geographic distribution largely depends on how the political-institutional environment absorbed traditional cleavages, thus largely shaping the response of political forces to new cleavages, especially the immigration and transnational cleavages that definitively emerged in the wake of the economic and social crisis:

> Because the expression of a cleavage depends on the institutionalization of prior conflicts, a uniform response to a new cleavage is unusual. The one exception in Lipset and Rokkan's (1967) account is the class cleavage, rooted in the industrial revolution, which produced major socialist different expressions across Europe. This reflects the contrasting effects and differential timing of the economic and migration crisis in the different regions of Europe which play out in the context of prior cleavages. The outcome, in broad terms, is that the South has seen radical left parties mobilize on the class divide. In most former communist countries, by contrast, the radical right has catalyzed the transnational cleavage, and the radical left is weak or absent. Most Central and Northern countries have seen radical right parties mobilize on the transnational cleavage, with green parties at the opposite pole and radical left parties pressing distributional issues. (Hooghe, Marks, 2018)

2.3 The case study: Podemos and the Spanish context

One of the most exemplary and interesting cases of left-wing populism in government is undoubtedly Podemos: from January 2020 until November 2023, the Spanish party was part of the Sánchez II government, the first coalition government in the Spanish context. During this time, the party's former secretary and founder, Pablo Iglesias, served as Vice-President of the Council and Minister of Social Policies until March 2021.

Podemos was launched as a top-down initiative led by a "mediatic leading figure" like Pablo Iglesias and a group of intellectuals mostly from the Faculty of Political Science and Sociology at the Complutense University of Madrid. The project was introduced on January 17, 2014, at the *Teatro del Barrio* in Madrid. *Izquierda Anticapitalista*, an organization of the Spanish communist left (of the Trotskyist tradition) that was not electorally significant but had a fair territorial organization, also attended the event.

Podemos was born and developed during a particularly delicate period in the Spanish context, during which two crises, independent yet closely related, took place: a political system crisis and an economic crisis that together created what has been called a "critical neoliberal conjuncture" (Della Porta et al., 2017: 46). A "lethal mix" that disrupted the Spanish political system, which had remained almost stable since the end of Francisco Franco's regime and the promulgation of the 1978 Spanish Constitution. That constitution established a parliamentary monarchy with a central role for the executive and parties, favoring a two-party system, political alternation, a decentralized state structure, and an electoral system ensuring stability and governing capacity. In fact, Spain's electoral system is a very fair proportional system with markedly two-party effects: it divides the country into many districts and calculates proportional representation within each district, without inter-district communication. In effect, this creates an implicit threshold (in addition to a formal 3% threshold) that benefits the largest political forces and does not penalize regional parties, since their broad support is concentrated in specific districts.

For more than forty years, the Spanish state showed very little political fragmentation and an electorate that was moderate, with limited party identity and participation, since electoral competition always occurred between the two main forces, the *Partido Socialista Obrero Español* (PSOE), in the social-democratic tradition, and the Partido Popular (PP), in the conservative-liberal tradition. Precisely for this reason, the emergence of other political entities gaining increasing support, such as Podemos, but also *Ciudadanos* (Cs) and later *Vox*, represented a real storm in the Spanish political system:

> With the emergence of Podemos (and *Ciudadanos* at the national level), the Spanish party system experienced a deep transformation as the crisis of bipartisanship in Spain led to a more fragmented political scenario and to political polarization, with a deep transformation of the party system. (Della Porta et al., 2017: 46)

When Podemos burst onto the scene, the party system was already experiencing a profound legitimacy crisis, with declining trust—and therefore support—for the two main parties, as evident from election results. The PSOE registered the most pronounced effects of this representation crisis, generating high voting volatility and political and electoral space for new parties. The PSOE's crisis is part of the broader decline of center-left and social democratic forces in Europe, especially in countries hardest hit by the 2008–2010 economic crisis and the resulting austerity policies.

For example, the PSOE's support fell from 43.8% in 2008 to 22% in 2015. A key reason for the crisis of social democratic forces was their inability to implement classic center-left policies. In Spain, for instance, the first austerity measures (identified by governments and international institutions at various levels as the "remedy" for the global crisis) were implemented by Zapatero's Socialist government from 2010 onwards—later than in other European countries. These measures included pension reforms, wage cuts, deteriorating working conditions for public employees, and a Labor Reform that "would have brought precarity, increased labor market instability and facilitated layoffs; likewise, it would have weakened workers' collective bargaining power" (Della Porta et al., 2017: 46).

Podemos found fertile ground for its project due to its *anti-austerity* stance and its break with the traditional party system, especially from the political and media dominance of the PSOE within the center-left. As Iglesias himself said, "the space of social democracy was empty and we occupied it" (Iglesias, 2015).

However, the fertile ground had been "prepared" by another event that shook Spanish political and social life. On May 15, 2011, a large national demonstration was organized by the digital platform *Democracia Real ¡Ya!* ("Real Democracy Now!") against the social and economic effects of the crisis and in response to the aforementioned austerity policies. This demonstration, convened under the slogan "We are not goods in the hands of politicians and banks", mobilized tens of thousands of people nationwide, giving rise to the *Indignados* movement, also known as 15M (*Quince M[ayo]*). The *Indignados* started from the premise that existing anti-establishment organizations and structures had failed to capture social discontent. This required a "new kind" of movement, new in terms of its organizational and communicative forms. "Participation" is central to 15M, becoming its programmatic element rather than merely a means to achieve goals. It is articulated both as an external demand and as an internal practice, serving as a tool and example of alternative political practice. From this perspective, it is essential to note a peculiar feature: the movement breaks with the traditional (and often stereotyped) leftist rhetoric of "demanding more state", while still defending and reclaiming the welfare state, seeking free spaces for self-management and recovering central issues of collective and individual life. The "public" is no longer just the state but a space of collective construction and co-creation.

I talked about these issues with some of the interviewees, and Pablo P. Gianfornina—an activist in the Andalusian 15M movement and the current leader of the *Anticapitalistas* party in Sevilla—confirmed what was stated in this paragraph.:

> 15M was not leftist: there was a 'political dispute'. Here in Andalusia, for example, the PSOE was governing with IU [*Izquierda Unida*]. So, they could not capitalize this movement. Who did capitalize for the left? The alternative left, but the movement was not leftist *per se*, it was against the parties and against the unions. It was not a right-wing movement, but it was a critical movement. (Ganfornina, 2022, Interview 5)[3]

---

3 Details of the interviews recalled in Tab.1. See the Introduction.

This analysis is shared by Clara Serra, an active member of Podemos since its inception, a former Podemos deputy in the Madrid Assembly, and later a member of *Más Madrid.* According to her:

> 15M is not a 'liquid' leftist thing, it is not something that is recognized as leftist. There is a rejection of the political class, there is a rejection of the existing parties. In this sense there is also an anti-political impulse that we would consider dangerous and reactionary. Therefore, at this moment there is a total conviction that questioning in a leftist language, as we speak in our own militant spaces and in our own political parties, is not feasible. That is to say, it deactivates this power and there is a populist reflection of this moment, as a populist moment of disruption, as an event that changes politics, but that requires, in this sense, a strategy of great amplitude and a certain distance from the language and discourse that the classical Spanish left has made. (Serra, 2024 Interview 10)

Through the 15M mobilization, a profound critique of traditional representative democracy emerged, proposing a model between radical democracy (self-management) and participatory democracy ("institutions that open political agendas"). Rather than moving along the left-right axis, the movement operated on the high-low axis. The idea of self-management is based on "cooperation", "mutual aid", and "spaces of shared knowledge". These words and practices rapidly spread among thousands of people in the squares and streets of the Spanish state. The "how" of participation becomes the defining axis, rather than the "what" to achieve. The participatory management of the famous *acampadas* itself became a laboratory and a metaphor for 15M's political proposal. The demand for self-management was not about creating new decision-making spaces or seeking representation in institutions; participation did not mean choosing who makes decisions, but rather "doing things".

> Participation was widespread. People debated whether to debate. There was a vote on whether to vote. Those who spoke were obviously the most politically framed. But a lot of 'normal' people started to get involved in politics. The middle-class dream was broken. It wasn't a middle-class movement, but it was very cross-cutting and representative. And it was not just a week of demonstrations and encampments. It was a moment that opened up to the neighborhoods: the housing rights movement, the health care movement, the Green Tide for education. The protagonists of the issues were mainly us, the university students from the middle class, but also people from the working-class sectors. The material motivation was the crisis. (Ganfornina, 2022, Interview 5)

To summarize, three main features of the *Indignados* movement's participatory method can be identified: the first is the assembly as the key structure of political participation. During *acampadas* and more organized phases, the assemblies were accompanied by a complex structure of committees and working groups that always referred back to the assembly's decisions. "How" to make decisions, that is, the decision-making method, is the second defining aspect of 15M. "We don't vote, we come to consensus" is a phrase found in many documents, statements, and activist interviews. The "consensus" method served as a tool and a distinguishing element of the 15M movement, expressing not only the desire to make decisions "by collective agreement" but also rejection of the decision-making methods typical of representative and parliamentary democracy. The last defining element is the "network" organizational structure: real and virtual networks built an organizational model seen as connections of nodes without central leadership or delegated functions and offices. This reaffirms the movement's inclusive nature, aiming to involve a cross-sectional majority—characteristics that set it apart from other social movements:

> I think there was an idealization of what happened in the squares, in the occupations, in the demonstrations. That was the radiating core, of course, but the most important was what happened in the bars, in the workplaces. People started talking about politics. In this country, people were not talking about politics. People were going to vote but they were not talking about politics. This is what was different. This is what Podemos is based on. Pablo Iglesias said the same things in 2011 as he did in 2014, but he didn't have the same impact as he did in 2014. There were three years in which people began to make politics about the right to housing, to their children's schools, to health care, to work. But the construction was more complex than a 'simple' class struggle. The 15M created a remobilization that went very well. The media defined Podemos as the party of 15M, and the moment Podemos crushed, also 15M crushed. It was a false correlation. You should not idealize. The 15M was something completely different, something that was not given. (Ganfornina, 2022, Interview 5)

In fact, Podemos is not the direct evolution of the *Indignados'* 15M movement. Precisely because of its characteristics and participatory practices, the movement never intended to merge into a political entity aimed at electoral representation. On the contrary, this premise gave birth to the new movement party: according to its leaders' analyses (Iglesias 2015b; Errejón 2015), Podemos is conceived as the political expression of a social movement that rejected political representation. From this movement, it draws its *relato* (political discourse) and imagery. In its first phase, Podemos acquired a sense of detachment from the traditional left's political identity, adopting the slogans, symbolic styles, and demands of 15M. It also partially integrated its activists and its participatory, organizational, and communicative practices. This is because "Podemos identifies very well that the existing left, for example *Izquierda Unida* and other political parties, do not know how to capture the political power of 15M" (Serra, 2024). The early founders of Podemos came from a militant leftist background but recognized in 15M the opportunity to build a "transformative" organization starting precisely from detaching themselves from the discourse and structures of the traditional left:

Our analysis is that this is obviously an artificial operation, in the sense that 15M is essentially nothing as far as we make it. We said that the political potential that exists could have many different possibilities. And so those of us who come from the organized and militant left want to put that political potential at the service of a transformative left project. What I mean by that is: the fact that it is very popular and very transversal, of course, means that there are policemen in the 15M demonstrations, but nevertheless we find an initial popular-elite discourse, for example, that targets not only the political caste, but also the economic caste. (Serra, 2024, Interview 10)

This is the phase that Juan-Carlos Monedero, Professor of Political Science at the Complutense University of Madrid and one of the founders and ideologues of Podemos, calls the "destituent phase":

When we achieved the first electoral result in the 2014 European elections, when we went back to the Reina Sofia Square, where we had put a stage if things went well, and it was full of people, when we went up, people greeted us shouting '*Que si, que si, que si nos rap-resentan*' [Yes, yes, they represent us], when the cry of 15M was '*Que no, Que no, Que no nos rapresentan*' [No, no, they don't represent us]. People greeted us with a cry of 'problem solving', it was not a cry of 'reinventing everything'. It was a cry of regeneration, not generation. [...]. What was the proposal with respect to party functioning? There was no proposal than regenerative. There is one very important thing: we must distinguish between the de-constituent moment and the constituent moment. The de-constituent moment is the moment of illusion, of generosity, it is the Laclausian moment, of the empty signifier, of 'us versus them', of chains of equivalence. There is a saying that 'happiness lies in the eve'. The constituent moment is the stage of the child who has to start learning about reality and that if he takes the game away from another child, the child will beat him up. It is the least exciting stage, unless you keep the enemy alive, a clear tension that positions you. (Monedero, 2022, Interview 8)

Podemos is not the evolution of 15M, of course, but it would not have been conceived without 15M. Although social movements do not generally have a long-term perspective, they have allowed traditional political actors to weaken in the political system, creating space for new actors challenging both the economic and political crises. The 15M was, in short, a "window of opportunity" ("*ventana de oportunidad*", as it is defined in many interviews we conducted) for the political system. Moreover, the themes and content of 15M produced new anti-austerity identities—a transversal and orphan dissent that Podemos easily intercepted, making it the core of the populist hypothesis:

In particular, the wave of protests allowed for the emergence of a new cleavage based on an anti-establishment dividing line, pitting 'new politics' against 'old politics'. This distinction was also used to transcend the classical left-right cleavage ('we are neither leftist nor rightist' was stated during the 15M protest), building a new one based on the distinction between those below (the ordinary people affected by the crisis) and those above. Podemos aimed

> at reorganizing the political map around this new axis and promoting a new double and
> mixed cleavage: 'the caste' against 'the people' and 'the old' against 'the new' politics.
> (Della Porta et al., 2017: 49)

Unlike social movements, however, Podemos entered the political arena with a
clear "will to win" (Monedero, 2018) and to enter government, opposing 15M's
anti-election spirit. As Monedero himself admits in his book *La izquierda que
asaltò l'algoritmo* ("The Left that Assaulted the Algorithm"):

> the electoral vector, with a large media presence of its leaders, with an executive power with
> many prerogatives (granted in the Party Congress where there was a discussion with those
> who demanded a more participatory and 'less Leninist' model), was designed to win elec-
> tions and allowed the Executive (composed of eleven people) to make a large number of de-
> cisions, including that of changing the order [sic!] of the lists elected compulsorily through a
> primary process. (Monedero 2018: 139)

This brief *excursus* on the genetic phase of Podemos is particularly important for
a better understanding of the features considered in analyzing its time in government, which is the focus of this analysis. The origin and birth of political subjects
and parties is one of the fundamental themes of Political Science, crucial to understanding not only their current evolutionary state but also the shifting historical
and institutional contexts to which they have contributed in a reciprocal process
of influence. As political scientist Angelo Panebianco states in *Party Models. Organization and Power in Political Parties:*

> But a party, any party—like any organization—is not a laboratory object that can be isolated
> from its context, nor is it a mechanism that, once inserted and set in motion, always contin-
> ues to function in the same way. [...] The organizational characteristics of any party, in ad-
> dition to other factors, depend on its history, on how the organization came into being and
> was consolidated. Indeed, the manner in which a party was formed, the main features of its
> genesis, are capable of exerting a weight on its organizational characters even decades later.
> (Panebianco 1982: 103–104)

2.3.1 From opposition to government

While the following chapters will delve into the detailed causes and consequences,
it is important to first provide a concise overview the chronicle of events that
marked the rise and conclusion of Podemos's initial experience in government.
On January 13, 2020, the Sánchez II government, the first coalition government
in the history of Spanish democracy, officially began. An "anomalous" government not only in its composition but also in its genesis. On January 7, 2020, the
government received the confidence of the Spanish State Parliament: 167 deputies

voted in favor of Premier Pedro Sánchez Castejòn, thus sanctioning the historic alliance between the *Partido Socialista Obrero Español* and *Unidas Podemos* (UP), which includes, among others, Podemos and *Izquierda Unida*. The opponents numbered 165, represented mainly by the *Partido Popular, Ciudadanos*, the center-right party that failed to meet expectations, and especially *Vox*, the example of Spanish right-wing populism, which emerged as the third party with 52 seats. As required by current legislation, the executive, although it did not reach the 176 votes needed for an absolute majority in Parliament, managed to gain confidence thanks to the abstention of the Catalan independents of *Esquerra Republicana de Catalunya* (ERC) and the Basque independents of *Euskal Herria Bildu* (EHB). In short, a coalition government without an absolute majority, built thanks to an alliance considered impossible just a few months earlier.

The November 2019 elections were in fact only the latest act in a complicated and ambivalent political relationship between the PSOE and UP. When the first Sánchez government was formed on June 2, 2018, following the no-confidence vote in Parliament against the Rajoi II government[4], the internal debate within Podemos led, at that stage, to the acceptance of a subordinate role and external support for the new government. These were months of radical upheaval within the movement and from outside: as will be analyzed in detail in Chapter 4, on January 17, 2019, the clash between the two founders, Iglesias and Errejón, finally exploded, leading to a genuine split and the birth of a new political movement, *Màs Paìs*, led by Errejón himself. At the same time, the Catalan crisis severely impacted Podemos's image, which gradually managed to halt its free fall in the polls only through continuous efforts to confront the single-party socialist government on social and economic issues (Caruso, Campolongo 2021).

In February 2019, the PSOE does not have the numbers in parliament to approve the financial measure (due to the defection of ERC, determined to show toughness toward the government's position on the Catalan crisis). As a result, Sánchez is forced to resign and call new elections. Podemos's political objective in these elections is clear: from both a communicative and programmatic perspective, they aim to appear as the only force capable of forming a government that opposes the elites and the growing far-right factions (*Vox* enters the field, in fact, with poll numbers comparable to Podemos's early days) by bringing issues of redistribution, feminism, environmentalism, and the fight against privilege to the executive level. The political goal was to build a coalition government with the PSOE: the tone of the campaign is never harsh, and Sánchez himself never re-

---

4 Thanks to the so-called "motion of censure": in the Spanish system, a majority vote of the parliament on an alternative government hypothesis is required to challenge a government.

jects the possibility of such an option. In the April 2019 elections, UP obtains 14.32% of the vote, losing 6.83% from the 2016 elections, but still managing to surpass poll predictions.

However, the PSOE seems to want to propose the same arrangement to UP again—a one-party government with outside support—while also negotiating with *Ciudadanos*, a center-right force that, in a notable feat, earns 15.86% of the vote. After months of fruitless negotiations, during which UP proposes various formulas for a coalition government (in which they are underrepresented in the number and quality of ministries), Sánchez remains closed to any reasonable proposal from UP, and they are thus forced to return to the polls.

The second electoral campaign in a few months is centered on mutual accusations over the failed negotiations, and UP, determined to achieve a coalition government, is forced to play on unfamiliar ground, with Pablo Iglesias adopting a somewhat effective "moderate and constitutional" stance (Caruso and Campolongo, 2021), again advocating a progressive coalition government. In the November 2019 elections, UP continues its downward trend, receiving 12.9% of the vote. The victor is *Vox*, which in just four months gains 4.8 percentage points, reaching 15.09% of the vote and becoming the third largest party. For these reasons, amid such a complex scenario, in less than 48 hours something previously impossible occurs: a legislative coalition agreement is reached, including Iglesias as Vice President, four ministries for UP, and a highly advanced program. At the same time, the PSOE softens its stance on the Catalan issue, opening up dialogue and abandoning centralist tones. Entering the government marks a historic step in Podemos's life, which—as repeatedly stated publicly and in the interviews we collected—has had the explicit strategic goal of joining the country's government from the very start.

2.3.2 The end of Podemos's experience in government

On 29 May 2023, the day after the autonomous and local elections in which the PP (as well as the centre-right) clearly outperformed the ruling party in terms of preferences, the government, at the behest of its president, who had accepted defeat, convened an extraordinary council of ministers to resign and call new elections. This was the end of Podemos's experience in government.

As we will analyze in detail in the following chapters[5], after the resignation of Pablo Iglesias as Vice-President the designation of Yolanda Díaz as a future candi-

---

5 In particular, see Chapter III.

date for the presidency of the government has changed the very nature of the UP coalition. Indeed, Yolanda Díaz, the Vice President and Minister of Labor, inaugurated in March 2022 a new political platform named *Sumar* that was "an initiative to promote the listening process that will take Yolanda Díaz around the country. It is about listening, dialogue, and building together a citizens' project for the next decade. In short, *Sumar* wants to organize hope so that the new country can make its way" (Sumar, 2022). *Sumar* appeared as an entirely new project built around the figure of Yolanda Díaz that aimed to overcome, or at least change, the very nature of UP. This was particularly evident at the first public event, called *proceso de escucha*, which took place on July 8 in the *Matadero* cultural space in Madrid. Nothing in that event referred to UP or its internal components: the logo, graphics, and aesthetics of the event were completely new. There were no flags or banners of IU (Yolanda Díaz's home organization), nor of UP, let alone Podemos. But even more noticeably, none of the Podemos leadership was present at the event, not even informally. In fact, Podemos will not announce that it will join the *Sumar* coalition until 10 June 2023, a few weeks before the national parliamentary elections in July. We will discuss in detail the electoral results in Chapter 3, but here we are interested in highlighting the practical and political implications.

On 24 October 2023 *Sumar* announced an investiture agreement with the PSOE to allow the birth of a new coalition government. On 11 November 2023, online voting among Podemos members ends. With 86.10 % (47,675) of the valid votes, Podemos decides to support the investiture of the Sánchez government. Subsequently, on 16 November, voting confidence for Pedro Sánchez as head of government, *Sumar* coalition became part of its third executive, expressing five ministers, none of whom were from Podemos.

Podemos, which remained outside the government, announced the passage of its five deputies to the mixed group in the Congress of Deputies to open a new stage in the search for political and parliamentary autonomy, with the votes of its seats and its own voice. Thus, officially ends the participation of Podemos in the governmental moment and begins a more complicated phase of external support of the Sánchez III government in which Yolanda Díaz, leader of the coalition with which Podemos had run for office, in the position of vice-president of the council. A new challenge for the *morada* formation, in a newly changed political space.

Chapter 3 – Podemos's Electoral Trajectory

3.1 The populist flow

As has been analyzed in other contexts (allow me to refer to Giardiello, 2022), if the 2014 European elections saw the entry and sudden support for many populist forces in the European context, the results of the 2019 European Parliament elections created a new, more fragmented, and more polarized political environment (Dennison, Leonard, et al., 2019), mirroring the political-institutional change in individual national contexts. Contrary to predictions, however, there has not been a clear victory for populisms of all types, but rather an increase in support for green and liberal forces. Populisms, however, have not disappeared, nor have they become a marginal phenomenon lacking electoral and institutional continuity; rather, they have been a reality in the European political system, especially regarding the far-right populist forces that made significant gains and advances in the 2024 European elections.

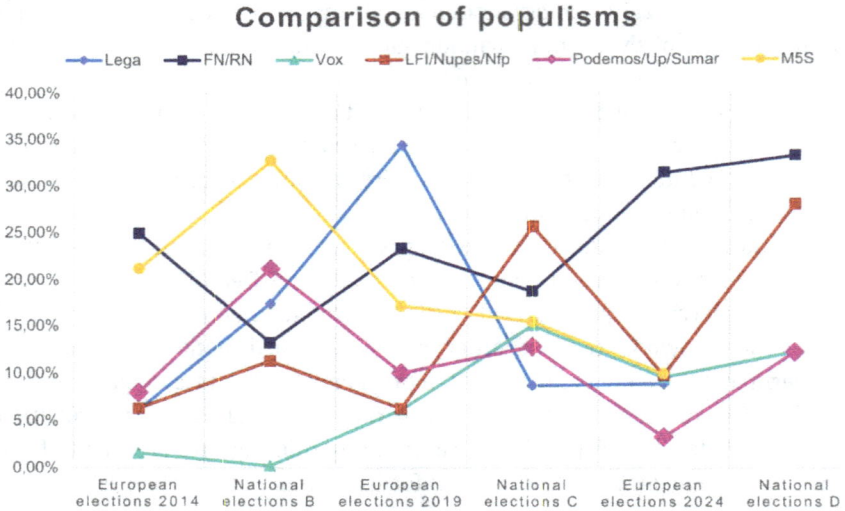

Fig. 3: The populist flow in Spain, Italy, France (2013-2023). Source: election results compiled by the author.

For these reasons, it is interesting to compare the "populist flux" that has occurred in three of the major European countries that have most prominently and enduringly displayed this phenomenon: Spain, France, and Italy.

https://doi.org/10.1515/9783111591537-007

Fig. 3 summarizes the electoral trends of six populist forces: for Italy, the *Movimento 5 Stelle* (M5S, an example of hybrid populism) and the *Lega* (an example of right-wing populism); for France, *La France Insoumise* (FI, an example of left-wing populism) and the *Front National* (now *Rassemblement National* -RN-, an example of right-wing populism); and finally, for Spain, Podemos (an example of left-wing populism) and *Vox* (an example of right-wing populism). In the graph, we compare the results obtained in the national election rounds (for Italy, the 2013, 2018, and 2022 legislative elections, considering results for the renewal of the Chamber of Deputies; for France, the 2012, 2017, 2022, and 2024 legislative elections, reporting the results of the first round; for Spain, the 2016, 2019, and 2023 legislative elections) with the results of the European elections of 2014, 2019, and 2024 in each national context.

Starting with Italy, Fig. 3 shows how the electoral performance of the two analyzed political forces diverges between the two levels considered. Specifically, the M5S displays a remarkable fluctuation in its support: in the context of national elections, it has experienced sudden growth since the beginning of the considered period, establishing itself as the leading force in both the 2013 elections—with the surprising 25.56 % in the Chamber of Deputies—and the 2018 elections—32.68 % of the vote. These results are not replicated at the European level in elections held just one year after the national contests. From 2013 to 2014, the M5S drops from 25.56 % to 21.15 %, losing 2,884,044 votes—a decline only partially attributable to lower turnout—while from 2018 to 2019 it goes from 32.68 % to 17.07 %, losing 6,162,977 votes. In the most recent national elections, the M5S records its worst electoral result within the selected period and among national general elections, obtaining 15.43 % of support or 4,285,894 absolute votes, losing 6,659,517 compared to 2018. The party's electoral decline continued in the 2024 European elections, where it received less than 10 % of the vote. The *Lega*, on the other hand, initially showed a decidedly upward *trend*, especially at the European level, where turnout is generally lower than in national contests. From 2013 to 2014, the League gains 297,663 votes, and from the 2018 general elections to the 2019 European elections —during which it participates in the Conte I government in alliance with M5S—it gains 3,476,521 votes, becoming Italy's leading force in the 2019 European elections. This positive trend abruptly ends in the 2022 general elections, where obtains 8.77 %, losing 3,238,512 votes compared to 2018, and is confirmed by the result of the last European elections. Obviously, the growth in support for Giorgia Meloni's *Fratelli d'Italia* has severely reduced the political and electoral space available to the *Lega.*

Regarding the French case, a similar phenomenon can be observed: the electoral performances of the two types of populism analyzed are antithetical. While left-wing populism garners more support during national elections, right-wing populism achieves its best results at the European level. Fig. 3 shows the fluctuating trend of the forces led by Jean-Luc Mélenchon, the French leftist leader who ran for the presidency in 2012 with the *Front de Gauche* coalition and later founded *La France Insoumise* in 2016. The latter experienced a significant loss of votes between national and European levels: although it obtained 7,059,951 votes in 2017, just two years later it loses 5,631,403 votes in the European elections. However, this *trend* is reversed in the last legislative elections, when Jean-Luc Mélenchon and *La France Insoumise* lead the *Nouvelle Union populaire écologique et sociale* (NUPES), an alliance uniting major French left forces, including the *Parti Socialiste*. The result is extremely positive: in the first round, NUPES obtains 25.66%, only 21,359 votes fewer than *Ensemble*, President Emmanuel Macron's coalition, making it the second largest force in the country. The same occurred in the 2024 European elections, where FI ran alone, and in the subsequent legislative elections, in which the left-wing populist force led the *Nouveau Front populaire* (NFP), obtaining 8,995,226 votes in the first round and winning the largest number of seats (178) in the National Assembly in the second round.

Marine Le Pen's *Rassemblement National (Front National* until 2018) confirms the trend for right-wing populisms: in both the 2014 and 2019 European elections, it outperforms its previous national election results, emerging each time as the leading French political force. Notably, RN achieves stable results at both European and national levels: 13.60% and 13.20% in the 2013 and 2017 legislative elections respectively, and 24.90% and 23.30% in the 2014 and 2019 European elections. There is a slight increase in the legislative elections of 2022, where Marine Le Pen's force obtains 18.68%, gaining 1,258,172 absolute votes compared to the previous legislative elections. In 2024, it achieves its highest results ever, with 28.75% in the June 2024 European elections and becoming the top political force in percentage terms (33.21% in the first round) in the subsequent legislative elections a month later.

We will provide a more detailed analysis of the Spanish case in the following paragraph, but even from these initial observations and from Fig. 3, some clear considerations arise. Right-wing populism generally performs better at the European level than at the national level: right-wing Euroscepticism thus attracts more support in second-tier elections than EU criticism originating from left-wing populism. The sovereigntist "us" vs. "them" based on ethnic and center-periphery divides (Treib, 2021) performs better at the European level than the people vs. elite approach grounded in the class and capital/labor cleavages typical of left-wing populisms and, in some cases, hybrid populisms.

Since 2014, European right-wing populism has shown a general upward trend in both first- and second-tier elections, while left-wing populism, after a sudden rise, is currently experiencing a phase of relative decline. The 2024 European elections did not substantially alter the majority supporting the von der Leyen-led European Commission. The "feared" advance of the radical right did not challenge the so-called "Ursula majority", but it cannot be denied that there was indeed an advance. Eurosceptic and far-right forces have steadily grown over the past quarter century: from around 8% (of seats) in the European Parliament in 1999 to 26% in the new Euro chamber (Ipsos, 2024).This trend has been offset not only (and not so much) by the decline of the European People's Party—down from 37% to 26% of seats over the same period—but also by that of the Socialist Group, which in 1994 led with 35% of the seats and today holds just over half that (around 19%).

3.2 The electoral flow of populist forces in Spain

For these reasons, it is important to closely examine the electoral flow of Podemos and *Vox* from their inception to the most recent general elections, in order to better understand the context in which Spain's first coalition government emerged and the subsequent developments. In this regard, it is necessary to combine two levels of analysis, the national level and the European elections. Fig. 4 summarizes the electoral flow of the two populist forces in the Spanish context. We have chosen to include all electoral moments that, although close in time and showing similar trends, are still independent measurements of each other.

The 2014 European elections were Podemos's first electoral appearance and marked the movement's consecration. Podemos presented itself five months after its founding as an outsider in the Spanish political system, featuring Pablo Iglesias's face in its symbol. All polls predicted a certain failure, giving Podemos between 2 and 3 percent. However, in the May 25, 2014 elections, it obtained 1,253,837 votes, 7.98 percent, becoming the fourth largest force in Spain and electing five MEPs, including Iglesias himself. In the following months, Podemos became central in the public narrative of Spanish politics, to the point that some editorials in major newspapers called 2014 *"El año de Podemos"* (Pérez Rojo, 2014; Machuca, 2015). The increased public and media attention corresponded to a rise in the polls: a few days before the 2015 national general elections, the Metroscopia Institute estimated Podemos at 27.7%, marking the first time since 1981 that a party other than the PP or PSOE ranked among the top two in voting intentions. March 2015 marked the start of a long electoral cycle leading up to the December general elections.

In the December 2015 national elections, Podemos refused to form a national coalition with either *Izquierda Unida* or other related political forces, choosing to run alone under its own symbol. The only exceptions were in Catalonia, Galicia,

SPAIN

	European elections 2014	National elections 2015	National elections 2016	European elections 2019	National elections 2019 (April)	National elections 2019 (November)	National elections 2023	European elections 2024
Podemos	7,98%	20,68%	21,15%	10,07%	14,32%	12,84%	12,33%	3,30%
Vox	1,57%	0,23%	0,20%	6,20%	10,26%	15,09%	12,38%	9,63%

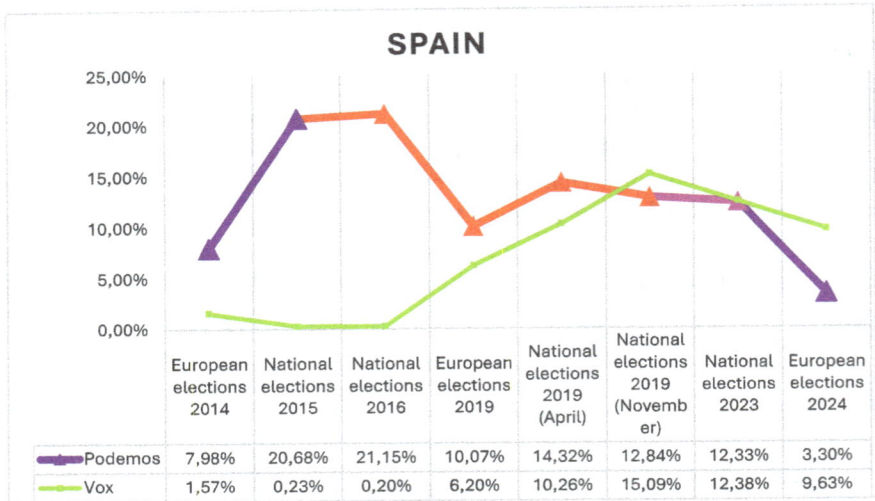

Fig. 4: Podemos/UP/Sumar and Vox electoral flow (2014-2019). Source: election results processed by the author.

and the Valencian Community, where it ran in coalition with local forces such as *En Comú Podem, En Marea,* and *Compromís-Podemos-És el Moment,* respectively.

This national strategy stemmed from an internal debate in which two different models emerged: on one hand, the line closer to Íñigo Errejón—applied in this election—viewed the party as an electoral machine, essentially a communicative party, a "Lacausian" magnet for social demands, but not inclined to form alliances with other political forces (especially the "traditional left") or to serve as a direct expression of collectives and social movements. On the other hand, there was the Iglesias-Monedero line, integrating this model with a vision of a party more present on the ground and in political and social dynamics, linked to mobilizations, social struggles, active involvement of the militant base, and the possibility of alliances with other political actors. In the 2015 general elections, Podemos and its local coalitions obtained 5,211,711 votes, 20.66 percent, just 300,000 votes behind the PSOE, confirming the positive trend of European left-wing populism at the time and establishing itself as the third force in Spain's political scenario.

The results of these elections, which shook Spain's two-party system, showed that forming a new government was impossible. Attempts began on January 22, 2016, with Pablo Iglesias's proposal for a PSOE-Podemos coalition government in which Pedro Sánchez would be president and Iglesias vice president. Both government partners would share ministries equally, giving one to IU. Sánchez decided not to accept, as the PSOE aimed to form a moderate government with *Ciudadanos*, the other outsider force in this election.

Elections were called again for June 2016, and this time the Iglesias-Monedero line prevailed: Podemos formed a national alliance with *Izquierda Unida* and *Equo*, the green party. However, the results fell short of polls and expectations: the new *Unidos Podemos*[1] took 21.15%, 5,087,538 votes, which was 1.1 million fewer than the sum of Podemos and IU in the December elections, failing to surpass the PSOE as hoped. Still, the outcome was historic for Spain, representing the highest result for a coalition outside PP and PSOE. The election, which saw a clear gain for the PP, led to Mariano Rajoy's second government. After these elections, as seen in Fig. 4, UP's election results began a downward trend. In addition to the April and November 2019 national elections mentioned in previous chapters, UP also saw a considerable drop in support in the May 2019 European elections, losing 2,355,713 votes compared to the 2016 national elections and obtaining 2,258,857 votes (10.07%), a result lower than the combined tally of Podemos and IU in the 2014 European elections.

Vox, on the other hand, exemplifies the upward trend of right-wing populism in the post-2008 European economic crisis. The 2014 European elections were its first electoral launch (1.57 percent), followed by two unsuccessful national election rounds, relegating the force to a marginal role in Spanish politics.

Following the 2017 Barcelona bombing, claimed by ISIS, and the broader spread of right-wing populist buzzwords in Europe, the xenophobic and Islamophobic content disseminated by *Vox* began to resonate with the Spanish electorate. As a result, Vox's support jumped to 10.26% in the April 2019 national elections (+2,640,910 in three years) and just seven months later reached 15.09% (+968,887 compared to April 2019), surpassing UP to become the third largest political force in the country. In the May 2019 European elections, *Vox* lost 1,294,408 votes compared to the national elections held only two months earlier.

In the 2023 national elections, Spain once again proved to be the exception among European democracies. Contrary to predictions and trends, the far-right lost ground, social-democratic forces held steady, and the pro-independence forces of the autonomous regions remained the balancing factor. After the July 24 elections, the situation resembled an almost symmetrical "bloc" system in a newly discovered bipolar—though not bipartisan—context: the "progressive" bloc led by the PSOE (31.7%) and Yolanda Díaz's *Sumar* coalition (12%), and the conservative bloc led by the PP (33%) and its "extreme" arm *Vox* (12.39%),

---

1 It will later change its name to *Unidas Podemos*.

along with the bloc of independence forces, which, though fragmented, again served as the deciding factor.

The PP emerged as the leading party, regaining significant support in just two years after one of its worst results ever (20.99 %). It recovered 47 seats (and over 3 million votes), partly through a clear strategy of using *Vox* as an "attack dog", employing populist agitation on issues dear to the right-wing electorate. At the same time, the PP appeared responsible, creating a climate of anxiety, fear, and disillusionment. Thus, it became the largest party but lacked the numbers to form a government, even though all polls (which proved wrong) predicted a clear lead over the PSOE. In fact, the Socialists gained nearly a million votes compared to the previous elections and increased their congressional seats by two.

Vox clearly lost out. Far-right populism did not make a breakthrough; instead, it lost 33 seats compared to 2019, reducing what was feared as a new threat to European democracy. The "right wing" of the PP was absorbed by its likely governing ally, and extreme nationalist positions did not pay off except in a few central areas of the country.

Sumar, the "new" left-wing coalition, failed to impress. In the 2023 national elections, Podemos participated in the *Sumar* Coalition, joining just a few weeks earlier (June 10, 2023). As we have seen, *Sumar* is a new personal political entity formed a year before the elections by Yolanda Díaz, taking over the electoral space previously occupied by UP and incorporating IU, *Verdes Equo*, and *Más País*. *Sumar*'s numbers fell short of expectations raised at its inception, a true rupture in the Spanish left. *Sumar* lost more than 700,000 votes and seven deputies compared to the 2019 results of the parties now united within it, considering that, as mentioned, more political forces were included compared to *Unidas Podemos*.

Finally, the 2024 European elections were the first national elections since 2015 in which Podemos ran alone, outside of a coalition. On December 5, 2023, Podemos left the coalition and the parliamentary group, joining the mixed group in strong criticism of the formation of the Sánchez III government. The new executive did not include any Podemos members and also vetoed the reappointment of Irene Montero as Minister of Equality, a crucial objective for Podemos.

Compared to the 2014 European elections (the only ones in which it participated alone, but when the Errejón component was still present), Podemos lost 675,830 votes, still electing two MEPs, Irene Montero and Isa Serra, who were key campaign figures. *Sumar* also did poorly, with 4.67 % of the vote, well below expectations.

Vox obtained 9.63 %, a better result than in previous European elections, but on a negative trend compared to the national elections. This is not only due to the climate of renewed bipolarity described earlier, but also to the sudden emergence

of a new political force, *Se Acabò la Fiesta*, with a clearly populist, far-right character. This electoral list, the brainchild of a very active social media influencer, Al-
vise Pérez, secured 803,545 votes in just two months (4.58%, +1.28% compared to
Podemos), in the most classic style of populist blitzkrieg. Has a new populist actor
emerged on the Spanish scene, or is it just a fleeting media phenomenon? It is too
early to say, but this again creates a new scenario worth analyzing.

3.3 Political Barometer

So far, we have analyzed the official electoral results—at both the European and
national levels—that led to the formation of the coalition government and those
that took place after its end. In this section, we will examine the electoral trends
that developed during Podemos' "governmental moment." In other words, we
want to observe the effects that left-wing populism in government had both on
the political system and on the force under study.

   This section analyzes changes in voting intentions in Spain from February
2020—the first month of the Sánchez II government—to May 2023—the last
month of the Sánchez II government—and the latest available data for UP, since
from June 2023 *Sumar* begins to be pooled as a unique coalition. Among the different survey institutes that describe Spanish political opinion trends, I decided to
use the estimated votes (as a percentage of valid votes) prepared by the *Centro
de Investigaciones Sociológicas* (CIS), the public research institute based in Madrid. Using these data, a series was constructed and is represented in Fig. 5.

   The first survey after the government's swearing-in on January 13, 2020,
shows growth of the coalition compared to the November 2019 election results:
the survey shows UP at 13.60% (+0.74%) and PSOE at 30.90% (+2.9%). This growth
visibly stops in the following months, leading to a slow loss of percentage points
for UP until March 2021, when it reaches 9.60%.

   That month, Pablo Iglesias resigns from the vice presidency of the Council,
causing a slight rise for the movement until June 2021 when it polls at 13%,
again above the levels achieved in the 2019 general elections. The coalition's support fluctuates between a high of 13.7% (December 2021) and a low of 9.6% (March
2021 and May 2022), with a rising trend in July 2022 that puts it ahead of *Vox*. In
January 2023, UP reaches 14.20% approval, its highest percentage in the survey period. This figure symbolizes voters' approval of government action and policies
implemented by the coalition's representative ministries in late 2022. From then
on, the polls begin to fall, especially from April 2023 when *Sumar* starts to be pol-
led by the CIS. In May 2023, the month the Sánchez II government ends, UP's last
recorded poll shows a drop to 6.10%. From the day of the swearing-in to Sánchez's

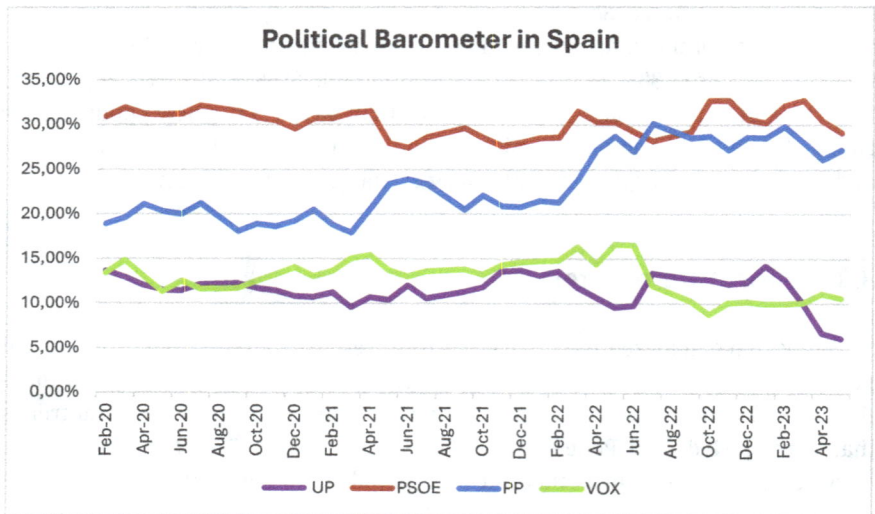

Fig. 5: Political barometer in Spain. Source: estimated CIS votes (in % of valid votes) prepared by the author.

resignation, trust in *Unidas Podemos* averages 11.86 %, one percentage point lower than the percentage of votes obtained in the last national election.

The PSOE initially shows an increase in support during the government's first months, peaking in July 2020. After that, it follows a generally negative trend until the symbolic overtaking by the PP in July 2022. From October 2022, there is a sudden increase in polls, finally settling at 32.70 % in March 2023. In the month of Sánchez's resignation, PSOE's support falls to 29.10 %. The average support during the Sánchez II government (30.24 %) is higher than the votes obtained in the November 2019 election.

The PP, the largest opposition party in Parliament, shows two opposite trends. In the early stage (February 2020-March 2021), it experiences a sharp decline, reaching a low of 17.90 %. After that, it undergoes a sudden growth, gaining momentum in the last year until it surpasses the PSOE in July-September 2022, peaking at 30.10 % in July 2022. In the latest surveys of May 2023, it stands at 27.20 %, two percentage points below the PSOE. However, the average support over the considered period (23.72 %) is higher than its November 2019 result.

Also in the opposition, *Vox* initially shows slow but steady growth until it emerges in October 2020 as the third force in the Spanish political scenario, peaking in May 2022 (16.5 %, compared to UP's 9.6 %). However, *Vox*'s fortunes seem to mirror those of the PP, confirming the electorate's contiguity between the two forces. As the PP gains support, *Vox* enters a negative trend (highlighted by many other polls), particularly evident from July 2022 when it is overtaken by UP and records, in October 2022, its worst detection (8.80 %). In May 2023, it stands at 10.6 %, slightly up from October 2022. Over the period, its average (12.91 %) is lower than the result obtained in the 2019 national election.

3.4 Autonomous community elections

	2015	2016	2017	2018	2019	2020	2021	2022	2023	2024
Parlamento de Andalucía	592.133			585.949				281.619		
Cortes de Aragón	137.325				54.252				26.923	
Junta General del Principado de Asturias	102.178				58.674				21.052	
Parlamento de las Islas Baleares	62.868				41.824				19.980	
Parlamento de Canarias	132.159				78.532				34.531	
Parlamento de Cantabria	28.272				10.224				13.395	
Asamblea de Ceuta	Did not run				505				186	
Cortes de Castilla-La Mancha	106.565				74.777				44.462	
Cortes de Castilla y León	163.637				68.869			62.138		
Asamblea de Extremadura	50.873				44.309				36.836	
Asamblea de Madrid	591.697				181.231		263.871		161.032	
Asamblea de Melilla	829				408				285	
Asamblea Regional de Murcia	83.133				36.486				32.173	
Parlamento de Navarra	45.848				16.518				20.095	
Parlamento de La Rioja	18.298				10.844				8.457	
Cortes Valencianas	279.596				215.392				88.152	
Parlamento de Cataluña	367.613		326.360				195.345			Did not run

Continued

	2015	2016	2017	2018	2019	2020	2021	2022	2023	2024
Parlamento de Galicia		271.418				51.360				4.420
Parlamento Vasco		157.334				72.113				23.888

Tab. 2: Podemos election results (in the different coalitions) in the autonomous communities. Source: Election results compiled by the author.

The third and final level to be analyzed concerns the autonomous communities, a territorial electoral field that holds particular value in the Spanish context, not only because of the nature of the institutions but also due to the identity and symbolic importance they carry. These elections were, among other things, the first territorial electoral challenge since the 2015 European elections. In fact, since March 2015, an intense electoral cycle had been underway before the December general elections analyzed in the previous paragraphs: elections in Andalucía in March, autonomous and local elections (in numerous municipalities, including major Spanish cities) in May, and elections in Catalunya in September. The clash between the two tactical models also emerged in these circumstances, leading Podemos to adopt differentiated approaches. In the initial phase, in most autonomous communities, Podemos chose to present itself independently, while in the cities it tried to build "popular unity coalitions", i. e., unified lists involving Podemos and other political movements (notably *Equo*, an ecological party, and *Izquierda Unida*) and organizations expressing social movements descending from 15M.

The second model, according to many analysts, proved more effective than the first (Caruso, Campolongo, 2021). As shown in Tab. 2, in the elections to the autonomous communities, the results ranged from 8.13 % in Extremadura to 21.15 % in Aragón, with a national average of about 13–14 %. In most cases, Podemos thus emerged as the third force. By contrast, "popular unity coalitions" managed to win in many key contexts, obtaining, for example, 25 % in Barcelona, 31 % in the city of Madrid, 30 % in La Coruña, 28 % in Cádiz, and 25 % in Zaragoza. This wave of victories led to the spread of the so-called "municipalist governments" (Martínez, Wissink, 2021).

However, the autonomous elections in Catalunya in 2017 and Andalucía in 2018 foreshadowed what would occur in all the other autonomous communities voting in 2019. Most notably, in Andalucía Podemos ran in coalition as *Unidas Podemos*, achieving a result far below the sum of the votes the individual forces had obtained separately in 2015, losing 6,184 votes compared to its previous result.

The year 2019 saw multiple local and autonomous community elections. But it was also the year of the internal clash within Podemos and the formal departure of Íñigo Errejón's faction. The conflict—which will be analyzed in detail in Chapter 4—began precisely regarding how to participate in the local elections in Madrid. Following the battle over the party statutes, Errejón secured his influence primarily in the Madrid community, working on the formation of lists as the party's unified candidate, in constant tension with Podemos's national leadership. On January 17—the anniversary of Podemos's launch—Errejón announced that he wanted to join outgoing mayor Manuela Carmena, a proposal unacceptable to Podemos due to strong tensions created throughout her administration. Even more so, because Errejón aimed to present the list without the Podemos symbol, but under a new acronym, *Más Madrid*, to move beyond the UP alliance in a more "transversal" direction and place himself at the head of the new Madrid component. For the Podemos leadership, the decision was inevitable: since he acted without the party membership's knowledge, which had already voted on candidate lists in the primaries, Errejón was removed from the organization. This effectively caused a split among militants and cadres in Madrid, divided between those following the national line and those joining the *Más Madrid* list. As a result, Podemos decided not to present any other candidate, effectively abstaining from the Madrid municipal elections.

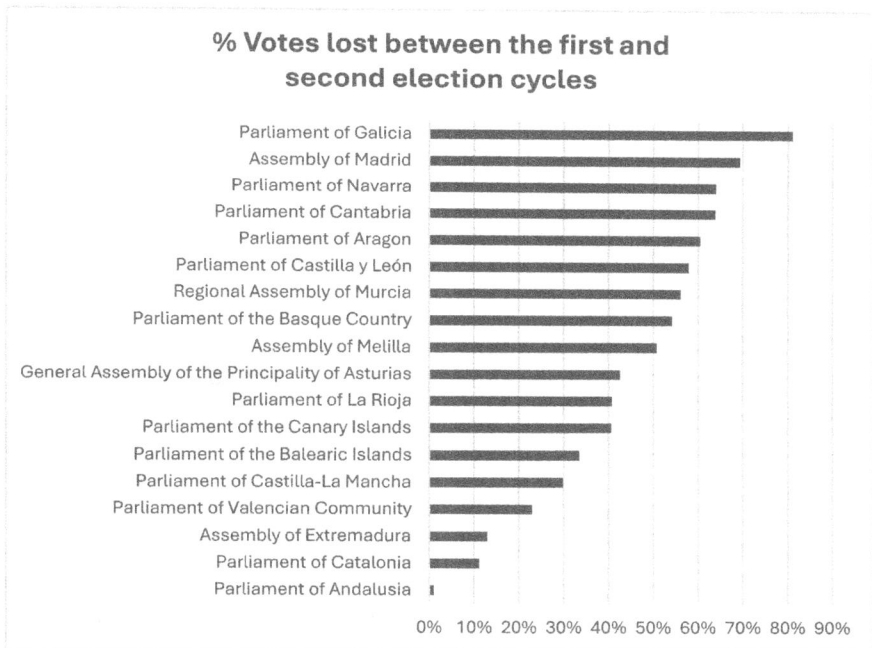

Fig. 6: Votes lost between the first and second election cycles. Source: election results compiled by the author.

For these reasons, the result obtained by Podemos with the *Unidas Podemos* coalition in the Madrid Community elections is one of the most severe: the coalition loses 69 % of the votes (equal to 410,466 absolute votes) compared to the result obtained by Podemos alone in 2015. As shown in Tab. 2 and Fig. 6, the trend is downward in all subsequent rounds of autonomous community elections. The most negative results appear in Galicia (-81 %), where voting took place in May 2020, along with *País Vasco* (-54 %), the first elections after the birth of the coalition government; in Navarra (-64 %) and in Cantabria (-64 %). In these cases as well, the internal earthquake within the organization partly explains the outcome. The split not only had serious internal repercussions, but also damaged the party's public image, creating an impression of conflict, internal fractures, and unreliability, leading to greater disillusionment among both militants and voters. In addition, in territories where parallel platforms to Podemos had been created—mainly representing local movements, organizations, and committees with their own autonomous community identity (such as *Las Mareas* in Galicia)—these decided to run independently in the new elections, refusing to join the UP coalition.

Also in Navarra and Cantabria, as in the previous electoral round, Podemos presents itself separately from IU. This tactic, adopted partly due to friction between the two local political forces, does not pay off, causing a 64 % drop in votes for the Podemos list. The only *trend* that appears positive in Tab. 2 is the election in the autonomous city of Ceuta, a territory in which Podemos had not previously run. Of the seven major cities where Podemos had governed since 2015, only Kichi González (from the *Anticapitalistas* area) in Cádiz and Ada Colau in Barcelona were confirmed.

The third territorial electoral round in which Podemos participated since its inception took place in 2021 in Catalunya and the Community of Madrid, and in 2022 in Andalucía. In the Catalan elections, Podemos ran with the *En Comú Podem* coalition, which included *Catalunya en Comú*, Ada Colau's force, and *Esquerra Unida Catalunya* (IU). Once again, the coalition's performance declined compared to its predecessors, losing 40 % of its vote compared to the 2017 elections.

The Andalusian elections were, perhaps, an even greater failure. Due to internal clashes within the UP coalition, Podemos failed to present its own list and placed some of its candidates within the *Por Andalucía* list (including former deputy and civil guard Juan Antonio Delgado[2]), led by *Izquierda Unida* representative Inmaculada Nieto and also including *Más Madrid*. The list obtained 7.68 % of the vote, winning only five seats in the entire Andalusian Parliament.

The 2021 Madrid community elections represent a turning point in Podemos' "governmental moment" and in its overall history. On March 15, 2021, in a video recorded in the office of the Vice-Presidency of the Council and addressed to Podemos militants and voters, Pablo Iglesias announced his resignation from the government post and his candidacy for the presidency of the Community of Ma-

---

2 See Interview 7.

drid. Reflecting on the first year of government, Iglesias stated, "We have achieved things that had never been achieved in politics [...]. It is the first time in more than 80 years that the transformative left in this country has participated in a state government[3]." According to Iglesias, the Spanish state was undergoing a period of major transition. If Podemos had succeeded in breaking the two-party system, it now had to serve as a defender of democracy and a barrier against the "Trumpist" right that was threatening the state's institutions, starting with *Vox*'s support for the PP in the Community of Madrid: "In politics you have to have courage, courage to fight the necessary battles and also to know when to make way for new leadership" (Iglesias, 2021). On March 15, 2021, in that same video, Iglesias argued that "May 4 will decide whether the ultra-right carries out its assault on Madrid or whether we stop them. We must prevent these thugs, these criminals, who claim dictatorship [...], from holding power in Madrid, with all that it means for the rest of the country" (Iglesias, 2021). That is why he proposed himself as a candidate for the presidency of the Community of Madrid, because "a militant has to be where he is most useful at all times", and he called for the left, starting with *Más Madrid*, despite "the scars", to form a single candidacy to confront "the great danger of the ultra-right".

This is the moment when, unexpectedly, Iglesias pointed to Yolanda Díaz, Minister of Labor and a member of *Izquierda Unida*, as the future leader of *Unidas Podemos*, as Vice President and candidate for the coalition in the next national elections. Iglesias argued that his political and media persona had become an obstacle to a future government led by *Unidas Podemos* and the development of new central figures, especially women, within the coalition. This, he maintained, resulted mainly from the relentless attacks he and his family had faced from the Spanish media system.

Indeed, strong media attacks have relentlessly targeted Iglesias's public and private persona, waging a war fueled by scoops about his personal life and fake news regarding his political and international dealings, nearly all of which were disproven by the courts. Despite this, these attacks have significantly eroded public opinion's judgment of the leader, thereby affecting Podemos's overall image.

A representation of this is Fig. 7, which graphically summarizes the series of results of polls from February 2019 to May 2021 (the month of his resignation from party and institutional offices) regarding the assessment of Pablo Iglesias. As can be seen, he is extremely well-known, with the sole exception of the countervailing

---

3 See *Pablo Iglesias deja el Gobierno para enfrentarse a Ayuso en las elecciones de la Comunidad de Madrid*, El Mundo, https://www.youtube.com/watch?v=xuKU8XQ0rjw

Knowledge and rating scale (1–10) of political leaders: Pablo Iglesias

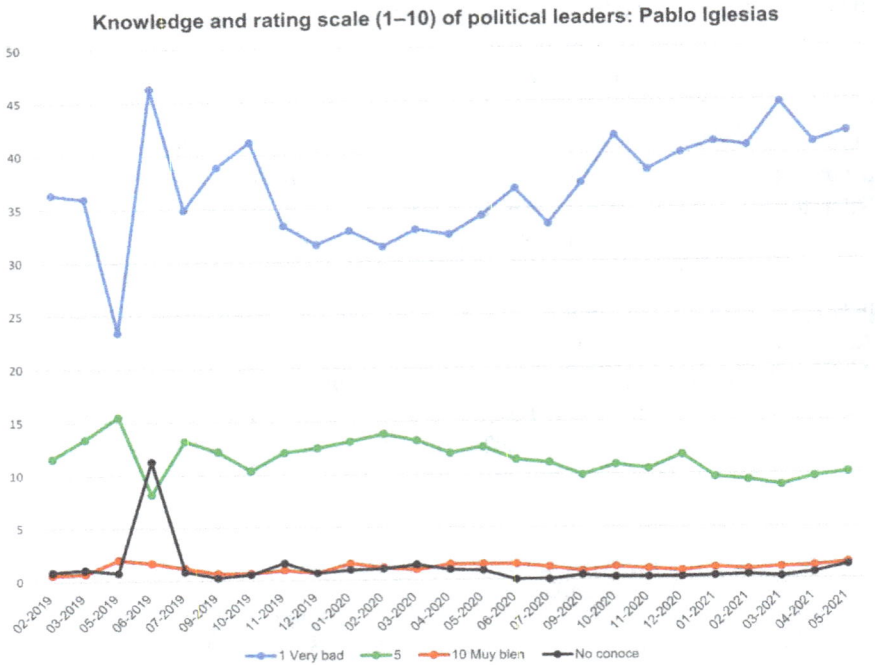

Fig. 7: Knowledge and rating scale (1-10) of political leaders: Pablo Iglesias (February 2019-May 2021). Source: CIS.

data from June 2019. Before his entry into government, his popularity showed fluctuating ratings, registering a sudden and steady improvement in October 2019 (corresponding to the second national elections of that year) and one of the lowest levels of negative ratings (31.4%) in February 2020, one month after the start of the coalition government. Afterwards, however, his approval ratings steadily declined, reaching the highest level of negative ratings in March 2021, the month in which he resigned from the vice presidency.

The results of the Madrid elections did not meet expectations: *Más Madrid*, running independently, obtains a historic 16.99% and establishes itself as the second force after the PP, which wins the elections. The *Unidas Podemos* coalition, while recovering 46% of the vote compared to the 2019 elections, obtains 7.24%. On May 4, 2021, in a press conference speech, Pablo Iglesias declares, "We have failed. We have been very far from achieving a sufficient majority to put together a decent government"[4]. Iglesias once again describes himself as a "scapegoat" who mobilizes "the darkest and most contrary affections of democracy". This does not help the UP's project of "consolidating its institutional weight". That is why on that date he decided to give up all his offices and leave politics, "understood as party and institutional politics". After seven years, the most iconic leadership of all European leftist populism ended.

In the last two electoral rounds of 2023 and 2024, Podemos returned to its initial strategy, participating in most of the elections with its own symbol (or that of the local branch linked to it) or, in some cases, with IU. In all cases, there is a deterioration compared to the results of the previous electoral rounds, except in the Autonomous Communities of Navarra and Cantabria, where the coalition with IU saw an increase in support.

3.5 A non-positive trend

It has long been claimed that there is generally a negative incumbency effect on parties in power in established parliamentary democracies (Rose, Mackie, 1983). More recent studies confirm that these negative incumbencies have persisted. Some authors (Wolfgang, Müller, Strøm, 2008) assert that government participation is electorally "more liability than an asset" for parties in Western European coalitions. It has been demonstrated that "governing parties considered collectively tend to lose votes" and "their average losses have become progressively larger over the last few decades" (Narud, Valen, 2008). Thus, government participation tends to cost votes in Western Europe.

The literature on the effects of incumbency on radical parties is scarce (Albertazzi, McDonnell, 2015). Of more relevance for this purpose is the study by Akkerman and de Lange (2017), which examines the effects of government participation on seven radical right parties:

> If one considers their post-incumbency electoral results, on average radical right parties appear to have been evaluated as normal parties by voters. Their results do not deviate from the general pattern of electoral results following incumbency. (Akkerman, de Lange, 2017)

For these authors, while "on average the incumbency effect has been negative", regarding most radical right parties, they have managed to win in post-incumben-

---

4 See *Pablo Iglesias abandona la política tras el "fracaso" de la izquierda en Madrid*, El País, https://elpais.com/espana/elecciones-madrid/2021 – 05 – 04/pablo-iglesias-anuncia-su-salida-de-la-politica-tras-el-fracaso-en-madrid.html

cy elections. Albertazzi and McDonnell also believe that "it is by no means a given that office is electorally damaging for populists. On the contrary, and especially when it is not their first time in government, populist parties may be well able to maintain, and even increase, their support". However, it is worth underscoring that "the radical right parties with a positive policy record that managed more or less to adapt to office organizationally were electorally rewarded", while at the same time, "in coalition governments, weak performance and internal conflicts not only were an obstacle to claiming policy results, but also might discredit parties as officeholders more generally" (Akkerman, de Lange, 2017).

From these analyses, there is interesting evidence for our study that right-wing radical parties generally performed better than left-wing radical parties, "a group in which no party at all managed to win votes after government participation" (Akkerman, de Lange, 2017). This is also confirmed by the research conducted by Dunphy and Bale, in which the authors highlight that from all interviews carried out for the study, "party leaders revealed, time and time again, that government participation may involve painful compromises and even short-to-medium term electoral losses" (Dunphy, Bale, 2011).

The analysis conducted here shows that right-wing populism in Europe generally performs better on the European level than on the national level. *Vox*, however, emerges as a borderline case, showing a divergent trend compared to that observed in other national contexts. In the European elections held in May 2019, *Vox* lost 1,294,408 votes compared to the national elections held only two months earlier, thus confirming the pervasiveness of its support within Spanish national issues. The most recent European elections, those of 2024, represented a significant defeat, marking the worst result for the radical right-wing Spanish party in the last five electoral cycles.

In general, right-wing European populism has shown a consistent upward trend since 2014 in both first- and second-tier elections. In contrast, left-wing populism, as exemplified by Podemos, experienced a sudden surge in support before entering a phase of stagnation or, in some cases, decline. Focusing specifically on our case study, Podemos has registered a negative trend in autonomous elections following its entry into government, despite using varied strategies (alliances or solo runs). The only exception to this trend was the 2021 Madrid Community elections, an isolated case due to the candidacy of Iglesias for president. Since entering government, Podemos has faced a largely negative electoral trend across almost all electoral rounds. While government participation may explain some of these losses, other contributing factors certainly exist.

Unlike other European contexts, such as France and Italy, Spain demonstrates resilience in its traditional liberal and social-democratic parties, which remain the strongest in polling results. What sets Spain apart, compared to its political landscape prior to the 2008 social and economic crisis, is the presence of other out-sider populist and radical forces that are now integrated into the Spanish system. These forces include *Vox* on the right and Podemos and *Sumar* on the left.

Since Podemos chose to leave *Sumar*, the latter has occupied the electoral space once held by Podemos, positioning itself closer to the PSOE's orbit. It is clear, therefore, that following the dissolution of the *Unidas Podemos* coalition, Podemos must rebuild its own autonomous electoral base. This is complicated by the presence of *Sumar*, which often appeals to the same electorate and address-es similar issues. As we will see in later chapters, this necessitates both organiza-tional and discursive changes. *Sumar* remains a necessary partner for the PSOE to govern. The 2023 national elections demonstrated that participation in the execu-tive did not appear to significantly penalize IU and Podemos at the national level. The results were only slightly below UP's performance in the previous national elections, although a stronger result might have been expected given the coali-tion's expanded membership and the robust political and media campaign led by Yolanda Díaz.

The *Partido Popular*, after its defeat in 2019, has re-emerged as a competitive force in national elections against the PSOE, gaining significant ground in the most recent national elections at the expense of *Vox*.

Vox, meanwhile, has shown a sharp decline in national polls since June 2022, returning to its position as Spain's fourth-largest political force behind *Sumar*. De-spite this, *Vox* remains a crucial ally for the PP in building majorities at both the local and national levels.

Following the July 2023 elections, the Spanish political system has evolved into an almost symmetrical bloc structure within a newly rediscovered bipolar—but not bipartisan—context. The "progressive" bloc is led by the PSOE and supported by *Sumar* and other forces to its left under Yolanda Díaz's leadership. The conser-vative bloc is led by the PP, supported by its "extreme" ally *Vox*, alongside the bloc of independence forces, which, although fragmented, continue to play the role of kingmakers. Populist forces, or so-called populisms, remain significant actors within the Spanish political system, even as traditional political forces regain cen-trality. In this context, Podemos must work to reclaim its electoral space at all lev-els.

Chapter 4 – Evolution of Organizational Structure

4.1 Introduction

What happens to an outsider force when it enters government from the perspective of its internal organizational structure? How does the participation of a populist force in government affect the structure of the party in office and its relationship with the party on the ground?

A leftist populist force is an interesting subject of study because it presents alternative and innovative forms of organization compared to the traditional party system. These organizational forms emerge as a response to social demands for participation and representation of new cleavages (Lipset, Rokkan, 1967: 1–64), which are either ignored or only weakly assimilated by European liberal democracies. The adaptation of these new organizational forms to the functions of government—the entry of the "new" into the traditional structure—is fundamentally important for analyzing not only the changing party system but also the very evolution of European democracies.

Indeed, it is intriguing to understand how political forces born out of the crisis of representation confront that crisis and become active participants in the system. In other words, parties and forces that once defined themselves as anti-system end up becoming part of the system. Moreover, once they are integrated into the system, it becomes important to analyze the roles they assume within the governmental chessboard and the practical outcomes they achieve. Reflecting on this type of political actor also allows us to continue analyzing the changing nature of progressive and leftist forces in the European context.

The crisis of social-democratic forces has paved the way for new political actors and the development of new forms of organization, such as movement parties (Kitschelt, 2006). These new forms have made it possible to capture emerging fractures, mistrust, and social discontent not represented by traditional political organizations (Damiani, 2016; Damiani, 2020; Ricolfi, 2017; Sassoon, 2020). Supporting this theory, Della Porta, Kouki, and Mosca reflect on the emergence of movement parties in their seminal volume *Movements Parties Against Austerity:*

> Movement parties emerged in fact as established parties were most dramatically losing citizens' trust and the relations of cooperation of center-left parties with social movements have been reduced as left-wing parties moved to the center, while movements increasingly addressed social issues. Similar to the Latin American cases, in Europe the movement parties seem therefore to have emerged and succeeded when center-left parties were perceived

https://doi.org/10.1515/9783111591537-008

as compromising with austerity policies. As we are going to see, during the economic crisis the PASOK in Greece, the Democratic Party in Italy, and the PSOE in Spain all turned toward neoliberal policies based on structural reforms and privatization programs which translated into cutting social spending, increasing the retirement age, reforming the labor market, reducing the public sector, and so on. (Della Porta et al., 2017: 10–11)

But when these actors enter institutions, what happens to them from an organizational perspective? In my opinion, focusing on leftist populist forces means analyzing some of the key political actors that have emerged in countries most affected by distrust and the crisis of legitimacy in European institutions. Understanding the role of these actors—now central to their respective institutional contexts—contributes to the analysis of the evolution of the European political system in the coming years, helping to map out future changes and trajectories. Additionally, this analysis provides a practical tool for evaluating the tangible effects of the crisis of representation in the European Union and contributing to the development of effective solutions.

Precisely because of its unique origins, which shape its current nature, Podemos serves as a paradigmatic case study for examining the changing nature of leftwing populism in Europe, particularly regarding institutionalization. The purpose of this chapter is to trace the evolution of Podemos by reconstructing its history and highlighting its key moments of transformation. In this chapter, the organizational dimension will be analyzed, while the communicative dimension will be addressed in the next chapter.

4.2 An organizational evolution

This chapter aims to analyze whether Podemos in government faces institutionalization pressures that alter its original organizational nature. Within scholarly literature, it is argued that movement parties—the typical organizational form of early populist leftist anti-austerity forces (Kitschelt, 2006; Della Porta et al., 2018)—experience strong pressures to structure themselves, or, as political scientist Panebianco defines it, to become more institutionalized, once they enter government. A movement party is often seen as a transitional phenomenon: it transforms when elected politicians act for opportunistic purposes or take up issues beyond their traditional ones, responding to changing voter preferences. This transition results in the loss of many of the party's initial organizational traits:

> Perversely, the more a movement party achieves in terms of procedural gains and/or substantive policy change, the more it may change its voters' preferences or salient interests such

that the party experiences growing pressure to abandon its existing profile of organization and policy appeal. (Kitschelt, 2006: 11)

This field of inquiry, however, remains insufficiently analyzed in the literature on populism in power. Albertazzi and McDonnell, who are among the leading theorists of this phenomenon, identify the organizational question as a central focus for future research in their work *Populists in Power* (2015), particularly concerning the structuring of political parties:

> As we explain below, several of our suggestions for future research focus on the need to better understand populist party organizations. [...] The study of this area should also explore [...] the extent to which populist parties that rely on a party model like 'mass party' are more likely to survive a change of leadership, or not. (Albertazzi, McDonnell, 2015: 177–178)

Subsequent research has moved in this direction. One of the most comprehensive texts is *Understanding Populist Party Organization* (2016) by political scientists Reinhard Heinisch and Oscar Mazzoleni. Focusing on the analysis of the "most successful" right-wing populist parties in Western Europe, the authors outline key organizational characteristics that are crucial for understanding the evolution and success of populist forces. However, their research does not address how the variable of government participation affects the evolution of these political forces. The authors argue that "the tendency [of the seven cases of populism analyzed] toward centralization can be considered the main feature we observed. Moreover, the concentration of power in leadership is frequently accompanied by formal or informal mechanisms designed to limit democracy within the party" (Heinisch, Mazzoleni, 2016: 227). The question of internal democracy within populist party organizations has recently gained significant interest among scholars. A recent article by Böhmelt, Ezrow, and Lehrer, titled *Populism and Intra-Party Democracy* (2022), addresses this issue through a compelling quantitative analysis, reaching conclusions similar to those of Heinisch and Mazzoleni. At the same time, however, the authors argue that:

> Our result that populism is associated with less democratic party organizations highlights possible extensions to understanding how these parties influence government formation and termination, and for considering how they respond to public opinion. (Böhmelt, Ezrow, Lehrer, 2022)

The focus of this research, however, will not be on the level of democracy within populist forces or the different forms of participation. Instead, it seeks to analyze the organizational patterns that leftist populist forces adopt when in government. In this respect, Heinisch and Mazzoleni argue that although right-wing populist

Fig. 8: *Timeline* of main events in the evolution of Podemos. Source: author's elaboration.

parties present themselves as outsider forces challenging the status quo, their appeal often lies in their anti-system discourse and style. Yet, "this perception hides the fact that, if we compare these parties in Europe, they conform to some extent to conventional forms of party organization. However, importantly, they also challenge party organizational models in important ways" (Heinisch, Mazzoleni, 2016: 238). Thus, as the authors argue, populist forces tend to move toward an "organizational normality"—a form of institutionalization that simultaneously incorporates strong elements of discontinuity, innovation, and model evolution. It is precisely this evolutionary trajectory that this research aims to follow.

4.3 The genetic structure: Vistalegre I

Why analyze Podemos' first process of organizational structuring if the purpose of this book is to analyze the effects of its governmental phase? What is the point of beginning to observe the dynamics that led to the formation of the first Podemos organization a full six years before the start of the Sánchez II government? The answer is simple: the initial "genetic" structure of a political force has concrete effects on its entire organizational evolution. It seems fitting to again quote the passage from the political scientist Panebianco that I used in the Introduction: "the organizational characteristics of any party, in addition to other factors, depend on its history, on how the organization came into being and was consolidated. Indeed, the way a party was formed, the main features of its genesis, are capable of exerting a weight on its organizational characters even decades later" (Panebianco, 1982: 104). Understanding the reasons that led to the first organizational structure of Podemos, and its main characteristics, will allow us to better comprehend the "legacies" that are still visible and decisive today. The first organizational structure, as we will see, was itself influenced by the context in which Podemos emerged—namely, the conclusion of the horizontal 15M social movement, which set the stage for Podemos' first launch as an electoral machine to compete in the 2014 European elections.

Let us start at the beginning: the first Podemos Congress took place on October 18–19, 2014, at the large Vistalegre Palace in Madrid, which from that moment on became the symbolic venue for Podemos' congresses. This event marked the beginning of the structuring process of what had, until then, been an outsider electoral list that achieved unexpected success in the 2014 European elections. The competition within the Congress centered on two main proposals—one led by Pablo Iglesias and the other by Pablo Echenique, the current Secretary of *Acción de Gobierno, Institucional y Programa* of Podemos. The main debate focused on the organizational model and strategic decisions regarding participation in future elections. These two proposals reflected two distinct visions of Podemos' organizational DNA—the mode of organization that would shape the evolution of the political project.

Claro que Podemos, the document proposed by Pablo Iglesias, Íñigo Errejón, Juan Carlos Monedero, Carolina Bescansa, and Luis Alegre, put forward a movement party structure that featured centralized power around Iglesias' leadership alongside diverse participatory mechanisms—both territorial (the *Círculos*) and online. This tension between horizontal and vertical dimensions would come to define the entire organizational history of Podemos. In contrast, *Sumando Podemos*, the document spearheaded by Echenique, proposed a far more horizontal structure with a *bottom-up* dynamic, decentralized decision-making within the territorial *Círculos*, and a "three-headed" leadership.

Voting concluded on November 15, 2014: the *Claro que Podemos* document won with 80.71% of the vote, compared to 12.37% for *Sumando Podemos*. Pablo Iglesias was thus elected general secretary with the participation of 112,070 people, representing 54% of the initial Podemos membership (205,750 members). However, the most significant aspect was not the result itself: for the first time in the history of the Spanish state, a political organization not only experimented with a collective decision-making method open to all its members but also implemented it using a digital platform. This decision broke new ground in the Spanish political and institutional context. It was both a practical tool and a political message, as

Raffaella Fittipaldi points out in her work *Podemos, an Organizational Profile* (2021):

> The decision to contemplate a digital channel from the very first congressional appointment responds to the platform society's imperative for connection and the decision to allow online voting takes on the contours of a political method entirely geared to exploiting its advantages. The connection and the web infrastructure thus become not only the vehicle of the programmatic proposals but even come to coincide with the message itself: connection and participation or, even better, connection is participation. (Fittipaldi, 2021: 38)

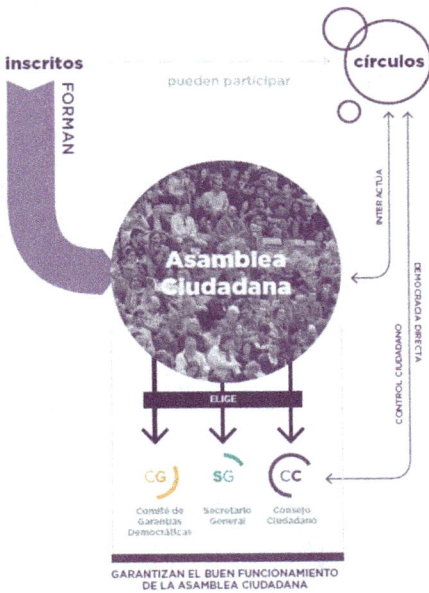

Fig. 9: Podemos organizational chart following *Vistalegre I*. Source: First Organizational Document, 2014: 14.

Fig. 9 represents the organigram that has shaped the organization of Podemos from the first *Asamblea Ciudadana* to the present day, undergoing several changes over the years that will be analyzed in the following paragraphs. It marks the first formal organizational systematization after a period of 'spontaneous' evolution, characterized by a constant struggle between the need for structure and the demands of electoral moments—a dynamic that has defined Podemos' entire trajectory. Using a metaphor often cited by its militants, "the party ties its shoes as it runs."

As shown in Fig. 2, at the national level, the *Asamblea Ciudadana Estatal* serves as the 'grassroots' unit around which the entire organization is built. As the Organizational Document defines it, it is "the highest decision-making body of Podemos" (First Organizational Document, 2014: 13). The *Asamblea Ciudadana* consists of all members registered on the Podemos digital platform, who are called upon to vote on decisions of national significance. Caruso and Campolongo describe this structure as both informal and participatory:

> Informal because the members are neither activists nor militants and entry into the grassroots decision-making audience has very low thresholds. Moreover, Podemos addresses this audience more as a slice of the electorate (a microcosm of the 'people') than as its base, thus more as a part of the external environment than an articulation of the internal system. It is an extroverted base, one might say, that meets the top leadership more through the media (television and social media) and in a unidirectional sense (top-down) than as actively involved in the life of the party. The characterization in the participatory sense derives instead from the fact that members are constantly consulted at the national, regional, or municipal level, on all the most important decisions and not always [...] the results of the consultations are those desired by the general secretary and the party leadership. (Caruso, Campolongo, 2021: 130)

This extroverted base has been central to Podemos from its inception. The so-called congressional appointments, where the *Asamblea Ciudadana* meets publicly (up to now, there have been four such events, as shown in Fig. 8), are meticulously planned down to the smallest details—from the stage design, graphics, and music to the distribution of speeches and messaging to the outside world. These events aim to inspire and energize the internal membership while also serving as a 'calling card' for the media and political opponents. The *Asamblea Ciudadana* directly elects the party's executive bodies: the General Secretary and the *Consejo Ciudadano*, the political governing body.

The *Consejo* consists of 81 members: the General Secretary, 17 regional secretaries, a member elected directly by Podemos members living abroad, and 62 members elected by the *Asamblea Ciudadana*. The *Consejo*'s role is to implement the lines of action approved in the Asamblea's documents. It can convene lower-level territorial assemblies and approve budgets and financial reports for those holding public office. The *Consejo* is also divided into specific areas, each led by a head responsible for building a team to work on particular issues[1]. While initial-

---

1 The minimum areas within which the *Consejo Ciudadano* must be divided are: "Strategy and campaigns; Social and political analysis; Studies and program; Outreach, territorial organization and circles; Relationship with civil society and social movements; Participation; Social networks; Press; Anti-corruption, Justice and governance; Social rights: Education, health and housing;

ly informal—with references to generic 'areas' and 'area managers'—this structure would later formalize into what is now recognized as a political secretariat. The final national body is the *Comité de Garantías Democráticas*, also elected by the *Asamblea*. Its role is to safeguard the rights of members and uphold the principles and norms on which the organization is founded. Sub-state levels mirror this structure at regional and municipal levels, replicating the organizational design on a smaller scale. These include regional and municipal assemblies of members, regional and municipal *Consejos Ciudadanos*, coordination groups, and general secretariats.

The organizational form closest to the grassroots level is the *Círculos*, defined in the organizational document as follows:

> *Círculos* are a voluntary and open group of people interested in social transformation based on respect for democracy, dignity, and human rights. The relationship formulas between the circles and the Councils and Citizens' Assemblies shall be in accordance with the provisions of this Statute and the Regulations that each Territorial Assembly may agree upon. The circles are the best guarantee for the control and evaluation of Podemos' organs and public officials, guarding against corruption, opacity, participation and guaranteeing all processes. (First Organizational Document, 2014: 30)

The *Círculos* perform three main functions. First, they serve as the smallest organizational unit for territorial visibility and contact with social movements, associations, and local committees. For this reason, a circle can only be established at the neighborhood (*barrio*) level and cannot be duplicated within the same area. Second, they act as *bottom-up* mechanisms of control and supervision over municipal, autonomous, and national bodies. This 'popular control' allows for procedures such as contesting and revoking decisions made by higher bodies. Third, they create spaces for participation, debate, and political mobilization—reflecting Podemos' origins as a movement party and its vision for an alternative democratic model.

At this stage, every organizational component serves a strategic goal: winning the 2015 general elections. To achieve this, the party must function as a streamlined electoral machine while maintaining the horizontal and participatory ethos central to its identity. The defining characteristic of this period is the uneasy integration of two axes: the horizontal-participatory axis and the vertical-decision-making axis. Participation in Podemos is shaped by its hybrid organizational nature. The party borrows democratic practices from the 15M movement, emphasiz-

---

Training and culture; Women and equality; Youth; Economy; Ecology and environment; International relations; Funding and transparency" (First Organizational Document, 2014: 18–19).

ing participation from those excluded from mainstream politics. The *Círculos* symbolize this grassroots organization, serving as spaces for discussion, debate, and policy proposals. Simultaneously, Podemos employs collective list-building for the 2014 European elections and program drafting.

From its inception, the digital environment has been central to Podemos, functioning not only as a communication and mobilization tool but also as a platform for participation and direct democracy. Early on, when other coordination infrastructure was lacking, online spaces like *Plaza Podemos* became critical for decision-making and consultation. However, over time, a split emerged between platform members and consultation participants, with voter turnout declining relative to membership numbers (Caruso, Campolongo, 2021). Moreover, party-platform models often reinforce plebiscitary dynamics, as consultation outcomes generally align with the leadership's decisions (Gerbaudo, 2020).

While horizontality defined Podemos' early phase, significant limits existed in its identification with horizontal movements (del Barrio, 2014). Podemos replicated the participatory practices and rhetoric of social movements, but it also developed a centralized leadership and vertical organizational structure. The electoral-hierarchical axis and the egalitarian-participatory axis coexisted within this hybrid organization, though in an imbalanced manner. At times, as acknowledged by Podemos leaders, the electoral-hierarchical component overshadowed the participatory role of the *Círculos* in decision-making, debate, and candidate selection.

This position is reflected in an interview with Ángela Rodríguez Martínez, former Vice-Minister and *Secretaria de Estado de Igualdad y contra la Violencia de Género* (2021–2023), known as Pam:

A: -How has grassroots political participation changed from the first Podemos to now?

ARM: -There is much less political participation. Podemos was a very horizontal structure; any person from any place could download materials from the internet to create their own Podemos space in their city, and little by little a more classic party structure was created with municipal, provincial, and regional groupings. There is difficulty in the participation of citizens. This is a mistake. Much horizontality has been lost. One of the virtues of Podemos was a very Yankee primary system, very American, big television scenarios where there was the primary debate that created a lot of participation, people saw an internal debate of a party from home, which if you think about it is incredible. [...] With *Vistalegre II* the type of participation changed. (Rodríguez Martínez A. R., 2022, Interview 2)

Rodríguez Martínez confirms that the main organizational shift occurred at the *Vistalegre II* Congress, marking a transition toward greater institutionalization. Podemos evolved from an electoral machine with broad horizontal participation into a more institutionalized party structure.

In conclusion, the First Podemos Congress established a vertical structure combined with a permeable, horizontally organized grassroots base. This dual structure was embodied in the central role of the *Asamblea Ciudadana*—composed of all adherents who voted on key decisions—and the *Círculos*, which functioned as spaces for grassroots debate, mobilization, and oversight. At the same time, the leadership of the *Secretario General* (Pablo Iglesias) and the *Consejo Ciudadano* introduced a clear vertical dimension. This "genetic" organizational approach would continue to shape Podemos' evolution, defining it as both a vertical electoral machine and a grassroots movement party. While still rooted in its horizontal origins, Podemos had already begun its institutionalization during this early phase.

4.4 Vistalegre II, the Watershed Congress

There are events in the history of a political organization that serve as real points of no return. The Second Congress of Podemos, known as *Vistalegre II*, is one such event, frequently mentioned in all the interviews I conducted. It took place on February 11–12, 2017 after Podemos' greatest electoral success (the 2016 legislative elections) and marked two significant developments: the first was an organizational, strategic, and discursive shift; the second was the exposure of divisions and fractures between the different factions within the party, which ultimately led to the departure of certain members. In short, *Vistalegre II* was a watershed moment for the organization. With the defeat of the faction led by Íñigo Errejón[2]—who advocated for a more transversal and populist option and a shift from an electoral machine to a decentralized, federal popular movement—the 'Pablist' organizational option became Podemos' strategic mantra. However, the practical realization of the principles expressed in the congress document was not necessarily effective.

To understand this, it is important to examine how the Congress emerged and the key points of contention between the proposed documents, particularly regarding political strategy and organizational aspects. The Congress occurred after an internal conflict that had already surfaced during the two national electoral rounds concerning Podemos' electoral positioning. As highlighted in Chapter III, Iglesias and Errejón had already demonstrated differing visions, not just tac-

---

2 A political scientist, he is among the first founders of Podemos. In 2014 he was appointed by Pablo Iglesias as campaign manager for the European elections, influencing Podemos' first speech. After Iglesias, he was therefore the best-known public profile and media presence. He has been a member of the Madrid Assembly and is currently a congressman for *Màs País*.

tically but also regarding the organization's strategic direction. Tensions escalated between March and April 2016 when ten Podemos leaders from the Community of Madrid—not coincidentally, Errejón's stronghold—resigned in protest against the Regional General Secretary, Luis Alegre, a close ally of Iglesias.

This conflict triggered upheaval within the national leadership. Sergio Pascual, head of the organization within the *Consejo Ciudadano* and aligned with Errejón, was dismissed and replaced by Echenique, who was now closer to the 'Pablist' faction. This change drew significant media attention, and political opponents seized the moment to launch a harsh communication campaign against Podemos, framing the events as evidence of inevitable disintegration. Tensions were further heightened by the results of the June 2016 elections. Despite achieving the best result ever in percentage terms for a political force outside the PSOE and PP, disappointment stemmed from Podemos' failure to surpass the Socialists—a goal predicted by many polls but unrealized, despite (or, depending on interpretation, because of) the creation of the *Unidas Podemos* coalition.

Errejón's faction had a clear position on the matter: the alliance with IU had confined Podemos to the radical left, forcing it into a left-right confrontation rather than enabling it to represent a broader social majority. For Errejón, *Unidas Podemos* was a phase to be left behind. As expressed in the document *Recuperar la Ilusión*, prepared for Vistalegre II, Podemos needed "to recover a transversal discourse that leaves behind the labels of left and right, not because of some kind of renunciation, but because it is assumed that the unity of the people is more ambitious, radical and transformative than the unity of the left" (Political Document *Recuperar la Ilusión*, 2017: 14). The period following the celebrated *Remontada* of December 20, 2015, was described as "the catastrophic impact and blizzard" (Ibid: 7). To recover, Errejón argued, Podemos needed to speak to a broader social base (not just the extreme left) by transitioning from an "electoral war machine" to a more plural, distributed popular movement:

> At the moment we believe that Podemos must adapt to the new situation because what has changed is the task. The task of a revolutionary force is not to always do the same thing but to be able to change as the balance of forces and terrain changes. In a nutshell: if yesterday it was a question of creating a concentrated electoral war machine for an immediate assault, today it is a question of generating a democratic and popular organization, distributed, territorialized, feminized, and complex. This is what we have called the transition from an electoral war machine to a popular movement. [...] Podemos must be a more open, non-resistant political force, but one that exploits the new opportunities of the new cycle to fulfill the tasks of becoming a governing force and building a people. [...] Today, for the first time in our accelerated history, we have the experience, time, and conditions to set ourselves the tasks, perhaps not so urgent, but essential to articulate a patriotic, democratic, more mature, and useful political force for our people. (Political Document *Recuperar la Ilusión*, 2017: 7–10)

The resulting proposal was to transform Podemos into a light and agile structure, one that would primarily act within institutions while maintaining a relationship of mutual autonomy with social movements. This vision, which balanced movement-building and electoral strategy, relied on a Laclausian populist framework and a transversal discourse constructed along the high-low axis. This perspective also allowed for a reconsideration of alliances with the PSOE—a contentious issue at the time, as the *Partido Socialista* was supporting Rajoy's PP government, backed by *Ciudadanos:*

> Approaching the relationship with the PSOE in an intelligent and secular way has always been much more productive for Podemos than obsessive denial and frontal clashes. [...] It is not a question of ideology; it is a question of political skill. Podemos' relationship with the PSOE must be skillful because it cannot ignore its historical importance, but neither can it make decisions based on its existence. It cannot ignore it, but neither can it systematically subordinate itself by defining itself in relation to it. The obsession with the *Partido Socialista* has more to do with the outstanding debts of a part of the left in our country than with the claims and aspirations Podemos should have in this new phase. Podemos doesn't have to choose between the dilemmas of the past, it doesn't have to decide between being the PCE or the PSOE: Podemos was born with a hypothesis that kicked those dilemmas, even though since 20D [20 December, election day] decisions have made it lean more towards one of these two options. If 15M has taught us anything, it is the importance of fighting the battle against the privileged on new ground. (Political Document *Recuperar la Ilusión*, 2017: 9)

In contrast, Iglesias and the *Podemos Para Todas* team interpreted the election results differently. For them, *Unidas Podemos* had demonstrated its ability to channel political protest, achieving the strongest electoral result ever for a force outside the two-party system. For Iglesias, the June 26 elections required a strategic shift: while the goal remained winning to govern, the strategy needed to pivot from a 'blitzkrieg' approach to a 'war of position', necessitating a more organized and socially rooted party. Iglesias's approach emphasized strengthening alliances, starting with IU, and building a "popular social bloc" through institutional representation and territorial presence. In *Plan 2020. Ganar al Partido Popular. Gobernar España*, Iglesias articulated this strategy:

> Podemos, which was born from the exhaustion of the two-party system and its supporters, must continue to build with other actors the political space for change in a country that is particularly complex due to the historical construction of our state and our plurinational nature. The logic must therefore be that of unity in diversity: a project shared by different political, social, and territorial identities, where what is reality in everyday life is articulated in the political sphere. (Plan 2020, 2017: 29)

Unlike Errejón's vision, which prioritized strategic alliances with the PSOE, Iglesias's proposal kept Podemos as an outsider party while collaborating with leftist forces and fostering the growth of a social bloc uniting sectors with shared interests and objectives. Iglesias emphasized the importance of institutional representation, particularly at municipal and regional levels, while also working to strengthen civil society and grassroots organizations:

> If we subordinate ourselves to institutional logic, we dissolve; and if, on the contrary, we limit ourselves to what is known and already transited, we exclude ourselves. The movement-institution dialectic (a permanently unstable equilibrium) never ends but must serve to advance the transformation and overcoming of the current institutional order. That is why we must continue to build the historical, social, and popular bloc – that union of sectors that meet because they coincide in their diagnoses, interests, and objectives – that does politics in institutions and non-institutional public spaces. (Plan 2020, 2017: 27)

Therefore, in the 'opposition-alternative dialectic' to the Rajoy government, Podemos needed to articulate an opposition policy that engaged broad social sectors to strengthen its political structure and the 'muscle' of civil society organizations. Iglesias believed there were widely unrepresented social sectors whose demands needed to be channeled through 'political and social figures of a new kind.' The role of Podemos, therefore, was to transfer initiatives from social movements into institutions while respecting the independence of civil society organizations, collaborating in their growth and social strengthening. A true movement party, with a robust organizational structure, would project itself not only through institutional representation but also through strong territorial and social roots.

The third main proposal at *Vistalegre II* came from the *Anticapitalistas* component, one of the founding factions of Podemos and the only one that had established structures and territorial presence from the outset, particularly in Andalusia. It is no coincidence that, as of 2015, the mayor of Cadiz was José María González Santos, known as Kichi, an *Anticapitalista* loyalist who continued governing his city even after *Unidas Podemos* suffered a setback, losing some municipalities. The *Anticapitalistas* officially left Podemos in 2020 following its decision to enter a coalition government with the PSOE. The hypothesis expressed in their document *Podemos en Movimiento* aligned with Iglesias's vision but placed stronger emphasis on relationships with social movements. For the *Anticapitalistas*, a movement party structure was also necessary, but with greater focus on grassroots participation and collaboration with movements and social forces. The party, they argued, should serve as an instrument for building a countervailing network of power, minimizing media reliance while fostering equal relationships with social movements. The organizational structure they proposed closely resembled the *Podemos Para Todas* document, with the notable difference of abolishing the General Secretary position—central to Iglesias's model—in favor of collective leadership represented by three spokespersons, an idea similar to Echenique's First Congress proposal.

The Asamblea Ciudadana Vistalegre II did not begin under the best circumstances. The media intensified its focus on the internal fractures within Podemos, and the party leaders exchanged public accusations. Errejón, through his clash with Iglesias, garnered significant media coverage, which opponents used to construct a narrative of a 'head-on clash' between the party's two main leaders[3]. On the day of the Congress, the atmosphere was tense but moderated by the careful discursive and scenographic construction of the event. The entrance of Podemos' leaders into the Vistalegre arena was met with the same enthusiasm as two years prior, but chants of *"¡Sí, se puede!"* were interspersed with shouts of *"Unidad, unidad!"* not only at the event's opening but also during speeches presenting the political documents. The event was stitched together with piano interludes and performances by the theater group *Improteatro*, which staged improvisational sketches between speeches[4]. The aim was to portray the Congress not as a deadly clash but as a stage in the party's evolution and growth. The speeches refrained from directly attacking other proposals, instead focusing on explaining the internal differences. At the same time, they clearly set out the direction to be taken. Iglesias, for his part, made it clear where he believed Podemos needed to evolve:

> To win, electoral victories are not enough; social victories are needed. We need to build a people that expresses from today the possibility of a new Spain [...]. We can be leaders together with the sister political forces and civil society of a historical bloc of change. But let us not confuse ourselves, let us not recognize the ideological geography of the parliament. We were born saying that the old categories were not always useful. I am a leftist, but I do not believe in the parliamentary geography according to which the *Partido Popular* is on the right and the *Partido Socialista* is on the left. They are the representatives of the project of the *elites*. (Iglesias, 2017)

Iglesias elaborated on two fundamental themes from his document that would shape Podemos's future. The first was the evolution from a *maquina de guerra electoral* (electoral war machine), focused solely on electoral victories, into a

---

3 I refer to the *'Cara a Cara'* ('face-to-face') interview published by *El Diario* (*Cara a cara entre Pablo Iglesias e Íñigo Errejón*, El Diario, https://www.youtube.com/watch?v=0Pn2nchxEJI) or to reports of mutual accusations published a few days before the Congress (*A dos días de Vistalegre II Iglesias y Errejón no rebajan la tension*, El Correo de AndalucíaTV, https://www.youtube.com/watch?v=_sRp62LRdbs).
4 All speeches are recorded in the live streaming of the event available here: *Vistalegre II – Sábado mañana #ÚltimoDíaVotaVA2*, Podemos, https://www.youtube.com/watch?v=a2RpjStPw7M.

structured movement-party that would organize and build the people in alliance with alternative political and social forces. The second theme was Iglesias's clear ideological positioning ("I am of the left") and his reiteration of the need to transcend the left-right axis by constructing a "high-low" social bloc to fight the *elites*. In an implicit critique of Errejón's populist hypothesis and his definition of 'transversality', Iglesias asserted:

> We can never forget who we are. Parliament is important, we must continue to do things well there, but we cannot resemble them in gait. Transversality, comrades, does not mean looking like *Ciudadanos* or looking like the PSOE. It means resembling the people, resembling Spain. (Iglesias, 2017)

This transversality, therefore, was not about diluting Podemos's identity or appealing to rival electorates. Instead, it was about representing a unified people —a concept typical of populist movements.

Regarding these divisions, Clara Serra—a member of Errejón's team at *Vistalegre II* who publicly supported his platform and later left Podemos when his faction split—offered an insightful perspective during the interview. Serra highlighted that the leadership struggle was shaped by both political and personal conflicts. She noted:

> There are also personal quarrels and that also explains things. I think Iñigo was wrong in many things, and I think many mistakes are explained by a management of Pablo and Iñigo that is catastrophic, very personal, very little political and very much of two friends fighting. (Serra, 2024, Interview 10)

From a political perspective, the 'Errejónista' faction advocated for greater democratization and horizontality, aimed at restructuring what Serra referred to as "a highly hierarchical structure" whose vertical approach—dating back to *Vistalegre I*—continued to shape its organizational structures and would later be inherited by and shape those of *Más Madrid* and *Sumar*:

> Podemos has been a highly vertical party from the very beginning—a centralist party that grants broad powers to the figure of the secretary-general and those around them while reserving for the party base the ability to either support or reject (through plebiscites) decisions that have already been made. At *Vistalegre II*, part of the leadership questioned the organizational model established at *Vistalegre I* and argued that the party needed to democratize, to take its governing bodies, regulations, institutions, grassroots membership, and territorial presence more seriously. What was born as a monarchy needed to be 'republicanized' and endowed with proper structures. In any case, this was about correcting a shared mistake, as the verticalist model upon which the party was founded was strongly supported by many of us, including those who later defended the need to move away

from it. Responsibility is collective and, of course, includes Iñigo, who, along with Pablo, was one of the main architects of the party's initial structure. The idea was to build an 'electoral machine' capable of quickly seizing state power—a machine that needed to make swift and bold decisions and could move more efficiently if it remained unburdened by internal organizational constraints. The debate over the limitations that this organizational model has imposed on the project has never been conducted honestly and still isn't today, as blame is assigned without any real self-criticism. Responsibility is widely shared, and in fact, the organizational design established at *Vistalegre I* is the same one found in Podemos, *Más Madrid*, and *Sumar*—that is, a mistake that has never been overcome or reformed (Serra, 2024, Interview 10).

Vistalegre II and its effects were thus the product of various interrelated factors. On one hand, it reflected differing visions of Podemos's evolution—organizationally, strategically, and discursively. These differences are significant not only for Podemos but also for understanding the broader evolution of European populist forces born in the aftermath of the 2008 crisis. This will be explored in greater detail in the following paragraphs. On the other hand, *Vistalegre II* revealed a political—and, in some cases, personal—clash between Iglesias's strong vertical leadership and Errejón's attempt to challenge it or create his own political space. This space would later manifest in Errejón's leadership of *Más País*, advancing his vision of the movement while positioning him as a leading figure. Whether political or personal factors predominated is difficult to determine. However, for the purposes of this study, it is essential to analyze the political differences between the factions in greater detail, which we will do in the following paragraphs.

4.5 The organizational and political results of Vistalegre II

Pablo Iglesias was re-elected Secretary General with 89.09 % of the vote. However, when it came to voting on the documents, the situation was not a complete plebiscite as in the case of leadership. Although the 'Pablistas' managed to win in all cases with a percentage greater than 50 %, the highest level of support was 56.04 % for the political document.

Errejón had not aimed to challenge Iglesias for the secretariat, a difficult undertaking that would have exposed him to a likely heavy defeat given Iglesias's leadership legitimacy and strong media presence. However, Errejón succeeded in 'counting' his supporters, strengthening his faction politically and ideologically, and placing a block opposed to the 'Pablista' line within the *Consejo Ciudadano*. As seen in the graphical representation of the results in Fig. 10, the 'Errejónista' line achieved more than 33 % support for all documents. The third proposal, the *Anticapitalista* option, garnered varying results ranging from 8.93 % for the political

Vistalegre II document results

■ Pablo Iglesias Team ■ Íñigo Errejón Team ■ Miguel Urbán Team ■ Others

Political Document	56,04%	33,71%	8,93%
Organizational Document	54,42%	34,86%	10,01%
Ethical Document	53,63%	33,90%	11,63%
Equality document	61,58% Iglesias and Urbán Team	35,60%	

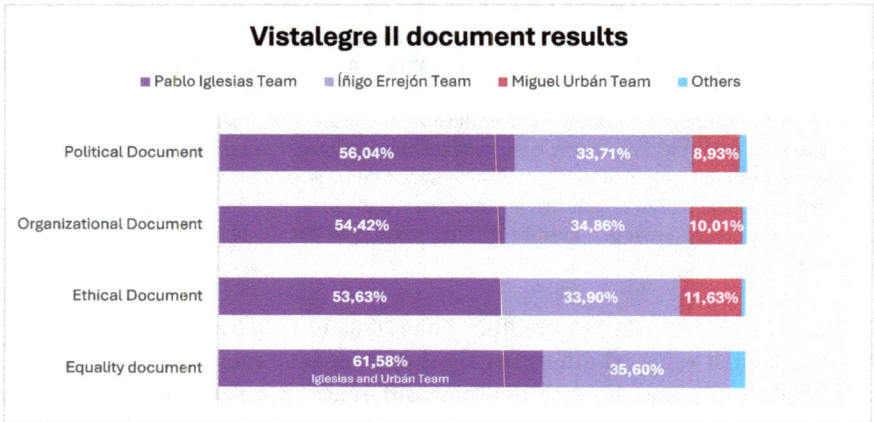

Fig. 10: *Vistalegre II* document results. Source: author's elaboration of data in Silva, El Païs, 2017.

document to 11.63% for the ethical document. Additionally, the *Documento de Igualdad* was voted on, which included a joint motion between the Pablistas and *Anticapitalistas* under the name *Feminismo En Movimiento Para Todas*, receiving 61.68% of the votes[5]. The *Consejo Ciudadano* was thus composed of 60% representatives from Pablo Iglesias's team (37 people), 37% from Errejón's faction (23 people), and 3% from the *Anticapitalista* faction (2 people).

The results, therefore, strongly reaffirmed Iglesias's leadership, although the party's internal divisions were evident. The party's base was split, yet Errejón successfully positioned his ideas within public debate beyond the organization, built a loyal team—primarily concentrated in the Spanish capital—and established himself as a strong media figure capable of challenging, albeit without hope of victory, the monolithic leadership of Pablo Iglesias.

For his part, Iglesias maintained control of the party's central organs during this delicate phase, pursuing his strategic vision for Podemos's evolution. Even though the definition of a movement party remained in the victorious organizational document, Podemos at this second constituent assembly already demonstrated significant attention to its internal structure, distancing itself from Kitschelt's (2006) classic definition of a movement party as a low-organizational-investment structure. *Vistalegre II* marked the beginning of Podemos's hybridization and progressive institutionalization. The main practical outcomes of the vic-

---

5 All results are available here: *Resultado de las votaciones de Vistalegre 2*, El País, www.el-pais.com/elpais/2017/02/12/media/1486905606_936694.html

tory of *Podemos Para Todas* followed this trajectory: at the central office level, the major change was the formalization of the *Consejo de Coordinación* or *Secretariado*. This body consisted of 10–15 members (later rising to 30 in subsequent congresses), with each member assigned specific competencies.

As previously noted, the first Political Document had already proposed subdividing the *Consejo Ciudadano* into working areas led by coordinators. This decision was institutionalized at *Vistalegre II*, creating an executive body for Podemos, elected by the *Consejo Ciudadano*, which effectively became its decision-making group. The vision of the *Organization of the 21st Century* described in the document highlighted a need for more structured leadership while also advancing participation and localization. The second key outcome occurred at the party's grassroots level through the strengthening of the *Círculos* and a reform of militancy. The affiliation system was changed, introducing a distinction (later formalized in the third Congress) between simple "members" and "militants." This differentiation established varying levels of participation, moving away from a fully horizontal and transversal structure to one closer to a traditional party membership system.

In the Organizational Document, Podemos committed to launching a membership campaign aiming to reach 100,000 militants and over 1,000,000 members. This double path of participation distinguished those registered on the website —who offered external support—from those actively engaged in the *Círculos*, who gained more responsibilities but not additional rights.

Furthermore, at *Vistalegre II*, Podemos declared for the first time that membership in the party was incompatible with membership in other political parties. This decision marked a shift towards greater structural organization and reduced fluidity in political participation, fostering stronger identification and loyalty to the organization. However, it also ended the porous boundaries characteristic of social movements. Regarding its relationship with social movements, Podemos launched a new campaign called *Vamos*, aimed at creating a shared space for dialogue and collaboration between the party and social movements. The goal was to develop a common discursive space and strengthen the relationship between institutions and grassroots movements, a central point of the 'Pablista' proposal.

In short, with this transition, Podemos became more structured in two directions: first, it focused on organizing the party on the ground (militants, members, *Círculos*, and relationships with movements) that had been sidelined during the construction of the electoral war machine. Second, it adopted a more vertical structure, where the Secretary General retained a central role but was now supported by an executive body capable of managing different thematic areas in a top-down manner, previously overseen by the collegial *Consejo Ciudadano*. In this regard, Raffaella Fittipaldi notes:

Podemos consolidates and enters fully into the institutional dynamic, with a process of adaptation to the political space and from a perspective that from destitute (of protest and opposition) and rupture with the Regime of '78 in crisis, increasingly takes on constituent traits, of acceptance and attention to the institutions and the challenges that these entail in terms of alliances and relations of political agonism. (Fittipaldi, 2021: 45)

4.6 The Comparison of the Documents

Table 3 summarizes the main differences between the three most discussed documents, dividing them according to six criteria considered fundamental for analyzing the discursive and organizational evolution of Podemos. These key issues, as will be analyzed in the following sections and the next chapter, continue to characterize Podemos's internal debates.

	Proposal 'Podemos para todas' (Iglesias Area)	Proposal 'Recuperar la ilusiòn' (Errejón Area)	'Podemos en movimiento' proposal (Area Anticapitalistas)
Organization	Movement party 'top-down'	Federal Movement + Electoral Organization	Movement party 'bottom-up'
External image of the party	Outsider Party	Responsible Party	Outsider Party
Right/left	Identification in the left-wing political space with a vocation for majority representation	Transversality and majority vocation	Sharing a common political space with left-wing and movement organizations
Social base	Social and popular blocs understood as a union of the 'people' and sectors that share the same goals.	Construction of the social majority through political discourse, attracting sectors of the electorate from other parties.	Social and popular bloc sharing the same class interests.
Dialectic square/ institutions	Party as a political instrument of civil society, representatives as 'institutional activists'. Construction of a territorial social bloc that does politics inside and outside the institutions.	Parliamentary opposition activities to advance innovative social demands. Construction of distributed and plural territorial links.	Party as a political instrument of civil society, representatives as 'institutional activists'. Reduction of media use in favor of a countervailing power network and equal relationship with social movements.

Continued

	Proposal 'Podemos para todas' (Iglesias Area)	Proposal 'Recuperar la ilusiòn' (Errejón Area)	'Podemos en movimiento' proposal (Area Anticapitalistas)
Alliances	Building alliances between the forces representing the social bloc of change. Strengthening *Unidas Podemos*.	Responsible party that can forge strategic electoral alliances without foreclosing any possibilities.	Building alliances between the forces representing the social bloc of change. Strengthening *Unidas Podemos* through a process of participation from below that involves the movements and social forces more closely.

Tab. 3 The differences between the three main Vistalegre II documents. Source: author's elaboration of Campolongo, Caruso, 2021.

The analysis of the different congressional positions was also conducted by comparing the contents of the two most voted documents examined with Nvivo software. Fig. 11 and Fig 12 represent the comparison of the two main documents, respectively *Podemos para todas* and *Recuperar la ilusiòn* from a discursive and lexical point of view using word clouds of the hundred most frequently used words longer than five characters[6].

Fig. 11: Word cloud *Podemos para todas*. Source: author's elaboration via Nvivo.

Fig. 12: Word cloud *Recuperar la ilusiòn*. Source: author's elaboration via Nvivo.

It is evident from this comparison that there are substantial differences between the two documents. The language used in the 'Pablista' document focuses on the

---

6 It was decided to exclude words common to both documents such as 'Podemos', 'politico/a', 'document'.

issue of *gobierno* (government, mentioned 55 times within the document) and thus on the concept of power, with two distinct connotations: it refers both to power as a target of criticism, such as *"gobierno del PSOE"*, *"gobierno de Rajoy"*, etc., accused of favoring the elites, and to the necessity of seizing power and exercising it to bring about a paradigmatic shift. The term *cambio* (change, used 43 times) is another central theme, often paired with adjectives like *nuevo/a* (new), to describe areas where change has occurred or is needed (town halls, society, etc.) or the actors responsible for driving it (forces, social blocs, movements, etc.). Two other frequently used terms are *transición* (transition, 42 times) and *elecciones* (elections, 45 times).

The document argues that the democratic transition that began after Francisco Franco's regime stalled due to a kind of social compromise between "those above and those below." The 15M movement "reshuffled the cards", opening up new possibilities for progress and initiating a new democratic transition in which Podemos, along with a clearly defined alternative social bloc, has played and can continue to play a decisive role. The elections demonstrated the need for institutional construction of this alternative, breaking through the wall of bipartisanship. However, this is not sufficient: without the continuous construction of a social *bloque* (bloc) that brings together increasingly broader *sectores* (sectors), the road to change cannot continue.

The concept of *cambio* (change) is also central to the second document, where it appears even more frequently (111 times) and is regarded as an essential and ongoing process initiated by 15M. However, the document warns that this process is at risk of being compromised, or failing to find an adequate *proyecto* (project) to guide and advance it. The primary objective of this change must be the recovery of social, economic, and cultural *derechos* (rights, mentioned 79 times) that the elites have taken from the Spanish people. To achieve this, it is necessary to "recover the illusion" of the original Podemos project, regaining the majority support that has been lost due to the current organizational formula, according to the document's supporters. A key tool in this process is *cultura* (culture, mentioned 103 times), described as the "key to change" because, as the document states, "culture must be a central axis in Podemos's discourse and policies, and this centrality is part of the originality of the project" (Political Document *Recuperar la ilusión*, 2017: 91). This emphasis reflects the Laclausian and post-Marxist nature of the document's approach. Laclau's theorization, in which French philosopher Chantal Mouffe also participated, frames populism as the very logic of "the political". As we have analyzed in the previous chapters, according to this theory it is meaningless to determine whether a political force or movement is populist or not; instead, one must analyze the degree of populism they embody. One important consequence of this theory is the acceptance of the vagueness and indeterminacy of social heterogeneity, which must be articulated through populist discourse. In this process, culture plays a crucial role. In Laclausian leftist populism, the approach is transversal, eschewing the traditional 'class' concept central to leftist movements and political forces. These movements, often anchored in Marxist theory, typically derive their identity (class consciousness) and their "us" from the capital-labor divide.

However, as is clear, neither document uses the traditional language of leftwing forces. The word "socialism" does not appear in either document, and the term 'class' is rarely used. In the first document, it appears only seven times, primarily in reference to the "middle classes", while alluding to the traditional meaning of class (e. g., the proletariat, the working class) through the term "popular sectors". In the second document, 'class' appears six times, also used to refer to the "popular classes" or working class. Similarly, the word 'left' is used sparingly: it appears six times in the first document and fourteen times in the second, mostly in references to the "traditional left" or the "right-left axis".

In the general voting at the Congress, which selected the internal organs and approved the political, organizational, and ethical documents, 155,190 voters participated out of a total membership of 456,878. In absolute terms, this means more people voted than at the First Congress. However, when considering the percentage of eligible voters, the situation is different: 54.46 % participated in approving the *Vistalegre I* documents, while only 33.98 % voted at *Vistalegre II.*

4.7 The *Terzera Asamblea Ciudadana:* Podemos institutionalizes itself

The *Tercera Asamblea Ciudadana* (Third Citizen Assembly) was organized three years after the previous one—three years that completely transformed the political and social landscape of Europe and the world, and which also saw significant internal upheavals within the *Morada*[7] formation. If we look again at Fig. 8, we can see that 2019 was a year in which Podemos faced no fewer than four major electoral appointments (two national, one municipal and regional, and one European), leading to the formation of the coalition government on January 13, 2020. These events, as previously noted, triggered strong internal tensions within Podemos, culminating in the departure of Errejón's faction in January 2019 and later the *Anticapitalistas* in February 2020 due to their opposition to joining the govern-

---

7 Named for its representative color, purple (esp. *morado*).

ment with the Socialists[8]. To complicate matters further, just days after the coalition government was formed, Spain—like the rest of the world—had to face the health, social, and economic emergency caused by the Covid-19 pandemic.

This was the political and social backdrop in which the 3rd Congress was organized. Initially scheduled for March 21, 2020, it was postponed due to the health emergency. Voting was ultimately conducted online from May 15 to May 21, 2020, through the platform *terceraasamblea.podemos.info*. The main aim of the III Congress was to continue evolving Podemos' organizational structure to adapt to the major internal and external changes that had occurred, particularly its new role in government.

The second key objective was to re-elect leadership positions following the exit of the 'Errejónista' and Anticapitalist factions. The problem of internal divisions and splintering had significantly impacted Podemos' organization and public image. From an organizational standpoint, some founding members of Podemos left the party. This prompted Clara Serra to comment, albeit critically:

> Today, we could say that 80% or 90% of the leadership that once existed in Podemos is no longer part of the party. Splits and ruptures within a party can always be attributed to power struggles or competition among leaders, and Podemos has certainly experienced those. However, a loss of leadership of such magnitude cannot be explained solely by betrayals, personal mistakes, or individual disputes; it stems from deeply structural causes and an organizational configuration that has imposed objective limits on the party's ability to integrate a leadership that was already heterogeneous from the outset. Ultimately, it is a political issue. If we want to learn from this experience politically, perhaps we need to move beyond explanations based on broken friendships and personal vendettas and instead question the kind of structure or framework within which these human conflicts unfold. Podemos was born with a fundamental design flaw—one that we should strive not to repeat. (Serra, 2024, Interview 10)

This division also had a major media impact, with campaigns in newspapers and on television covering every detail—based more on "broken friendships and personal vendettas" than on the important political issues—of the internal fractures, reinforcing the perception of a "quarrelsome left" splintering into countless factions.

The results of the vote effectively consolidated Pablo Iglesias' leadership. He was re-elected Secretary General for the third time. His list, *Un Podemos contigo*, won all 89 seats on the *Consejo Ciudadano Estatal* with 93.7% of the votes, while the list *Nuevo Impulso por la Democracia Interna en Podemos*, led by well-known critical activist Fernando Barredo, received 3.57%. The *Lista Blanca para Tercera*

---

8 For the details of this election phase, please refer to Chapter 3.

Asamblea Ciudadana, which lacked a candidate for Secretary General, received 2.73% and did not secure any seats.

However, the most notable figure was the low level of participation—or rather, non-participation—in the process. Likely due to the perception that the outcome was predetermined, as there was no viable alternative to Iglesias' leadership, only 59,190 people voted. Out of 516,492 members—219,158 considered active—this represents 11.46% of total membership and 27% of active members. This level of participation stood in stark contrast to the more competitive *Vistalegre II*, where the clash between the three main documents and Podemos' electoral growth drove greater engagement.

The main reform emerging from the III Congress is already clear from the title of the new Organizational Document: "The New Militant Organizational Model". In its opening paragraph, Podemos is defined as "A political instrument that aims to change the lives of the popular classes in this country of countries through social mobilization and entry into the institutions so that they are finally useful to the majorities and not to a few privileged elites" (Organizational Document, 2020:7). Notably, the term "class" is paired with the adjective "popular", signaling a rhetorical shift toward a more inclusive leftist discourse. Additionally, the emphasis on Spain's plurinational character (*"este país de países"*) reflects the political centrality of the Catalan crisis from 2017 to 2019.

The reform of Podemos' participation system, which began with the II Congress, takes its final form here. The document highlights the need to consolidate Podemos' organization at the local level—its "weakest link"—by strengthening its *Círculos:*

> Militancy will be more than ever a key player in the present and future of our organization. From now on, we will provide them with all the tools at our disposal to ensure that their voice gets the echo it deserves. The militants will be the ones who can exclusively choose their local leadership, and they will always refer to a *Círculo.* [...] In short, as we will see in the following pages, it is a matter of giving meaning, power, and collective action to the organic tools that our base must empower itself and do politics externally, outlining the political line that the organization will pursue in its territory and building a common future together with the sister forces of change. (Organizational Document, 2020: 7–8)

The militant thus becomes the key agent within the *Círculo* to which they belong, actively participating and determining the political line, particularly at the local level. The subscriber, on the other hand, is someone who supports the party without making a personal commitment but retains the ability to express their opinion through the online platform on macro-level issues defined by the executive bodies (such as municipal primaries, program development, decisions on alliances, and the composition of state and regional bodies).

Another notable change is that to become a full member of the organization—and thus a militant—it is now mandatory to pay a "popular quota" (deemed essential "for a project that supports itself outside the banks"). Additionally, this militancy must be linked to a single *Círculo*. This marks a significant shift in Podemos' concept of *membership*. The previous model, characterized by free and fluid participation with highly permeable boundaries, which allowed for varying degrees of engagement and largely relied on online platforms, has evolved into a system with clearly defined limits. Militancy now becomes a conscious choice and a personal commitment, formalized through the payment of a fee and deeply connected to practical activities at the local level. This transition moves Podemos from a participation model more akin to that of a social movement to one closer to a mass-party structure.

As Raffaella Fittipaldi (2021) observes, the *multi-speed membership* model proposed by political scientist Susan Scarrow (2015) aligned well with Podemos' original organizational identity: diverse forms of participation, undefined contours, engagement from different types of members and activists, and the use of horizontal and innovative practices were all crucial to Podemos' early success. What is now taking shape with the III Congress is a model that more closely aligns with Duverger's "concentric circles" concept (1961): an inner core of militants, a wider group of interested members who participate in macro-level decisions, and the outermost circle of voters. However, despite moving toward this form of institutionalization (and not simply "normalization"), Podemos' genetic nature still influences participation methods, which remain varied and innovative. For example, there are cyber-members who engage exclusively through the party's digital tools; supporters who contribute financially; social media followers or cyber activists who interact primarily through digital communication channels; and the news audience, who consume party messaging unidirectionally via social media, television, or articles. Thus, participation is becoming increasingly institutionalized but remains shaped by Podemos' foundational innovations.

Another key development in Podemos' evolution is the reform of the *Círculos*. While *Vistalegre II* had already positioned the *Círculos* as significant actors in the party's new territorial rooting strategy, the III Congress formally elevated them to a fundamental role as territorial decision-making hubs for local political practice. As stated in the new Organizational Document:

> The *Círculos* at the state level are the pillar on which Podemos' deployment is based and constitute an additional actor participating in the popular movement in our country. They are, in short, an instrument designed for direct action from their proximity to their territorial sphere. Support for the *Círculos* must be strengthened to maintain and increase our strength in the cities and towns. (Organizational Document, 2020: 58)

The *Círculos* also become Podemos' means of maintaining proximity to social movements while in government, acting as active agents of the popular movement in which Podemos is embedded. The objective is to create "capillarity" within the organization while listening to and supporting the needs of social forces. This dynamic fosters a continuous exchange between the top and grassroots levels while preserving the independence of the movements—a contact described as "fluid and permanent". Words like "fraternity, sisterhood, democracy, dignity, and identification" appear repeatedly in the section outlining the tasks of the *Círculos*. Their primary goal is to disseminate these principles, contributing to the "effective construction of the people" and fostering the "construction of a participative, critical, and autonomous society together with the rest of the social fabric".

The new strategy explicitly emphasizes long-term construction and societal transformation, grounded in the rhetoric of "position warfare". This marks Podemos' "new culture of militancy". The local organization is no longer structured to mirror the national model but is instead built around the *Círculos*. To bridge the gap between the autonomous level (comprising the *Asamblea Ciudadana Autonómica* and *Consejo Ciudadano Autonómico*) and the local level, intermediate provincial structures known as *Redes de Círculos Provinciales* are introduced:

> New intermediate structures are indispensable for militancy, through the *Círculos*, to be able to play a leading role and do politics at both local and regional levels, offering their representatives forums for discussion, proposals, debates, and socio-political interventions in their closest reality: neighborhoods, villages, or cities, and bringing these voices to the *Consejo Ciudadano Autonómico*. For this reason, in the case of communities with several provinces or on islands, we propose the creation of a *Red de Círculos* that would be a space of greater proximity than the autonomous one, from which to raise questions to the *Consejos Ciudadanos* and, at the same time, debate the solutions and policies that are given in these, as the highest organs among the assemblies of the territories. (Organizational Document, 2020: 39)

At the municipal level, structural changes were also introduced. In municipalities with 50 or fewer militants (or more, but with only one *Círculo*), new discussion forums called *Plenarias* were established, where a Municipal Spokesperson is elected to replace the previous *Secretarías Generales Municipales*. This spokesperson can propose forming a *Consejo de Coordinación Municipal* (Municipal Coordination Council), whose size will correspond to the number of militants. In municipalities with 51 or more militants and multiple *Círculos* (neighborhood or district-based), a new body, the *Consejo de Círculos*, replaces the *Consejo Ciudadano Municipal* and assumes its responsibilities. This *Consejo* consists of two members—at least one of whom must be a woman—from each *Círculo* in the municipality. Militants also elect a municipal spokesperson, who can propose forming their *Conse-*

jo de Coordinación Municipal. At the autonomous level, the structure remains largely the same, although the title of *Secretaría General Autonómica* is replaced by *Coordinación Autonómica*, which is responsible for political and institutional representation and ensuring strategic coherence with the national leadership.

On the one hand, this reform reorganizes Podemos' grassroots structure, strengthening territorial ties and clarifying boundaries and responsibilities. On the other hand, the *central office structure* remains largely unchanged, except for the expansion of executive bodies: the *Consejo Ciudadano Estatal* grows from 62 to 89 members, and the *Secretariado* increases from 15 members to a maximum of 30, forming the party's executive leadership.

The victory of the 'pablista' proposal in *Vistalegre II* marked the beginning of Podemos' organizational structuring. From that point onward, the party began to resemble a "top-down movement party". The III Congress finalized this transformation, adopting a bureaucratic, task-oriented structure at all levels—national, autonomous, and local—while maintaining the party's innovative roots. At the same time, participation evolved significantly. While the early Podemos relied on horizontal platforms and grassroots engagement, the III Congress introduced a more traditional, party-like participation model with "concentric circles" (Duverger, 1961). Militants with defined rights and responsibilities, including fee-based membership, now occupy the core of the organization, distinct from simple adherents who remain peripheral supporters.

4.8 The *Cuarta Asamblea Ciudadana:* the absent omnipresent

The *Cuarta Asamblea Ciudadana* (Fourth Citizen Assembly) was held on June 12–13, 2021, following the resignation of Pablo Iglesias on May 4, 2021, and his departure from political and institutional life. After seven years of undisputed leadership, Podemos needed to reorganize itself around a new central figure, both organizationally and in terms of media and discourse. This is why, little more than a month later, the assembly was organized at the *Auditorio Paco de Lucía* near the Madrid town of Alcorcón. The atmosphere was unique: the usual "crowd bath" of past congresses was absent due to the social distancing measures imposed by the pandemic. Under the summer sun, shaded by purple umbrellas, the audience did not witness the usual opening address from Pablo Iglesias but instead a video tribute recounting his political journey, concluding with the large inscription *"Gracias Pablo"*. The organization appeared "orphaned" of the central pivot of its structure, image, and identity.

There were three candidates to succeed Iglesias. The favorite from the outset was Ione Belarra, appointed *Ministra de Derechos Sociales y Agenda 2030* after

Iglesias' resignation. Her candidacy, *Crecer*, brought together most of Podemos' leadership, including Irene Montero, *Ministra de Igualdad*, and 11 Autonomous Co-ordinators. Belarra's leadership represented the continuity of the 'pablista' team, symbolizing the party's role in government. She was also a reassuring figure for the decisions Iglesias declared upon his resignation—namely, that he would "give his all" to ensure that Vice-President Yolanda Díaz (IU), *Ministra del Trabajo*, would become the country's first female President in the next general elections. In other words, Belarra's leadership of Podemos would honor the agreements made before Iglesias' departure.

The other two, more minor candidates were Esteban Tettamanti, a Podemos councilor in San Lorenzo de El Escorial (Madrid), who ran with the list *Podemos Horizontal*, and Fernando Barredo (who had also run against Iglesias in the III Congress) with the list *Nuevo Impulso*. According to the data, active voters were reduced to 138,457 (a sharp drop from previous consultations), with 53,443 votes cast, or 39.32 %. This figure was similar to the participation level in the III Congress just a year earlier, demonstrating resilient participation despite the declining trend in prior congresses. As expected, Ione Belarra won with an overwhelming majority, securing 45,753 votes, or 86.61 % of the total. Barredo obtained 3,106 votes (5.8 %), while Tettamanti received 2,730 votes (5.1 %).

Ione Belarra thus became the new General Secretary of Podemos—the first woman to take on the weighty legacy of Pablo Iglesias. Her first public speech[9] at the *Asamblea Ciudadana* was paradigmatic of Podemos' new course. Belarra began by thanking a wide range of individuals and groups, including *"sister"* forces of the European and global left (such as *La France Insoumise, Bloque de Izquierda, Die Linke, SYRIZA, Mas Bolivia*, the Party of the European Left, *Parti du travail de Belgique*, etc.), as well as national and regional actors with whom Podemos had built electoral alliances and the *UP* coalition. These included Alberto Garzón, leader of *Izquierda Unida* and *Ministro de Consumo*, Yolanda Díaz, and Enrique Santiago, Secretary General of the Communist Party of Spain and *Secretario de Estado para la Agenda 2030* until July 2022. She also thanked representatives of trade unions, collectives, and social committees. This was more than a list of acknowledgments; it underscored the political and ideological space in which her discourse would move—much more connoted on the right-left axis than others analyzed in the previous paragraphs.

Belarra's first acknowledgment, however, was for Pablo Iglesias, the ever-present absentee throughout the Congress: "Thank you for teaching us that a militant

---

9 All the interventions of the *Cuarta Asamblea Ciudadana* are available here: *Directo #Podemos | IV Asamblea Ciudadana en Alcorcón*, El País, https://www.youtube.com/watch?v=zPM5 t5NEyqs.

must be where he is most useful. [...] This will always be your home" (Belarra, 2021). Belarra spoke as both a minister and the leader of a governing party, a rhetoric that was new for Podemos in a public forum. She listed achievements from the first year of the coalition government, such as the Social Shield, the *Ley Rider*, the *Ley contra la violencia de la infancia*, and the upcoming *Ley de vivienda*. These accomplishments, she argued, demonstrated the political and historical significance of breaking the bipartisan system and building the first coalition government. However, the core of her speech was dedicated to the militants—the "heart of Podemos"—those who not only register but sustain the organization on the ground and within social movements, "taking time out of their lives and enduring insults". According to Belarra, it was thanks to them that the coalition government had been possible. The tone of the speech, however, was distinct: it did not speak of a militant "we" but a "you", addressing a central group external to the leadership. This was further emphasized by the prominent presence behind her of Podemos' new female leadership: Lilith Verstrynge, future *Secretaria de Organización y Formación*; Isa Serra, spokesperson; and Idoia Villanueva, future *Secretaria Internacional y Relación con Otras Fuerzas*.

From an organizational perspective, the IV Congress introduced no significant changes, as the party's structural reform had been completed only a year earlier to align Podemos with its new role in government. The only notable modification was an increase in the number of members of the national leadership bodies: the *Consejo Ciudadano Estatal* grew from 89 to 97 members, and the *Consejo de Coordinación* retained its maximum limit of 30 members.

The IV Congress thus served primarily to establish a new leadership following Iglesias' resignation and to further consolidate the state-level coordinating bodies, including the political leadership and executive (or political secretariat). The latest Congress (at the time of writing) marks the culmination of Podemos' evolutionary path, resulting in a fully institutionalized structure. The party has transitioned from a loosely defined organizational form to one comparable to a traditional political party. However, Podemos retains some of its nontraditional features inherited from its origins, such as the centrality of the *Asamblea Ciudadana*.

4.9 The next step: strengthening the organization

As is evident from the results presented and the statements in the semi-structured interviews, since the "blitzkrieg", Podemos has not been able to fully complete the process that began with the III Congress: establishing a strong territorial presence and building intermediate cadres on the ground capable of sustaining the organization beyond electoral moments. In short, the goal was to transition to "position warfare", involving a slow accumulation and gradual weakening of the political enemy (Gramsci, 1975). This is now Podemos' primary objective, with organizational strengthening being the core focus of the latest policy document (Political Document, *La fuerza para seguir transformando*, 2023). The document drafting process began on September 16, 2023, while consultations for government formation following the July general elections were still ongoing, during a public assembly titled *Con Vostras, Podemos* ("With you, we can"). At that event, Ione Belarra launched a process of collective debate among all local assemblies and militants. It was a process of "collective reflection" that allowed discussion and amendments to the document proposed by the executive, aiming to collectively redefine Podemos' course within the changing political landscape. The document was then presented at a political conference on November 4, 2023 (called with the same name), and became the party's political line. According to the General Secretary, over "5900 militants participated in more than 30 territorial meetings, with more than 2000 amendments, of which we incorporated more than 80 %".

The need to launch a long-term process of further organizational structuring was confirmed by former Organization Secretary (2022) Lilith Verstrynge in the following interview:

> A: I think Podemos now aims to have a different, more long-term perspective. If before it was a blitzkrieg to get to government, Podemos now has the perspective of building more organization.
>
> L.V.: Exactly, and safeguard us, because it is a cold period and what needs to be done is to stabilize, not disappear. I think we are not at the point of disappearing, but I think that is the doubt that the right has. So, stabilize and wait while you continue to do politics. (Verstrynge L., 2002, Interview 3)

This process will take time, especially because it started on a foundation with significantly different characteristics: strong horizontality and permeability, little territorial structure, and broad transversal participation, coupled with a decisive vertical organization and strong top-down leadership. In this regard, Pablo Iglesias confirmed in an interview that organizing Podemos served to move from a highly hierarchical structure to a more "collegial and democratic" one:

> A: Has the organizational form of Podemos changed for you? From a more horizontal organization to one that is more structured like a traditional party?
>
> P.I.: On the contrary, it started by being enormously vertical. In the beginning, Podemos was Iglesias, also betting on plebiscitary mechanisms, and just when it became a party it became a more collegial structure, with organs, democratic procedures, with accountability mechanisms. When Podemos was more hierarchical it was at the beginning. (Iglesias, 2022, Interview 1)

That type of organization was originally conceived as an electoral war machine for the central objective since its creation: becoming the first party and forming a Podemos-driven government. For this reason, Iglesias argued that after over-coming this contingency, the organization needed to be further structured and in-stitutionalized:

> P.I.: The electoral war machine responded to the contingency, to a moment in which there was no time to build the party and it was necessary to compete, to compete in elections. But of course, when time slows down, we say that the organization must be built with its democratic spaces, with its participatory spaces, with its territorial reality, etc. (Iglesias, 2022, Interview 1)

The current phase of organizational construction therefore focuses on defining local positions, training political cadres, and establishing more direct and consis-tent contact between national and territorial levels. Upon assuming the role of Or-ganization Secretary in June 2021, Lilith Verstrynge identified this as her top pri-ority:

> L.V.: [...] When we started working in the Secretariat of the Organization, we strengthened the regional level, which I think was necessary to do. We need to train the regional cadres, we must not treat them as if they were evil. I think we must work with them, be in good contact with them, and train them. But, above all, we tried to make the contact between the state level and the other levels more direct. And the other levels had to be created. (Verst-rynge L., 2002, Interview 3)

As Verstrynge continued, Podemos' organizational structure is being equipped with practical tools to reconnect the party's base with the national leadership while training intermediate cadres to lead on the ground. These tools include opening a Telegram chat for municipal and regional leaders ("an absurd thing, which had never been done before"), enabling them to share information directly; organizing assemblies or meetings on municipalism; and increasing the physical presence of national leaders in different territories. Previously, "Pablo went little to the places in general; people came to see him in Madrid." Other initiatives in-clude national 'milestone' events like the municipalist meetings, the *Universidad De Verano*, the *Uni de Otoño*, and the *Fiesta de la Primavera*. These gatherings allow militants to connect and engage, fostering political, emotional, and senti-mental ties to the organization. Verstrynge also emphasized a robust militant training program: "online and face-to-face training and, above all, organic train-ing. To explain to people how to build a party, how to do it." (Verstrynge L., 2002,

Interview 2). I personally participated in all the national events of 2022[10], observing firsthand the organizational, economic, and militant investment Podemos devoted to such meetings. The research strategy included participatory observation of public events and gatherings with party activists. This method was essential for understanding Podemos' "performative" aspect—its deliberate construction of a political community through collective events, whether public or exclusive to militants and activists. These events revealed key information from within, rather than relying solely on secondary sources, which aided in conducting the in-depth interviews.

The event structure is consistent: highly captivating and evocative videos and graphics promoted through social channels; a packed calendar of debates and training sessions on key political themes featuring members of the Secretariat or prominent institutional representatives; cultural, musical, and leisure activities to build a sense of community; and general assemblies recreating the atmosphere of the early *Asambleas Ciudadanas*, often attended by European and international political representatives.

These events also highlighted the emergence of new leadership figures associated with specific issues, a trend reflected in both media and digital communication. While Ione Belarra remains the General Secretary and central leader, other political figures—primarily women—have taken on prominent roles. Irene Montero, in addition to serving as a minister (2020–2023) and as MEP from 2024, has become the face of Podemos' gender equality discourse. Ángela Rodríguez Martínez has gained visibility over the past year, particularly on LGBTI+ issues. Idoia Villanueva, a Podemos MEP (2019–2014), has represented the party internationally, participating in global events and maintaining relations with foreign political forces. Lilith Verstrynge was a key figure in Podemos until her resignation in January 2024, known for her territorial outreach and her appointment as *Secretaria de Estado para la Agenda 2030*, a role that enhanced her institutional and media presence.

This model of "shared leadership" has elevated recognizable figures within the party and projected them to the broader electorate and Spanish public. However, the reliance on a single central leader has never been fully offset by the rise of figures capable of inheriting Iglesias' significant political legacy without internal turmoil or serving as strong territorial references. This was evident when Iglesias himself ran in the Madrid regional elections, stepping down as vice president

---

10 *Fiesta de la Primavera*, held in Valencia from 20 to 22 May 2022; *Cursos Complutense de Verano* held in San Lorenzo de El Escorial on 18 and 19 July 2022, *Uni de Otoño*, held at the *Facultad de Ciencias Políticas y Sociología UCM* in Madrid from 4 to 6 November 2022.

to reinvigorate the movement during a critical electoral period. The near-inevitable defeat forced Iglesias to resign as Secretary General and withdraw—at least temporarily—from political life.

Podemos' current objective is to consolidate its political and electoral space as an autonomous force while maintaining external support for the government. This involves both organizational and ideological strengthening. Organizationally, the party acknowledges weaknesses in its territorial presence, base organization, and relationships with social movements and other local forces:

> A plan to strengthen the organization with a clear militant protagonism. In the new phase, we need all the hands and all the intelligence of the people of Podemos in the task of leading the progressive bloc. This plan will include autonomous, provincial, island and district plans, taking into account the uniqueness of rural areas. New channels of political participation will be created with a focus on digital militants. The militant protagonism will be strengthened in all the activities of our organization, such as the 'Uni de otoño', the 'Fiesta de la Primavera' or the municipalist meeting. Likewise, activities will be carried out with the objective of strengthening the formation of the cadres of the party. (Political Document, *La fuerza para seguir transformando*, 2023: 39)

In terms of leadership, the "shared leadership" dynamic has continued beyond the government experience. Since the 2024 European elections, Irene Montero has resumed a central leadership role within the party. While she has always been a prominent figure, her exclusion from the general elections and government team of *Sumar* further elevated her symbolic and political prominence, leading to her appointment as Political Secretary within the *Consejo de Coordinación*. The party's two spokespersons, Pablo Fernández Santos—who became Secretary of Organization after Lilith Verstrynge's departure—and Isa Serra, also play significant media

4.10 Conclusion: the evolution of the organization

	Podemos I (2014– 2017)	Podemos II (2017–2020)	Podemos III (from 2020)
Participation	Horizontal participatory platform	Multi-speed membership	Militancy in concentric circles
Organization	Electoral war machine + Movement party	Top-down movement party	Hybrid Party

Tab. 4: Evolution of Podemos participation and organization. Source: author's elaboration.

Pablo was interested in a new type of party from a discursive point of view, but in practice he was interested in a party that would act as a transmission belt for his decisions, which were brilliant and very challenging. But we never managed to square the circle between a party that functions as an electoral machine and a party that functions democratically on the ground. And only now, when he is replaced by Ione Belarra, who has less charisma and less media capacity than Iglesias, the only way to articulate it is to build a party from the bottom up. And so, the new leadership, for the first time in eight years, has started to build a party. (Monedero, 2022, Interview 4)

As we have shown in the previous paragraphs, the attempt to combine the horizontal-participatory axis and the vertical-decisional axis has always been the omnipresent tension in the organizational life of Podemos. Monedero, with his characteristic rhetoric, is particularly clear in this excerpt from the interview: at first, the necessity of the nascent movement was to face the European elections a few months after its birth, when Podemos was only a participatory and media platform. Therefore, it was necessary to have an agile structure that could act as a fast transmission belt for the leadership's decisions. As Iglesias points out in his interview, Podemos' first "people" were mainly built around its media power:

It is the result, on one hand, of my presence in the media. So, the television audience is made up of people who watch Iglesias on television programs but who have a very specific ideological background, identifiable through the average of opinion polls. These include voters of leftist parties, such as Izquierda Unida, the PSOE, and pro-independence left-wing parties in Catalonia, the Basque Country, and Galicia, as well as left-wing abstentionists. In other words, it is a culturally progressive base, broader than that of the traditional left, but still operating within these parameters. (Iglesias, 2022, Interview 1).

An electorate was thus mobilized primarily through the top-down action of its leader, omnipresent in the media and effective as the party's internal leadership, while being simultaneously activated by the bottom-up thrusts of horizontal participation forms in territories and digital tools. Digital tools, however, did not evolve linearly, suffering significant setbacks in some cases. As highlighted by Meloni and Lupato (2023) in their *Two steps forward, one step back: the evolution of democratic digital innovations in Podemos:*

Contrary to studies that equate party change and democratization, we highlight the importance of setbacks as a possible outcome of the process of change. While some procedures were consolidated (e.g., microcredits and primaries), other well-known ones experienced hard setbacks such as elimination (e.g., *Plaza Podemos, BdT,* and *Impulsa*) or soft setbacks such as mutation (e.g., Citizens' Consultations and membership). (Meloni, Lupato, 2023)

Podemos, as an extremely permeable organization, experimented with practices and participatory modes inherited from 15M while showing a clear vertical leadership to act quickly in a scenario where the main objective was to "lift the table" and gain as much support as possible to reach the government. This organizational form epitomized the tension between the need for top-down direction and participatory impulses. The first Podemos can therefore be defined by the dyad "electoral war machine + movement party" using a "horizontal participatory platform". As Lilith Verstrynge argues in the interview:

> And in fact, the idea, within this tribune of the plebs, was to give the people a say and therefore to organize the Spanish people among the Spanish citizens and to make them participate in politics through a very horizontal organization. Then it is true that, of course, when you build a party, you must establish a series of hierarchies or axes, not fronts. (Verstrynge L., 2022, Interview 3)

Contrary to initial expectations before conducting this research—based on Podemos' horizontally participatory discourse—the party had already assumed a clear structure from its First Congress. While this structure still allowed permeable boundaries and base maneuverability, it revealed a strong vertical organization that would shape its entire evolution. Even though it retained its horizontal roots, Podemos began a process of institutionalization.

This process became one of the key points of conflict during *Vistalegre II.* Of course, this was not the only issue: as some interviews reveal, alongside an organizational and strategic-discursive clash, a struggle for leadership was at the heart of the conflictual relationship between Iglesias and Errejón. The victory of the 'pablista' hypothesis initiated a process of organizational institutionalization, strengthening the executive organs and building the political Secretariat while simultaneously focusing on reorganizing the grassroots and enhancing participation. At the local level, the centrality of the *Círculos* was strengthened, and the reform of militancy—more formal than substantial—began. This reform introduced a distinction between "members" and "militants" and provided opportunities for both digital participation and engagement with social movements through the *"Vamos"* platform. A *multi-speed membership* (Scarrow, 2015) was thus balanced with a more stable leadership structure, including a well-defined General Secretariat and an executive with specific roles and assignments. As a result, the organization took on the form of a "top-down movement party", underscoring its progressive institutionalization.

The III Congress further solidified Podemos' organizational structure. Boundaries were now clearly defined, culminating in the reform of militancy and the adoption of a participative form based on "concentric circles" (Duverger, 1961). This model established militants with well-defined rights and responsibilities, including the payment of a fee as a commitment to active participation. Despite this shift, the participatory origins of Podemos were preserved through the

Asamblea Ciudadana, an institution that remained a central feature of the party. This assembly—comprising members and militants—continued to elect the main offices and decide on significant issues. However, Podemos' leadership, in practice, centered on the General Secretariat and the *Consejo de Coordinación*, with the various Secretariats becoming increasingly personalized. Podemos thus adopted a formal party structure with an internal bureaucracy and clear divisions of power at the national, regional, and local levels while retaining its innovative participatory roots.

It can therefore be concluded that the institutionalization process has transformed Podemos into a genuine political party, albeit one with unconventional characteristics, which can be defined as a "party". This definition is supported in most interviews conducted. In this regard, Iglesias himself states:

> P.I.: Podemos is a party. It is a party with a party organization, with its territorial organization and leadership. Here I think the fundamental challenge is to understand that parties serve for what they serve. Parties serve to run for elections. Parties are for governing. Parties need to organize their presence on the ground. But parties need to be part of a broader political and cultural will, where the key is their relationship with social movements and their relationship with key ideological actors. But I believe that there is no magic, in the sense that there is no organizational formula that can make the difference. The organizational form of Podemos is a party form. (Iglesias, 2022, Interview 1)

This statement by Iglesias is particularly significant. The former leader identifies Podemos' organizational form as a political party—a term initially avoided during its early days, when Podemos was more closely associated with social movements. He clarifies that the party is not the ultimate goal but rather one of many tools for achieving transformative political change. This tool must operate alongside broader cultural and political forces, such as social movements and the media, forming part of a cohesive and independent strategy. However, Iglesias insists that the party remains a necessary organizational form that cannot be replaced by any "magic formula".

Podemos is a continuously evolving organization that successfully leveraged the "populist moment" for electoral and media success. Internal and external factors have driven Podemos, particularly since its time in government, toward an organizational shift that aligns with a "hybrid party model". While it has become more institutionalized, it has not been "normalized" into traditional party forms. Podemos now exhibits a higher level of institutionalization compared to its early days as a movement party, transitioning from weak boundaries and low bureaucracy to a fully structured political party. At the same time, the party retains certain participatory and structural inheritances from its horizontal origins. Thus, it can be hypothesized that Podemos' current organizational form can best be described as a "hybrid party". The hybrid and highly open organizational form allowed the early Podemos to channel the mobilization of those who sought active participation. The need for engagement, discussion, and visible territorial structures was a tangible legacy of the 15M movement in Spain. Podemos could never be solely a vertical cartel party (Katz, Mair, 1995), calling on followers merely to vote, nor exclusively a personal party (Calise, 2000) centered on Iglesias. It had to provide tools for participation that reflected its core values of participatory democracy while serving as a practical means to maintain support and build territorial presence. Its genetic organizational form was, therefore, not only a strategic machine for securing consensus but also a practical expression of its long-term vision. This research aligns with the findings of Daniela Chironi and Raffaella Fittipaldi in their *Social movements and new forms of political organization: Podemos as a hybrid party* (2017), where they define Podemos' "hybrid" nature as follows:

> In sum, our analysis suggests that movement mobilization played a large role in shaping Podemos' foundational choices. The result is a "hybrid" party that, to flourish in times of crisis of representation, has found a balance between the horizontalism of social movements and the efficiency of a party that aims to manage a share of state power. Overall, its genesis, as well as its evolution and organizational features, confirm our evaluation of the crucial nature of this case study. We believe indeed that other new parties, born under conditions of protest and crisis, may have followed similar paths of emergence and organizational development. (Chironi, Fittipaldi, 2021)

As discussed in previous chapters, the end of the *Unidas Podemos* coalition and the emergence of *Sumar* have further disrupted Podemos' fragile organizational development. The formation of the Sánchez III government marked the end of Podemos' governmental experience: although the government was established in coalition with Sumar—an alliance that included Podemos—none of its members were appointed to government positions. On December 5, 2023, Podemos withdrew from the Sumar parliamentary group. As a result, Podemos' parliamentary strength now relies solely on its 5 deputies, who will join the mixed group. This marks a sharp decline in Podemos' institutional strength at the national level compared to the previous legislature. The party's organizational evolution is therefore accompanied by a significant decline in its institutional influence and electoral support, as reflected in the results of the last *autonomicas* elections analyzed in Chapter 3. On January 26, 2024, Lilith Verstrynge announced via her social networks that she was resigning from all her positions within Podemos, including her seat in Congress. The current organizational setup discussed here faces yet another setback to its implementation, becoming redundant—or at least provisional—at a time when Podemos is reconfiguring its role in the Spanish political landscape, and perhaps its very identity.

The analysis of Podemos' case provides key insights into the organizational development of left-populist parties. It demonstrates the significant organizational challenges faced by left-populist forces. Their emergence, often rooted in social movements or horizontal participation, leads to a light and decentralized organizational structure with permeable boundaries. Simultaneously, the need to represent these demands electorally necessitates the creation of vertical, national structures to manage the electoral war machine that fuels the populist strategy.

The electoral success of these forces generates two critical demands: first, the creation of an organizational apparatus capable of sustaining institutional or governmental participation, and second, the need for deeper structuring to ensure long-term organizational stability. The main challenge lies within the party's grassroots level, which is often underdeveloped due to the party's rapid rise and the vertical organization initially designed to maximize the populist strategy. Entering government represents a strong institutionalizing force for these parties, often leading them to adopt organizational forms similar to those of traditional political parties.

This chapter has identified the changes and evolution of the internal structure. In the following chapter, it will be necessary to analyze the changes that occur in the discursive and communicative dimension directed outward, which, as highlighted, strongly defines the very nature of populist forces. At the end of the analysis of these two dimensions, the conclusions will present the results obtained within the proposed theoretical framework, identifying the direction of Podemos' evolution in government.

Chapter 5 – Transitioning from Challenger to Governing Party: The Evolution of Discourse

5.1 Introduction

The analysis of the evolution of political communication regarding ruling populist forces has significantly developed in recent years. Some scholars (Akkerman 2016; Bernhard 2020; Krause, Wagner 2019) have theorized that ruling populist forces adapt their discourse according to the so-called "inclusion-moderation thesis", originally used to explain the moderating effects experienced by parties with religious origins. Akkerman, for instance, explains that this thesis "argues that participation in democratic institutions and procedures will change the radical nature and ideology of political parties" (Akkerman et al. 2016:3). This occurs due to two main factors: first, populist parties in power tend to soften their discourse and demands to appeal to a broader electorate, which allows them to maintain power. Second, participation in government office is often linked to a moderating effect when these parties engage in coalition governments (Akkerman et al. 2016; Bernhard 2020). In this sense, negotiation and compromise with coalition partners become essential for their survival as a governing force.

Political scientist Jakob Schwörer tests these theories in his insightful research *Less Populist in Power? Online Communication of Populist Parties in Coalition Governments.* Schwörer notes, "we are faced with a growing number of studies dealing with the outcomes and consequences of populist participation in government, but with very little empirical evidence on the validity of the inclusion-moderation thesis for populist communication" (Schwörer, 2021: 472). However, Schwörer's analysis reveals a countertrend to the theories mentioned above. He finds no clear evidence that populist parties systematically tone down their rhetoric once they enter a governing coalition. Additionally, electoral setbacks and shifts in public opinion, often associated with changes in communication strategies, do not fully explain these changes. Schwörer argues that the quality and quantity of populist messages are influenced more by developments in each country's political and institutional context. Specifically, "the discourses of populist parties should not be expected to be tamed by offering them participation in a coalition government" (Schwörer, 2021: 486).

The shift in populist communication when in government is, therefore, a crucial aspect to examine. This chapter contends that it is inaccurate to describe this shift as a moderation of populist language. Instead, the change involves a transformation in characteristics: moving from a more transversal form of communica-

https://doi.org/10.1515/9783111591537-009

tion that relied on the 'high-low' axis as the central rhetorical tool of opposition to power, to a communication style that is more responsive to specific issues and the ideological traits of the political force. In essence, this is not merely a shift in content but also a redefinition of 'the people' and the target electorate, which incorporates a greater emphasis on the left-right axis. This perspective aligns with the research using Podemos as a case study, as it highlights unique features and lines of evolution while identifying digital communication as one of its key strategic tools. For instance, Campolongo, Raniolo, and Tarditi (2021), in their work *Podemos' Online Communication in the Time of Government*, present the following hypothesis:

> Our second hypothesis is that Podemos representatives have focused their communication on issues about government activity, promoting the party no longer as a protest actor, but rather as a responsive governmental force and, at the same time, able to hold itself accountable. (Campolongo, Raniolo, Tarditi, 2021)

5.2 The leader's speeches

Para dialogar, preguntad primero; después..., escuchad.

With this quote from the Spanish poet Antonio Machado, Pablo Iglesias ends his first inaugural speech as Vice-President of the Government of Spain. A speech that, despite its brevity, contains many significant elements. The choice of quotation is particularly notable: Iglesias chooses, at the height of Podemos' institutional power, to quote a poet who symbolizes the republican struggle against the monarchy. Furthermore, he selects a phrase that reflects the challenges of dialogue between UP and PSOE, while simultaneously expressing a willingness to engage and listen. It marks the beginning of a tense relationship, shaped by clear vetoes from the PSOE after Podemos' relentless campaign to forge a coalition government for change. Iglesias, in fact, describes the task ahead as "difficult" but takes the time to thank "the comrades and companions" of the PSOE for enabling a collaboration rooted in the principles of *"compañerismo"* and teamwork.

"Trabajo" and *"trabajadores"* are the recurring words in his speech, referring not only to the government's actions but also to the people he most wants to acknowledge, particularly the workers and officials of the ministry who will work alongside him. One of the first videos produced by Podemos[1]' communication

---

1 The video is available here: *Día 1: PABLO se presenta A TODO EL EQUIPO del Ministerio (Vídeo Inédito), Podemos,* https://www.youtube.com/watch?v=2Azjvz7Puds.

team shows Iglesias entering the Ministry of Social Rights building, personally greeting and thanking all the workers, from accounting officials to cleaning staff. While this video may seem trivial, it effectively identifies the communicative and discursive framework in which Podemos' governmental action—and specifically Iglesias' role—will take place. It is no coincidence that Iglesias begins his speech by noting the "irony" that his governmental journey begins in the very building that once housed the *Sindicato Vertical* (Vertical Trade Union), the only union permitted under Francisco Franco's dictatorship: "It speaks well of our history that we are here today" (Iglesias, 2020).

Iglesias defines the key characteristics of his ministry's mandate as those of "democratic constitutionalism", which he explains as "guaranteeing, securing, and expanding social rights". Achieving this, he emphasizes, requires a dynamic relationship between institutions and grassroots movements—one of mutual listening and pressure, as previously outlined in Podemos' political documents. Once again, Machado's quote perfectly encapsulates the essence of this relationship for Podemos. Iglesias makes it clear from the outset who his social referents are, and they are not "transversal" actors:

> I also want to refer to social movements, tenants' unions, workers' unions, civil society. Thank you for defending social justice over the last ten years. You will be the reference for this vice presidency. Don't stop criticizing us, don't stop lobbying us. This will allow us to do the best things. (Iglesias, 2020)

This concept is reiterated in a tweet from February 4, 2020:

> The social movements that have been saying '*Sí se puede*' for years are the real architects of this agreement. Now their pressure and vigilance will be essential for the new government to fulfill its historic mission: to transform this '*Sí se puede*' into real and concrete policies. (Iglesias, 2020)

The analysis of Iglesias' communication strategy is important for several reasons. First, his figure embodies the defining characteristics of the left-wing populist leader, serving simultaneously as party secretary and digital prince (Calise, Musella, 2019). Second, within Podemos, he is widely regarded as the most decisive figure to date, with his communicative style shaping both the organization and development of the party. As Lilith Verstrynge confirms early in her interview:

> The political bet that Podemos made when Pablo was leading the space in the first months, even in the dynamics of the European elections and then in everything that followed, was that the growth of the party was mainly focused on communication. So, first and foremost, everything revolved around the figure of that small leadership that came from the Complu-

tense University, which was a series of indignant professors who accompanied *juventud sin futuro*, etc., and around the figure of Pablo [...]. What my father [Jorge Verstrynge] used to say was that Pablo had to act as a tribune of the plebs. Pablo was indeed like the replica of the working class brought to indignation, to political contestation, who becomes a leader. So, the whole discourse of *Vallecano Coleta*[2], in other words, ordinary people suddenly decided to get involved in politics. So, at that time it is true that all that gave us militancy, and participation, that filled our meetings and assemblies, was basically the communicative power he had. In the beginning Pablo was very committed to going on television and, above all, to going to the right-wing media and confronting the right directly, telling a series of things that until then had never been told on television, let alone by a young university professor from a middle-class working-class background. It was around this that the growth of the party was built. (Verstrynge L., 2022, Interview 2)

Since the leader's discursive strategies are a defining feature of populist political forces and play a major role in determining their key characteristics, I have chosen to analyze two aspects of Iglesias' communication. First, I will examine two public speeches delivered by the Podemos leader: his first closing campaign[3] speech during the 2014 European elections and his final campaign speech for the 2021 local elections in Madrid. Second, I will analyze the evolution of Iglesias' digital communication from August 2019[4], during his last national election campaign, until August 2021, when he made his first public reappearance after resigning from his party and governmental roles.

5.3 The First and Last Speech

The closing of the European election campaign in the square in front of the *Reina Sofía* Museum in Madrid on May 23, 2014, was the first true display of strength for Podemos. The party had only been founded a few months earlier but had achieved media attention and growth at an incredible speed for an outsider force presenting itself for the first time, without any funding or organizational structures, at an election. Iglesias' figure was so central at the time that it was decided to place his face on the ballot symbol, as shown in Fig. 13.

---

2 Iglesias had this nickname because of his neighborhood in Madrid (*Vallecas*, a working-class neighborhood) and his famous long hair, which was always pulled back in a ponytail (esp. *coleta*).
3 The full speech is available here: *DIRECTO: Cierre de Campaña Europeas 2014 PODEMOS*, Canal 33, https://www.youtube.com/watch?v=DipcspGXx7k
4 The full speech is available here: *APOTEÓSICO cierre de campaña de Pablo Iglesias en Madrid | #QueVoteLaMayoría*, Podemos, https://www.youtube.com/watch?v=dfG5N0v_x_4

ELECCIONES AL PARLAMENTO EUROPEO 2014
ELECCIONS AL PARLAMENT EUROPEU 2014
DIPUTADOS/AS / DIPUTATS/ADES

PODEMOS-PODEM

(PODEMOS)

PODEMOS

Pablo Iglesias Turrión (Podemos).
María Teresa Rodríguez-Rubio Vázquez (Podemos).
Carlos Jiménez Villarejo (Podemos).
María Dolores Lola Sánchez Caldentey (Podemos).
Pablo Echenique Robba (Podemos).
Tania González Peñas (Podemos).
Miguel Urban Crespo (Podemos).
Estefanía Torres Martínez (Podemos).
Xabier Benito Ziluaga (Podemos).
Esperanza Jubera García (Podemos).
Daniel Mari Ripa (Podemos).
Ana Villaverde Valenciano (Podemos).
Jesús Manuel Castillo Segura (Podemos).

Fig. 13: Podemos ballot paper in the 2014 European elections.

Iglesias' speech was by far the most anticipated of the rally and encapsulated the entire essence of the early Podemos public discourse. *El Coleta* did not begin in the style of traditional political speeches but by telling a story, the story of *"Rattolandia"*. In this city, rats "like us" lived, and every time they went to vote, they elected a party of cats. They could change the color of the cats, but they were still cats. The problems of Rattolandia's inhabitants were never solved and only worsened because "the problem was not the color of the cats, whether they were black, whether they were white, whether they were magenta. It didn't matter what color they were. The problem was that they were cats, and cats make laws for cats and against rats!" (Iglesias, 2014b). That is why one little rat decided to gather with other rats to form the first circles of a political force that would solely defend the interests of rats. This story is symbolically important not only because, for Iglesias, it "describes what Podemos is" but also because it explains, more than many analyses, the vision of 'them', the caste, in the early Podemos. *"Casta"* is one of the most recurrent terms in the discourse, referring to economic and media powers, bipartisan deputies, MEPs, and above all political parties without distinction: between the PP and PSOE, "who is a copy of them. What is the difference? They are cats!". The attack is primarily against the PSOE, which, according to Iglesias, does not represent the history of socialism in Spain (Iglesias claims to be part of a family of socialists, "the originals") because they are part of the European *"casta"*, governing alongside Merkel and Hollande against the interests of the European people. This is why he returns to the theme of ideology, using concepts he would later revisit, as became clear in the first Congress. Although Podemos has a leftist soul, its aim is not to be recognized as the "left-left of I don't know who", but to represent the majority against the caste:

> I am of the left because I have it tattooed in my DNA. Because I am the son of who I am, the grandson of who I am. But they no longer make fun of me: the problem of this country is neither the center-right nor the center-left, it is the caste! [...] How short-sighted are those who believe that power fears the left! How little they have understood the history of the 20th century. Power fears the people, power fears the people! And we are a social majority! (Iglesias, 2014b)

For Iglesias, the important thing is not ideology but action: "program, program, program!" is his mantra, echoing former PCE secretary Julio Anguita. One of the first points of Podemos' program for the European elections was precisely the limitation of MEP salaries and ensuring equal judicial treatment—proposals common among populist, especially left-wing and hybrid, movements. The program, however, was not leftist; it was a "social majority" program:

> This is a social majority program. Whatever people voted for, come what may, get excited with the symbols they get excited with... end the caste, ban boards of directors, let the banks pay their debts through an audit, wage restraint, that we can democratize the economy, social rights... this forms a social majority, a popular majority, the majority of the people. The 20th century taught us this. That history is changed like this: when the people say 'we are here, we are a people, we are masters of our history'! That's why they are afraid of Podemos, that's why! (Iglesias, 2014b)

This excerpt is symbolic of the 'leftist transversality' of the first Podemos—at this stage much more transversal than leftist. It is transversal because it appeals to a broad majority beyond ideological, political, or geographical boundaries. It mobilizes participation, popular consciousness, and practical actions against a recognizable enemy. It is also leftist, however, because the program's themes belong to a clear value system and because of certain terms and symbols used during the event. For instance, Iglesias ends his speech by emphasizing that the scariest part of Podemos is not its content but its method. The Podemos method is its primary distinction from other political forces: participation, grassroots citizen activation, open primaries, and people power. This, he argues, is the only way to fight the *caste* and restore the interests of "those from below". Iglesias ends by quoting Chilean President Salvador Allende: "*La historia es nuestra, pero la hacen los pue-*

blos. El pueblo unido jamás será vencido!"[5], leading into the iconic song composed by Sergio Ortega, part of the historical repertoire of the global left.

The last campaign closure where Pablo Iglesias spoke as a candidate was during the elections for the Community of Madrid. The climate was entirely different from 2014. Podemos was in its first year of governing alongside PSOE, facing the difficult management of the pandemic, which delayed its governing party strategy. Furthermore, Iglesias had just stepped down as Vice-President of the Council, leaving his role to Yolanda Díaz, whom Iglesias himself designated as the future UP candidate. Iglesias focused his efforts where they were "most useful" namely in the strategic Madrid elections, where Podemos sought to recover from its earlier defeat and stop a potential PP government with the far-right *Vox*. It was framed as a battle for democracy and the party's survival. The campaign slogan *"Que hable la mayoría"* ('Let the majority speak') encapsulated the divide: "they" were the minority pushing for far-right governance, privatizing essential public services, and mishandling the pandemic in favor of the few, while *"we"* were the majority fighting for rights, public health, women's and LGBTQI+ rights, and solidarity during the pandemic's mismanagement by the right.

Unlike in 2014, Iglesias avoids the term 'caste' in both opening and closing remarks. The enemy is no longer politicians or parties but a media and economic power working to halt progress through a right-wing victory. The discourse revolves around the "battle for democracy", positioning *Unidas Podemos* as the sole democratic defense against the far-right threat:

> The phenomenon of the ultra-right in Spain is an anti-democratic reaction to what Unidas Podemos implies as a political force that demonstrated that things could be changed in this country. Precisely because we have shown that democracy can work, precisely because we have shown that by respecting the rules of the game you can make policies that change people's lives. So, to those who only respect democracy when they win and when they leave the privileges of the rich untouched, then they stop liking democracy and have no problem calling themselves fascists. [...] Precisely because the mask falls off and they reveal what they have always been. They have never believed in democracy. They have always believed in power. (Iglesias, 2021b)

The discourse leans more on the left-right axis, though references to "privileges of the rich", "elites", and "economic powers" persist, warning of the consequences of a further rightward advance in Spain. The right, Iglesias argues, serves to protect the few's privileges against the majority and the democratic forces like *Unidas Podemos*. In the closing section, Iglesias revisits the events that brought Podemos to government, describing how media attacks, fake news, and the creation of *Ci-*

---

5 "History is ours, but it is made by the people. The people united will never be defeated".

udadanos—"the Podemos of the elites"—were used to prevent Podemos from governing.

For Iglesias, entering government was essential: "The fundamental thing is not what you sign in the document, it is whether it is realized afterward. And the only way to check that it is realized is to be in the Council of Ministers". This sentence captures Podemos' strategic vision, born to govern and implement its program. Iglesias frames the historical choices of Podemos as a political testament before resigning days later. The speech revisits high-low rhetoric but increasingly reflects the left-right axis. Iglesias highlights Podemos' disruption of elite power, noting that the powerful never imagined "those at the bottom" would hold power: a supermarket cashier like Irene Montero becoming Minister, a militant trade unionist like Yolanda Díaz becoming Vice-President, or austerity being replaced with neo-Keynesian policies during the pandemic. Iglesias warns the far-right threat undermines democracy and politics itself:

> Politics is an asset of those at the bottom to set limits to those at the top. The politically illiterate is the worst enemy of the working class. The political illiterate is the greatest enemy of the fact that there is public health, public education, and public services. When workers' organizations, when women's movements began to organize politically, the word 'democracy' began to make sense. That is why democracy must be defended in this campaign. Democracy is not just a process, it is not just changing the rules of the chess game, democracy is a historical movement. It is needed so that the social majority can do politics. [...] For people like us to be in the Council of Ministers, you need democracy, you need to do politics. They don't need it, they have money, big business power, media power. (Iglesias, 2021b).

In the final part of the speech, alongside the use of the 'high-low' frontier that underscores the "very meaning of doing politics", Iglesias builds to a discursive climax where the concept of the working class takes center stage. The Podemos leader repeats the term multiple times to highlight that "sovereignty does not belong to the King of Spain, but to the Spanish people. [...] The working class embodies the state, it embodies the institutions, it embodies sovereignty, against the elites who believe that the state is theirs. No! The State belongs to the common people" (Iglesias, 2021b).

As is evident, this passage clearly reflects the typical discourse of left-wing populism. "The people", defined as a socio-economically characterized subject, embody the very notion of sovereignty, uniting the first two traits of the populist people as described by Cas Mudde. Furthermore, reinforcing the left-right axis is the symbolic choice of the closing song of the rally, *Bella Ciao*, a traditional anthem of the Italian Resistance, which has become an iconic symbol for the global left.

Pablo Iglesias (@PabloIglesias) - Twitter mentions by month

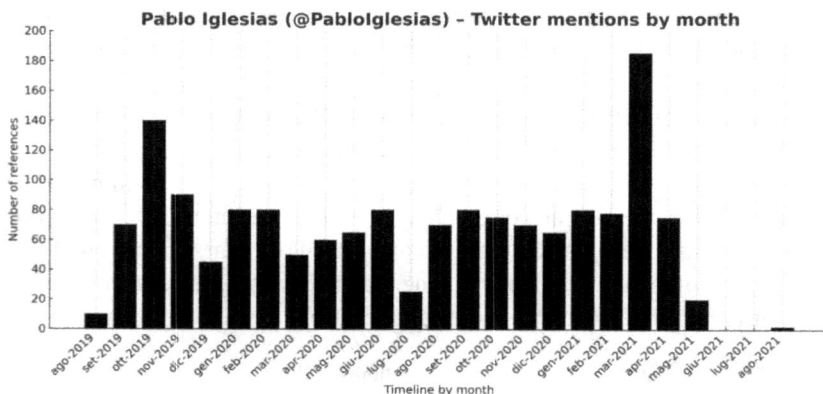

Fig. 14: Number of *tweets* per month by @PabloIglesias. Source: processed through Nvivo.

5.4 Iglesias' digital communication in the government

After analyzing two specific speeches, it is interesting at this point to observe the evolution of Iglesias' digital communication while in government. Fig. 14 graphically summarizes the Podemos leader's Twitter activity from August 2019 (the start of the electoral campaign for the November 2019 elections) to August 2021. This data is notable for several reasons: it is clear, first, that Iglesias' digital communication is an especially frequent and indispensable tool during election periods.

The leader's communication machine was significantly more active in October 2019, during the political election campaign for November, and particularly in April 2021, when Iglesias had already resigned from the government to personally focus on the election campaign for the Community of Madrid. The personal and organizational investment becomes evident when one considers that, in April 2021 alone, the number of posts published was more than three times the average.

Following the defeat in the regional elections, in which UP secured 7.24 %, and Iglesias' subsequent announcement of his departure from politics, he completely shut down all communication with the outside world, both on social media and in traditional media. After three months of silence, on August 30, 2021, Iglesias made his first public intervention—a phone-in participation in a debate on disinformation promoted by the media and the extreme right[6]. This marked the reemergence of Pablo Iglesias' social and media presence. Then, on September 4, he published an article in the magazine *Ctxt* titled *What if PP and Vox governed? The forces to the left of the PSOE should increase their collaboration throughout the state, share spaces for strategic reflection, and explore confederal paths*[7].

This programmatic article reiterates the need for a tactical alliance with the PSOE to prevent the extreme right from taking power. It reopens dialogue with the independence movements and levels strong criticism against the Spanish Crown, which Iglesias describes as an accomplice of a reactionary economic and media system. More importantly, the article lays the groundwork for strategic reflection on the future of UP and the broader Spanish left:

> What is to be done? In my opinion, the lefts other than the PSOE throughout the state must increase their collaboration and share spaces for strategic reflection. I believe they should assume that the government alliance with the PSOE is, at this juncture, necessary to protect democracy and implement social justice through public policies. The pandemic has reinforced a transversal sense of pride in the public sector, and, in a sense, the Keynesian turn that the EU has been forced to take is an opportunity with few precedents. At the same time, in the face of the reactionary project that, if it comes to government, will combine the most ferocious neoliberalism with the assault on autonomous powers and the persecution of independence advocates, the left must explore confederal paths for the reorganization of a shared state, more in line with national plurality and the will of the different peoples of the state. [...] Furthermore, I believe that the left must assume that the terrain of culture and ideology is as decisive as that of institutional and social mobilization. [...] What we have been losing for so many years in Madrid is not just elections, but a cultural and ideological battle. (Iglesias, 2021c)

---

6 The full speech is available here: https://x.com/PabloIglesias/status/1432416818996686855
7 Original title: *¿Y si gobernaran PP y Vox? Las fuerzas a la izquierda del PSOE deberían aumentar su colaboración en todo el Estado, compartir espacios de reflexión estratégica y explorar vías confederales,* https://ctxt.es/es/20210901/Firmas/37096/Pablo-Iglesias-tribuna-politica-izquierda-PSOE-gobierno-Vox-PP-ultraderecha.htm

Fig. 15: Word cloud @PabloIglesias. Source: author's elaboration via Nvivo. Note: The reference period is August 1, 2019 – November 10, 2019.

Fig. 16: Word cloud @PabloIglesias. Source: author's elaboration via Nvivo. Note: The reference period is November 11, 2019 – January 12, 2020.

Fig. 17: Word cloud @PabloIglesias. Source: author's elaboration via Nvivo. Note: The reference period is January 13, 2020 – August 31, 2021.

Continuing with the analysis of Pablo Iglesias's social networks during the period when he was leader of Podemos, Fig. 15, 16, and 17 graphically represent the words most frequently used on his Twitter (from 2023 "X") profile as word clouds. These correspond to three distinct periods: August to November 2019 (election campaign), November to January 2020 (coalition agreement period), and January 13, 2020, to August 2021 (governmental period). As can be easily observed, the theme of government dominates all three periods, reflecting Podemos' desire, from the election campaign onward, to achieve a result that would compel the PSOE into a coalition. The electoral campaign, though conducted with more moderate tones than previous ones, was still marked by strong rhetoric emphasizing the need to build a coalition government to finally represent "the people" or common citizens, and to establish *"#ungobiernocontigo"* ('a government with you') that defends *"derechos sociales"* ('social rights'). The campaign saw no shortage of mutual accusations between PSOE and UP regarding the failure of earlier negotiations. The slogan of one video commercial released by Podemos, *"Las cosas importantes nunca salen a la primera"* ('Important things never work out on the first try'), depicted individuals initially failing at common tasks—team sports, riding a bicycle, or performing an ice-skating pirouette—but ultimately succeeding through perseverance, unity, and collective strength, symbolized by images of protests and social movements. The message was emotional, impactful, and highly rhetorical.

After the election results and the swearing-in of the government, Iglesias's rhetoric shifted. While continuing to highlight *"personas"* ('individuals')—a term deliberately replacing 'people'—the vice-president adopted a more programmatic tone, presenting himself as a leftist voice within the government. He emphasized policies promoting social justice, wealth redistribution, and attention to society's most vulnerable. Above all, Iglesias framed himself as a defender of *"democracia"* ('democracy'), a necessary counterbalance against the looming threat of *"la ultraderecha y de la ultraultraderecha"* ('the far-right and ultra-far-right'), whom he targeted with sharp and sarcastic rhetoric during his investiture speech.

Since September 2021, Iglesias has steadily re-established his presence in social and traditional media, appearing regularly on radio and television programs as a political commentator on current affairs. His primary focus lies in analyzing the deeply political dynamics that exist within national and supranational media powers, particularly how these dynamics influence democratic processes. This interest led him to publish two books in 2022. The first, *Verdades a la cara. Recuerdos de los años salvajes* ('Truths to the Face: Memories of the Wild Years'), is an interview-based work in which Iglesias recounts the harshest years of his political career, including the personal and family repercussions of his time in government, as well as the decisions that led to his departure from institutional politics. The second book, *Medios y cloacas: Así conspira el Estado profundo contra la democracia* ('Media and Sewers: How the Deep State Conspires Against Democracy'), reflects on the role of media in Western political systems, as the title suggests.

Iglesias has also adopted strategies to counter what he describes as the "extra-power" of the media system, which, in his view, disproportionately targets political movements seeking to build "an alternative". In January 2022, he launched a podcast called *La Base*, where he delivers daily political commentary on current issues. The podcast serves as a counter-information platform, created alongside Manu Levin, a philologist and former vice-presidential speechwriter; Sara Serrano, a mathematician; and Inna Afinogenova, a Russian journalist specializing in Latin American affairs. Furthermore, in November 2022, Iglesias initiated a fundraiser to establish *Canal Red*, a television channel dedicated to counter-information, culture, politics, and entertainment.

In conclusion, Iglesias's early rhetorical style can be described as 'left-wing transversal populist'. At its outset, Iglesias emerged as one of Europe's most prominent left-wing populist figures. His rhetoric relied on a broad conception of "we", transcending ideological, political, and geographical divisions. He mobilized people around themes of participation, popular consciousness, and concrete actions against a clearly defined opponent. In this framework, "they" represented the elite, situated on a high-low axis of power. Yet Iglesias's rhetoric was distinctly leftist, not only because of the themes addressed in his program but also due to the specific terminology and symbols embedded in his communication.

After entering government, Podemos gradually reduced or, in some cases, abandoned populist Manichean rhetoric in favor of explicitly leftist messaging. The discourse shifted towards a more traditional left-right framework, with "we" increasingly defined in socio-economic terms. Iglesias and Podemos positioned themselves as a leftist voice driving government policies focused on social justice, redistribution, and protection for society's most vulnerable groups. This strategic communication embraced leftist values while innovating and modernizing the language and symbols traditionally associated with the radical left.

5.5 Ione Belarra and Irene Montero's digital communication in the government

Fig. 18: *Word cloud* @IoneBelarra. Source: author's elaboration via Nvivo. Note: reference period is March 30, 2021- January 2023.

Fig. 19: *Word cloud* @IreneMontero. Source: author's elaboration via Nvivo. Note: reference period is February 2021- January 2023.

This section will analyze the digital communication of the two highest representatives of Podemos in government: Ione Belarra, Secretary General of Podemos and *Ministra de Derechos Sociales y Agenda 2030*, and Irene Montero, *Ministra de Igualdad*. Fig. 18 represents the word cloud of the most frequently used words by Ione Belarra from March 30, 2021, the day she announced she would succeed Pablo Iglesias as the new *Ministra*, to the latest available data in January 2023. For both word clouds, stop words (such as *'http'*, *'gracias'*, etc.) were identified and eliminated from the count, considering only words with more than five characters. Fig. 19 depicts the word cloud of Irene Montero's most frequently used words from February 2021 (the first available data of her ministry period) to the last available data in January 2023.

At first glance, it is evident that the communication in both cases is strictly responsive to the issues addressed within their respective ministries. Regarding Irene Montero, the most frequently used word is *"mujers"* ('women'), which appeared 485 times during the analyzed period, reflecting the core 'we' in both her rhetoric and that of Podemos in government.

An analysis of Podemos' Twitter profile reveals that in six months (from September 2022 to February 2023), *"mujeres"* has been among the top ten most used words, and Montero's profile has been quoted the most (151 times since September), far exceeding Ione Belarra's (66 times, following Pablo Echenique, who was quoted 73 times). This indicates that gender issues and the defense of LGBTQI+ rights are central to Podemos' government actions and overall discourse.

Terms like *"violencia"* (311) and *"machista"* (185) are also prevalent in Montero's communication, symbolizing her 'they'.

Numerous tweets denounce patriarchal violence, which is not only the focus of a carefully crafted media campaign featuring elaborate graphics, photos, data, and videos, but also the central theme of one of Podemos' most significant laws addressing gender violence. From a communicative perspective, the official videos of the *Ministry of Equality* stand out: Podemos utilizes social media to disseminate messages of great political relevance concerning these issues.

This creates a form of 'institutional education' regarding political and cultural disputes, where the use of communication and information as a field of political and ideological agitation has always been a core aspect of Podemos' identity. A notable example occurred on December 23, when the *Ministerio De Igualidad* released a video on its Facebook profile titled *Charo, Navidades Corresponsables*[8], named after the woman protagonist. In the video, an adult woman is shown preparing Christmas lunch alone, while her husband lounges on the sofa. Overwhelmed by her efforts, she decides for the first time to 'boycott' the preparations and take a day for fun and celebration. The subsequent scenes unfold in a tragicomic manner: the chicken in the oven, set to a high temperature, begins to burn; her niece and husband attempt to salvage the meal, creating further chaos and food waste; meanwhile, the woman begins to relax, dance, enjoy wine, and play with her niece. The video concludes with an image of the family around a messy but joyful table, especially the woman. Irene Montero's voice then chimes in: "This Christmas, let's not leave it all to the same. Let them, apart from being happy, be co-responsible parties". The significance of this communication style is clear: a high-quality video, almost akin to a short film, conveys a message aligned with one of Podemos' principal concerns—combating discrimination and gender violence. This entire effort was broadcast through the official channel of a Spanish government ministry, representing a form of institutional digital populism.

"Derechos" ('rights') is another key term in the communication of Podemos' institutional figures. While it ranks as the fourth most used term by Irene Montero (284 times), it is the most frequently used by Ione Belarra (270 times), reflecting the specificity of her ministry. It is no coincidence that social rights, alongside gender issues, have consistently been central to Podemos' discourse and political strategy. At his inauguration, Iglesias emphasized that his vice-presidency would focus on "guaranteeing, securing, and expanding social rights". In contrast to

---

8 The video is available here: *Charo | Navidades Corresponsables*, Ministerio de Igualdad, https://www.youtube.com/watch?v=ur-d3dTEnmA.

Irene Montero, Ione Belarra frequently uses the term *"gobierno"* ('government', 161 times), underscoring her more 'institutional' role as the official voice of Podemos in government. While Montero is more connected to social movements (evidenced by the popular hashtag *"#niunamenos"*), Belarra adopts a more moderate communication style, primarily using the term *"people"* (141 times) as a discursive device to construct a sense of 'we'. Notably, "Podemos" (154 times) and *"puede"* (118 times) are among her most frequently used words. It is interesting to note that in Ione Belarra's social communication, her activity as Minister always shines through more than that as General Secretary of the party.

Although the communicative *framework* is embedded in a clear positioning on the left-right axis, there is no use of a lexicon belonging to the traditional left. For example, in the period considered the term 'class' is used five times by Ione Belarra and only three times by Irene Montero, while it is only present twice on the official profile of Podemos. It is also true, however, that when it is used it is not about the middle class or the political class, but to the concept used in the Marxist tradition. To give an example, in a tweet of 24 January 2022 Irene Montero recalls the five lawyers belonging to the PCE killed in 1977 by far-right terrorists in the so-called *Matanza de Atocha*. The Minister ends that tweet with the exclamation "It is thanks to them that we are here today. Long live the struggle of the working class. Let us not forget". The same expression can be found in one of her tweets on 1 May, Workers' Day. Similarly, in some tweets Ione Belarra explicitly refers to the "working class", but it is still a concept that from a communicative point of view is little used, or rather, is not communicated through this specific lemma.

Similarly, the term 'left' is not very present: the profile that uses it most is that of Podemos, which from September 2022 to February 2023 has included it in ten of its tweets, most of which are the sharing of speeches or interviews by Pablo Iglesias. On the other hand, the profile that uses the term *"trabajadores"* ('workers') the most is that of Ione Belarra, who addresses the issue in 49 tweets in the period under consideration. The term is mainly used in two contexts: the first refers to the support of mobilizations, strikes, and trade union victories in the world of work, thus highlighting the relationship of reciprocal support institutions/places that, as already pointed out, Podemos wants to build. The second context is specifically related to the work of her ministry, very often linked to that of Yolanda Díaz's work.

Finally, it is interesting to note that in both analyzed profiles the word *"todas"*, i.e. 'all of them' (women), is used a lot. It is a symbol of the attention to the use of gender in language that is very present in Podemos' political culture. Often, even in official and institutional communications, the two Ministers use both male and female genders or, in some cases, we can also witness the use of

Profiles with the most followers

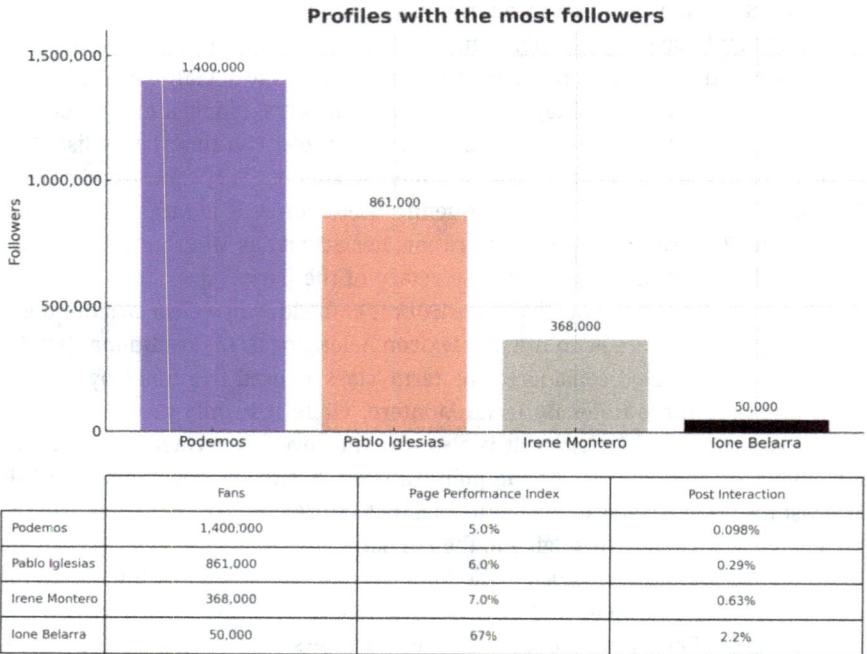

	Fans	Page Performance Index	Post Interaction
Podemos	1,400,000	5.0%	0.098%
Pablo Iglesias	861,000	6.0%	0.29%
Irene Montero	368,000	7.0%	0.63%
Ione Belarra	50,000	67%	2.2%

Fig. 20: Performance Facebook pages of Podemos, Pablo Iglesias, Irene Montero and Ione Belarra. Source: author's elaboration by Fanpage Karma.

the female gender only, especially by Minister Irene Montero even when she refers to a wide plurality. In other cases, we also witness the use of the ending *"-es"*, which does not exist in Spanish and indicates the use of 'neutral' language (e. g., *"justicia para todes"*, i. e. 'justice for all') that also includes those who do not identify with either the female or the male gender. This is also an absolute novelty in the Spanish, indeed, European institutional context.

Finally, the Fanpage Karma platform was used to analyze the performance of the profiles under study. This platform allowed the investigation to be extended to the Facebook social network, which is more suitable for observing the use of different communication tools such as images, videos, etc. The profiles of Pablo Iglesias (@iglesiasturrionpablo), Ione Belarra (@ionebelarra), Irene Montero (@irene.montero.5070), and the official Podemos page (@ahorapodemos) were taken into account. Fig. 20 graphically summarizes the performance of the pages under analysis at the moment I'm writing. Podemos turns out to be one of the pages with the most followers of all the European political organizations: if we consider only the Spanish context, Podemos (1.4 million followers) far exceeds that of the PSOE (232,199 followers), that of the PP (282,200 followers), and even that of *Vox* (491,852 followers), which has made right-wing digital populism one of its main propaganda weapons. Podemos thus confirms itself as unique at the European level in the way it uses digital tools, which create direct contact between the party in the central and public office and the party on the ground. As far as personal profiles are concerned, Pablo Iglesias confirms himself as the most followed public figure, with 860,672 followers, followed by Irene Montero (368,174) and Ione Belarra (49,694) who, despite being the Secretary-General, has a much smaller number of followers on Facebook than her party colleagues. Quantity, in this case, does not correspond to quality: according to the index compiled by Fanpage Karma, Ione Belarra's page performs significantly better than the other pages, with a post interaction level of 2.2%. This indicates that, in proportion to the number of followers, the General Secretary's page manages to maintain a very good level of interaction and sharing from its audience, also considering that she is a central public figure within Podemos' discourse from the moment she enters the government, when she is appointed Secretary of State for the ministry led by Pablo Iglesias.

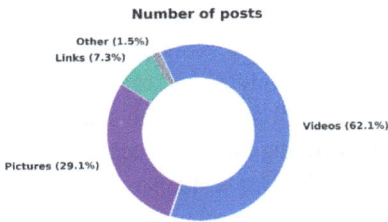

Number of posts

Other (1.5%)
Links (7.3%)

Videos (62.1%)

Pictures (29.1%)

Fig. 21: Content type analysis of the Facebook pages of Podemos, Pablo Iglesias, Irene Montero and Ione Belarra. Source: author's elaboration by Fanpage Karma.

Top 50 Words: Post interaction
The bigger the word, the more it was used. The greener, the more these posts were interacted with.

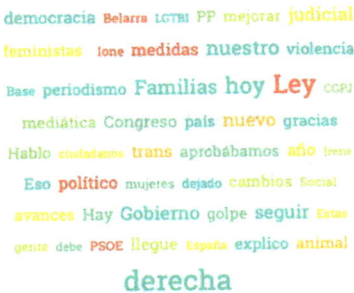

democracia Belarra LGTBI PP mejorar judicial
feministas Ione medidas nuestro violencia
Base periodismo Familias hoy Ley CGPJ
mediática Congreso país nuevo gracias
Hablo ciudadanos trans aprobábamos año Irene
Eso político mujeres dejado cambios social
avances Hay Gobierno golpe seguir Estas
gente debe PSOE llegue España explico animal
derecha

Fig. 22: Content analysis and interactions of the Facebook pages of Podemos, Pablo Iglesias, Irene Montero and Ione Belarra. Source: author's elaboration by Fanpage Karma.

Turning to content analysis, Fig. 21 graphically represents the analysis of the types of posts on the four pages under investigation. As can be seen, more than half of the published posts, i. e., 62%, are videos, thus confirming the special attention Podemos pays to this type of communicative production. Looking at individual pages, Iglesias is the profile that publishes the most videos (81.3% of the total), also due to his recent activity in *Canal Red*. The account of the activities of the former Ministry of *Igualdad* is also composed of 79.4% videos. The Podemos page, on the other hand, uses images more than the others (37.4%), although videos and live broadcasts (58.2%) are still predominant.

Fig. 22 summarizes the contents most frequently addressed on the four pages under study in the last month: the larger the word is represented, the more it was used; at the same time, the more it is colored green, the more it received interactions. As can be seen, the word that is most used and at the same time has had the most interactions is *"derecha"* ('right'): this confirms what was argued in the previous paragraphs regarding the systematization, within Podemos' discourse, of the creation of the enemy, of 'them', through the demonization of the right and the extreme right. Even *"democracia"* ('democracy'), although to a lesser extent, is a concept that resonates in Podemos' communication, both in its framing as an 'attack on democracy,' which the party claims to foil, and in the sense of the 'advancement of democracy,' the main task of Podemos' presence in government. In the period under consideration, the focus of the party's communication has been around the approval of two central laws: the family law and the law on trans rights. *"Ley"*, *"Familia"*, and *"Trans"* are indeed widely used terms. The peculiarity is, however, that the term *"Ley"* ('law') has not achieved the same number of interactions as *"Familia"* ('family'), which is among the most successful. The content of the law, rather than the means of the law itself, resonates more with an audience, such as that of Podemos, not 'genetically' accustomed to institutional instruments as a means of solving problems. Similarly, references to the PSOE, which, despite being a coalition partner, are often critical or harsh exhortations, do not receive the same level of interaction as the creation of the 'external enemy' of the right-wing threat. The left-right axis is therefore not only more utilized but also more appreciated by Podemos' digital audience.

This analysis shows a change, or rather an evolution, in the communication of Podemos in government. The figures in institutional positions have responsive communication on issues related to their ministries. However, the change is not a decrease in the degree of radicality but rather a shift in characteristics: from a more transversal communication, in which the 'high-low' axis was the dominant rhetoric of opposition to power, to a communication that is more responsive to the issues and ideological characteristics of the political force. This is not only a change in content but also a change in "the people", and therefore the target electorate, making greater use of the differences arising from positioning on the left-right axis. Digital communication is one of the main strategic assets of the junior partner in the government, which is often used as a "push from the left" for government action, especially against the majority partner.

5.6 The evolution of discourse: the abandonment of ideological transversality and firm placement on the left

> Political speeches are not made in a *vacuum*, they are not made regardless of the situation. You make a speech that works or doesn't work depending on the situation of the country. To think that you can say the same thing regardless of what happens when there are two parties in Spain as when there are five, or when there is no extreme right-wing party in Spain, or when there is, or when the PSOE is in government in Spain or when the PP is in government, or when the PSOE goes left or right...I think it's like a cretinism of political discourse, as if all politics is what you say and what you say is independent of material conditions. It's not like that. (Levin, 2022, Interview 3)

Manu Levin was responsible for the speeches of Pablo Iglesias, Secretary of the Podemos Speech and Head of Communication of the Vice-Presidency of the Council. He therefore oversaw all the stages of Podemos' communication, from being the main opposition actor to becoming a governing force. In the semi-structured interview that greatly enriched the analysis of the evolution of Podemos' discourse in this work, Manu Levin admits that, from this perspective, it is indeed possible to observe a change in communication strategy following Podemos' entry into government. Levin argues that such a change, albeit rapid, is a natural part of a political force's evolution. When the social, political, and institutional context shifts, it becomes necessary to adapt the discourse, which does not necessarily imply a change in strategic objectives. "Political discourses are not made in a vacuum", Levin emphasizes multiple times, listing the numerous contextual changes that led to what he calls "a moderation" of political discourse. He adds that there was an institutionalization not only at the organizational level but also at the discursive level. The first significant shift in context was transitioning from an oppositional discourse, which Levin terms "de-constituent", to one of government:

> On the one hand, there is an obvious difference in role. Whether you are in opposition or in government makes a huge difference. This has very significant repercussions on your discourse and political practice—it's not the same. I remember when I used to write speeches for Pablo during Rajoy's government. It was very simple. They were thieves, corrupt [...]. When there is no longer an enemy in government, it becomes harder. You have to construct a different discourse. So, there's an obvious difference because being in opposition is completely different from being in government. In opposition, the discourse is purely derogatory. You can say whatever you want because you don't have to act on it. But when you're in

> government, especially as a minority, it opens certain spaces for you, but it also closes others for political action and discourse. (Levin, 2022, Interview 3)

Additionally, the broader national context has changed. New forces outside the traditional bipartisan framework emerged to compete for the same discursive space as Podemos, such as *Vox* and *Ciudadanos*. "It's like a tool that the right and power also use to break this axis", Levin explains, referring to the 'new-old' dichotomy. According to Levin, Podemos' initial discourse resonated not only because of its appeal to the 'high-low' axis—speaking to those who felt unrepresented—but also through its renewal-oriented messaging, where 'the old' represented political parties unable to address the social demands of the 15M mobilization. This framework was disrupted by the emergence of a new right-wing force, a sort of "right-wing Podemos", which prevented Podemos from continuing its innovative discourse. Combined with other factors, such as the Catalan crisis, the end of social mobilization, and European political-institutional changes, these developments pushed Podemos to moderate its discourse, aligning it more closely with that of a governing force "to the left" of the PSOE. Levin does not fully agree with this moderation, as he argues that Iglesias, despite shifting his discourse, still maintained elements of rupture and revolution:

> But I would also say that, while Pablo Iglesias was at the helm, there was a discourse from the government with messages that no one had ever said from that position. Namely, questioning the monarchy, questioning the media, and asserting that the government is a political battleground where we don't always agree with the PSOE. [...] I think that while Pablo was there, despite everything I said earlier about being in government imposing certain changes, a radical spirit was preserved, and only later did this evolve further. (Levin, 2022, Interview 3)

From this perspective, Levin provides a critical reflection for the purpose of this research. On the one hand, he acknowledges that occupying government positions played a significant role in what he calls the 'moderation' of Podemos' discourse. However, he also insists that Iglesias managed to retain his *uniqueness* by introducing novel elements into both Spanish and European institutional discourse. Although a visible moderation of Iglesias' discourse occurred after Podemos joined the coalition government, he simultaneously maintained a radical and disruptive tone (as demonstrated in the analysis of his government inauguration speech). This suggests that the question should not be framed along the 'moderation-radicality' axis but instead focuses on the nature of the pursued discourse. Levin himself disagrees with the moderation in UP's rhetoric, particularly under Yolanda Díaz, whose discourse he describes as "much softer and closer to the PSOE, of course. Yes, I think this is a mistake. I think it all stems from a debate about analyzing what worked. I believe what worked and allowed Podemos to break through was its radicalism—the fact that it said things using new language and terms without resorting to defeated words." (Levin, 2022, Interview 4).

From another perspective, Clara Serra, one of the supporters of Inigo Errejon's position during *Vistalegre II*, asserts that positioning Podemos as "left" was never an option at the party's inception, especially not as an actor merely to the left of the PSOE:

> One of the possible paths for Podemos was to become nothing more than the left wing of the PSOE. In the early days of the party, we analyzed this option as something that would limit the project. That was not the role we wanted to play, and on this, there was broad agreement among most of us who were part of Podemos' first leadership core—except for some colleagues who saw it as a necessary moderation and a betrayal of our objectives. Our initial political analysis was that we did not want to be merely the left flank of the PSOE and, as a result, be defined by it—becoming an actor that is built subordinately to or in response to the PSOE's actions, positioning ourselves as just a little further to the left or slightly beyond but still moving in the same general direction. In other words, this would ultimately place us within an ideological framework that, at its core, remained functional to the *Partido Socialista* (Serra, 2024, Interview 10)

According to Serra, the origins of this shift are evident in *Vistalegre II*, where Podemos began to pivot toward the left-right axis. Interestingly, Serra does not interpret this as a move toward more radical or transformative positions:

> In a certain sense, we can indeed say that Podemos has become more left-wing since Vistalegre II. We can say this if we mean that it has appeared that way, that it has been perceived as such. But in part this has to do with the fact that it coincided with the entire imaginary of the left that existed before the 15M movement and our emergence. It is partly related to the restoration of symbols, language, and positions that we had precisely questioned—elements that were previously considered essential and non-negotiable. So, if your question is whether Podemos has become more left-wing in a truly transformative, revolutionary, or radical sense, then I would say no. I would argue that the original Podemos was more disruptive and posed a radical challenge to the culture of the transition and its core institutions, pushing for a new constitution. I think it would be unfair to say that Podemos' ideological definition is simply a domestication or that it should have remained undefined—because, under the argument of openness, there were times when a lack of courage was masked, something that, for example, *Sumar* has clearly demonstrated. On the one hand, Podemos has become more ideologically defined (which, to some extent, is inevitable and, in certain aspects, even defensible). But at the same time, it has lost political imagination. It has sought to differentiate itself from the PSOE in a way that has been largely reactive—focused on opposition and negation rather than proactive definition. As a result, it has lost its capacity to lead, meaning its ability to initiate or shape debates beyond merely countering the positions of others. Of course, any political force in a position of absolute disadvantage—Podemos has been the target of relentless attacks from some of the most powerful political, economic, and media forces for years—suffers enormous exhaustion simply from surviving, and we should not

overlook what that entails. We must understand the many reasons behind this weakness, beyond individual mistakes or personal decisions. But the fact remains that, compared to its early years, Podemos has been losing its ability to generate conflicts and oppositional dynamics that could reshape the political landscape. That means losing a kind of radicalism that defined Podemos in its beginnings—not in the sense of remaining undefined or empty, but rather in the sense of not aligning exactly with what came before it, including the traditional left as it existed prior to Podemos. (Serra, 2024, Interview 10)

Clara Serra adds another crucial point. In the interview, she highlights that the change in discourse, particularly that of Iglesias, occurred not only for "external" reasons but also for "internal" ones. At a time of significant fragmentation and division within the party, Iglesias opted for a more leftist language to consolidate his leadership and base, using both ideological and identification strategies. Serra argues that this was because the party's militants were further to the left than its broader voter base and therefore more receptive to such discourse:

> Podemos' return to a more traditional leftist imaginary, language, and symbolism is, in part, a consequence of the fact that the populist strategy of its initial expansionary phase did not allow for the construction of a stable identity. It is important to recognize that such an identity is, to some extent, necessary to sustain the party's activist base during difficult times. In a climate of discouragement, with fractures, divisions, and debates over the reasons for Podemos' failure compared to its initial ambitions, there was a process of closing ranks, and Pablo's discourse began to focus more on Podemos' militants rather than the broader public. However, in an internally fragmented environment, this shift also served to draw internal divisions, reinforcing the idea of a 'true' and radical Podemos versus a more moderate version that was seen as a betrayal of the project's spirit. *Vistalegre II* marked an identity-based closure of Podemos, which internally consolidated the activist base around Pablo's leadership while seeking a classic leftist identity as if it were the true essence of the project—when, in reality, it meant leaving behind part of Podemos' original DNA. Given that Podemos' core activists have always been further to the left than its broader electoral base, this return to a more traditional left was satisfying for them, as they had always been asked to make an effort in the opposite direction. These activists had been encouraged not to use Podemos as a means of self-affirmation but rather to help expand a political movement by reaching out to those who had yet to join. The rhetorical shift at *Vistalegre II* represented a kind of 'return home' for the most loyal militants. As a result, Podemos became less internally plural, less capable of engaging outwardly, smaller—but also more cohesive. (Serra, 2024, Interview 10)

To summarize, based on the analysis and interviews conducted, the discourse of the first Podemos can be described as 'left-wing transversal populist'. It is populist because, as repeatedly emphasized, it exemplifies the Manichean construction of society based on socio-economic and power dynamics. The 'high-low' and 'new-old' axes, along with the use of vocabulary such as 'majority' and 'people' to represent the mobilizing 'we' against the enemy 'caste', form the core of its populist rhetoric. At the same time, it is transversal because it provides an opportunity to speak to a broader social base:

> Transversality is an opportunity. It is a moment in which several ideological consensuses are being altered. Therefore, your discourse has the capacity to be effective on a broader basis than the traditional ones, to which you can refer to your own cultural identity. Transversality, like populism, is a moment. It is a moment in which certain discourses cross the traditional frontiers of ideology. (Iglesias, 2022, Interview 1)

Transversality, as Clara Serra points out, has a direct impact on political aggregation, the type of activism, and the electoral audience a political force can reach. While Podemos' founding core clearly had leftist roots and traditions, many new members of Podemos came from non-politicized backgrounds or entirely different political traditions:

> Transversality is both external and internal. We can define transversality as an extremely broad political appeal—one that allows people who once voted for the Partido Popular, but now feel betrayed, to connect with the anti-crisis discourse we are advancing. In the early days of the party, working-class right-wing voters could look at Podemos with interest and even consider voting for it. But transversality also relates to the heterogeneity within Podemos' own activist base. In its early stages, Podemos attracted people with no prior political experience, or individuals who, for example, did not identify as feminists and would say, 'I am neither a feminist nor a sexist'. It was not a left-wing activist base—at least not clearly, or not in many aspects. (Serra, 2024, Interview 10)

From both the analysis and the voices of its key figures, it is clear that the first Podemos was indeed transversal. Many consider this strategy to have allowed Podemos to capture the support of a large portion of the electorate disillusioned with the traditional political system and the spirit of renewal and horizontal participation that characterized the 15M movement. Initially, aligning on the left-right spectrum would have forced Podemos into the dynamics of bipartisanship, associating it with what was then perceived as 'the Spanish left', namely the PSOE. As emphasized in interviews and public speeches, Iglesias identified the media as a primary battleground to "turn the table" and avoid appearing as "the left of someone else", instead positioning Podemos as the voice of a broader social majority ignored by the political system. This strategy can be characterized as a catch-all approach (Fittipaldi, 2021), seeking to appeal to a larger segment of the electorate beyond the traditional left. However, a distinction must be made between Podemos and other transversal populist movements, such as Italy's *Movimento 5 Stelle*. Unlike hybrid populisms, Podemos had a clear ideological foundation rooted in the radical left. Its leaders never denied their leftist origins, often employing symbolic gestures, rhetoric, and cultural references aligned with that tradition. Podemos can therefore be described as embracing a left-wing transversality, or as Monedero calls it, a 'critical transversality' (Monedero, 2022). As Manu Levin points out, despite these elements of transversality, Podemos still resonated with a defined segment of the Spanish left:

> All this stems from the fact that the transversal and populist discourse has been, in my opinion, a successful discourse, which has allowed the left to grow, but which has never really been true in terms of social support. Podemos has never been a transversal party; it has always been a party supported by the left. Former PSOE voters, former Catalan and Basque left voters, and former *Izquierda Unida* voters. And at most, if you like, abstentionists, but not right-wingers. (Levin, 2022, Interview 3)

Transversality thus had a dual effect: it broadened the electorate while creating tensions within the party between those with a clearly radical leftist identity and those who identified as "neutral" or transversal— tensions that, as noted in the interview, could be seen either as a threat or as an opportunity for growth and politicization. These tensions and frictions culminated in the Second Congress, *Vistalegre II*. As has been noted repeatedly, this congress marked a shift not only in Podemos' organizational structure but also in its electoral positioning and discourse. *Unidas Podemos* emerged as a strategic perspective, firmly positioning Podemos on the left of Spain's political spectrum. The growth of other forces, such as *Ciudadanos* and *Vox*, necessitated clearer ideological identification, with Podemos aligning as a leftist force. Additionally, Podemos' governance in symbolic territories like Barcelona and Madrid diminished its outsider image within the institutional political system. The term 'caste' was gradually replaced by 'Trama' ('the plot'), referring to a network of political, economic, cultural, and media powers working to prevent the social majority from exercising true power. At this point, Podemos' "left-wing populism" became most pronounced, further accentuated by the departure of Errejón, who had championed the more transversal approach.

5.7 Is Podemos still populist?

A: Do you think the populist moment is over? And with it also the populist discourse of Podemos?

ML: Yes, I think so. I think if you look at 2011–2012 and now 2021–2022, any analyst realizes that the axis of Spanish politics is the 'left-right' axis. Again, it is not the 'high-low' or 'low-high' axis as it was then. Some will think, the reformist side, let's say, will think that this is the result of our mistakes for not opting for this, for not following this line. I don't think so, I think it is the result of the weight of the political events themselves, not of our mistakes. (Levin, 2022, Interview 3)

For the current Podemos leadership, or rather, for those who formally or informally have an influential role within it, 'populism' is not understood as the essence of the party that determines its very nature or as a 'thin-centered ideology' that complements its main one. In most of the interviews collected, populism is viewed, much like transversality, as a 'moment' shaped by the social, economic, and political context. A 'moment' that, if exploited—that is, if tactics and discursive practices capable of mobilizing a social majority are used—can help gain significant consensus and achieve governmental positions. In this regard, it is particularly interesting to quote Pablo Iglesias' response to this issue in full:

A: The first question is whether for you Podemos was a left-wing populist subject and whether today it resorts to such practices or whether its populist moment is over.

P.I.: So, in my opinion, populism is not a category that can be applied to political actors, but to political moments. A populist political moment can exist when there is a transformation in the ideological structure and suddenly, let's say, one can cross ideological borders with a discourse more effectively than at other moments. This is what makes some people believe that this has to do with the fact that there is no longer a left and a right or with the supposed transversality. The key is these types of moments that alter the ideological structure. Podemos, like the *Movimento 5 Stelle*, is the result of one of these moments. But Podemos can be a clearly left-wing force both in its program and its identity. Another thing is that Podemos can say that the left-right geography does not explain everything, and still does not explain everything. However, I would not assume that the notion of populism serves to describe the characteristics of a political actor. Indeed, when reading Laclau's *The Populist Reason*, it would be absurd to describe as ideologically populist all the plurality of political actors that Laclau includes in it. So, I think that the term has more to do with the moment, with a moment of crisis and a moment, let's say, in which non-institutional politics acquires different possibilities for the transformation of the ideological structure. In this sense, Podemos is the result of a populist moment. But I do not believe that there are populist organizations, considering, moreover, that this term has a strictly academic meaning different from the journalistic one. (Iglesias, 2022, Interview 1)

As is evident, this conception aligns with neither Cas Mudde's definition of populism as a "thin-centerd ideology" nor Laclau's understanding of populism as the "essence of political discourse", even though the first internal debate on the subject within Podemos originated from Laclau's framework. Iglesias, drawing on Chantal Mouffe's concept of the 'populist moment', generalizes its meaning, arguing that this label cannot describe a political subject. This interpretation has notable practical implications. By asserting that it is moments, not political actors, that are populist, Iglesias opens the door to the cyclical use of populist strategies depending on the socio-political and economic context:

> I think there are populist moments and moments of going back to the old axes, and I think this is one of them. I think it is a mistake to think that we can maintain the same discourse regardless of what is happening outside; regardless of whether people are in the streets or not; regardless of whether there are two parties or five; regardless of whether there is an extreme right or not; regardless of what is happening in Catalonia and everything that has happened. And I think we are now in a phase of a clear return of the 'left-right' axis, but that doesn't mean that there can't be a moment when it breaks down again. (Levin, 2022, Interview 3)

Because populism is understood as a moment, most interviewees believe that this discursive strategy is less suited to government. First, occupying institutional positions disrupts the ability to construct the Manichean division between the people and the elite—a key feature of the populist discourse used in the 2019 election campaign. Lilith Verstrynge explains in her interview that the primary issue is that, from a mainstream perspective, "normal people" now see Podemos as a governmental force, no different from other political parties:

> Politicians are identified as all the same. There is no difference between the politician who strives for decent pensions and the one who cuts them. They are all the same and they are all profiteers because this political class is far removed from the people. This shows that the populist moment has arrived because clearly the denunciation is there, there continues to be an elite that is disconnected from its people and does not pay attention, and that is becoming more and more independent from its people. We have talked about it many times: they have their schools, their banks, their circles. And we politicians are part of this elite that is being singled out. I think that when we entered government, we knew that it was a possibility, something that could happen, that we would be identified as part of the system, it is true that when you enter government you have to change certain things, including the way you dress. (Verstrynge L., 2022, Interview 2)

This interview is insightful for several reasons. First, it succinctly captures the discursive challenges faced by a populist movement when adapting its messaging to governance. Second, unlike Iglesias and Levin, Verstrynge believes that a populist moment is still ongoing and that Podemos should continue to leverage it, despite its role in government. Verstrynge highlights that the communication style and discourse adopted during the early years of Podemos' governmental participation distinguish it sharply from IU and other extreme-left experiences, such as the Portuguese Communist Party. Podemos, she argues, still manages to challenge power from within government by emphasizing the limitations of the coalition and publicly expressing disagreements with the PSOE. This approach positions Podemos as a disruptive and innovative force—one that asserts leadership not only within the Council of Ministers but also in public and media debates.

> There are differences, and we make them public. It is true that for a long time, we have been accused of being noisy, of not knowing how to govern, of annoying the PSOE, of always demanding too much. But the reality is that I believe that at the end of the road those who must vote know what some have asked for and what others have asked for. [...] It is true that this [being in government] forces you to blur your way of expressing yourself and your discourse. You must find a balance and understand when you can contest radically and when you must be a bit more polite or moderate. You have to dance; you have to learn to dance. (Verstrynge L., 2022, Interview 2)

Changing the 'point of observation', the series of CIS polls regarding the ideological perception of Podemos is particularly interesting—specifically, how Podemos is perceived by the Spanish electorate. The results confirm what has been discussed so far: at the time the Sánchez II government was formed, 30 % of respondents considered Podemos a communist political force, while 22.7 %, a significant number, could not answer the question. Meanwhile, 18.9 % viewed it as socialist. Nearly all respondents classified Podemos as a force belonging to the radical left, albeit in different variations. Another set of data compiled by the CIS highlights Pablo Iglesias' ideological rating scale from April 2020 (his fourth month in government) to May 2021 (the month of his departure from institutional and party life). The majority of respondents gave Iglesias a rating of '1', equivalent to the extreme left. During the first year of government, the leader's 'radical left' rating continued to rise, reaching its highest peak in April 2021, just weeks before the local elections in Madrid.

5.8 Conclusion: the evolution of the discourse

	Podemos I (2014–2017)	Podemos II (2017–2020)	Podemos III (from 2020)
Discourse	Left-wing transversal populist	Left-wing populist	Innovative Left

Tab. 5: Podemos discourse evolution. Source: author's elaboration.

In conclusion, the last "stage" in the evolution of the Podemos discourse has been examined from three points of observation: first, through the analysis of public speeches and digital communication, particularly those of Secretary General Ione Belarra, which revealed a moderation of language and a progressive focus on the right-left axis; second, this process was confirmed by both institutional and non-institutional actors of Podemos, who, in most interviews, recognized a change brought about by the party's entry into government and the altered context in which it operates; finally, "the people", represented by a sample of citizens in CIS polls, also identify Podemos as a force increasingly associated with the radical left. This perception is further supported by Iglesias:

> P.I.: I think Podemos is clearly left-wing, but it is not traditional or classical. It is radical, unlike much of the classical left, which is very conservative, and enormously secular in its symbolism, in its alliances, in its communicative senses, as opposed to the traditional left, even in the communist tradition, which has become very conservative both in its political praxis and in its styles and aesthetics. Podemos is a left that was born as a consequence of 15M, with a series of references, let's say, of leaders and younger thinking that is obviously left-wing, but which is very radical, very innovative, and which has been clear from the beginning that the fundamental terrain of the political struggle is ideology and communication. (Iglesias, 2022, Interview 1)

From the analysis conducted and the findings derived from semi-structured interviews, I demonstrated that Podemos has reduced, or in some cases eliminated, the use of populist Manichean discourse in favor of a left-wing but innovative style of communication. On the one hand, as pointed out, Podemos has not adopted the language and symbols of the traditional radical left. Instead, through a long process of debate and negotiation, including within UP, it remains one of the most innovative forces in terms of public discourse and communication, which continues to be one of its primary battlegrounds. At the same time, however, there is a clear shift away from the "critical transversality" of Podemos' initial phase, largely due to the challenge of sustaining a classically populist discourse while in government. For Juan Carlos Monedero, this is simply impossible:

> A: The question is: can there be populism in government or a populist practice in government?
>
> J.C.M.: No, I think it cannot exist. Nobody has ever explained it. You can read Chantal Mouffe or anyone else and they won't tell you what government populism consists of. It is an oxymoron. Institutional populism does not exist. It is a mental masturbation. It does not exist. So, populism only works in the destitute phase. [...] In the constituent part, the problem is that we live in very complex states, where the State—this is very important—manages between 40 and 50 percent of the Gross Domestic Product of a country. This means that states are run by parties. This is what Katz and Mair say in the book we have just translated, is it not? So, obviously, when parties are already part of the state and not part of society, it is incongruous to think that populism, which is purely social, should be exercised by someone who is part of the state. (Monedero, 2022, Interview 4)

We cannot assume that Monedero's statement is universally applicable without careful comparative analysis. What is important here is that one of Podemos' major intellectual figures believes that pursuing a populist strategy while in government is impossible. As we observed in the previous chapter, this perspective was not shared by Íñigo Errejón's team and was one of the main areas of contention.

Podemos is no longer a governing force. The results of the general elections in July 2023, the subsequent regional elections, the withdrawal from the governing coalition, and the loss of significant institutional positions in the Council of Ministers have all pushed Podemos into a more marginal political and media role. These events have sparked a reevaluation of its role within Spain's political landscape. This will inevitably influence not only its organizational development but also its choice of communicative and discursive strategies, which may deviate from those analyzed here.

More broadly, the analysis of Podemos' discursive evolution offers valuable insights for the study of other left-wing populist movements. It has become clear that the rise of such forces has been characterized by a highly polarizing populist discourse centered on the high-low axis. The creation of the populist "we" relied on a transversal discourse that defined "the people" in socio-economic terms, rather than nationalistic or ethnic ones, as seen in other forms of populism. This populist strategy was bolstered by the heavy use of social media and the prominence of a charismatic, recognizable leader. The entry into government was one of the main factors driving a shift in discourse—from a broader, transversal communication style to one that was more focused on the recipients of specific policies. But this was not the only reason: joining the government also required clearer ideological positioning, leading to the dominance of the left-right axis over the high-low axis. This shift occurred partly due to the need for clearer identification of both the party's target audience and the beneficiaries of its policies, and partly due to the internal dynamics of the governing coalition. When a political force is a junior partner in a coalition, it must differentiate itself from the majority partner and radicalize its discourse to act as a "push"—in this case, pushing the government's actions further to the left.

Chapter 6 – Conclusions

6.1 Podemos and the relationship with the government

"La fuerza que transforma. Un país feminista e donde nadie quede afuera" ('The force that transforms. A feminist country where no one is left out') is the new slogan Podemos has been using since November 2022, when the new communication campaign was launched on its social pages. This campaign also included a variation of the historical symbol of the Morada formation. It is interesting to analyze this slogan because, more than many other analyses, it encapsulates Podemos' strategic vision in government and the kind of governmental action it aims to pursue.

First, Podemos sees itself as a transforming force—a force that can practically change and improve reality. *"Sí, se puede!"*, the slogan most frequently used in public speeches, rallies, and in the chants of its militant base, expressed a condition of possibility: the ability to change things, to get into government, to represent the will of the majority. In government, Podemos presents itself in a new light, as a force that has already succeeded in transforming society, achieving significant advances for the social majority, and standing against forces that aim to halt change. It reflects a present reality, not just a future aspiration.

A video[1] that circulated on the party's official social pages in early January 2023 summarizes this vision with simple, effective language and minimal graphics representing the expressed concepts. Politics is defined as "a matter of forces. That is why we talk about political forces. There are forces that conserve, forces that restrain, and forces that transform". Politics can be visualized as the image shown in Fig. 23: a tug of war, a left-right axis, with two groups pulling in opposite directions.

The restraining forces are the right and the far right, who aim to pull the rope to the right and bring about retreats in the rights of the social majority. The conserving forces are those who want to hold the handkerchief firmly in the center, ensuring the rope doesn't shift to the right while also keeping the situation unchanged. The reference here is explicitly to the PSOE: in fact, when "forces that conserve" are mentioned, images of socialist leaders and Sánchez himself scroll by. The task for forces like Podemos is not to "hold the handkerchief steady", but to pull hard to the left to organize society in a "more just, more effective,

---

1 The video is available here: *Vamos a seguir siendo lo que somos: #LaFuerzaQueTransforma*, Podemos, https://www.youtube.com/watch?v=1xzJkV5JXlI

https://doi.org/10.1515/9783111591537-010

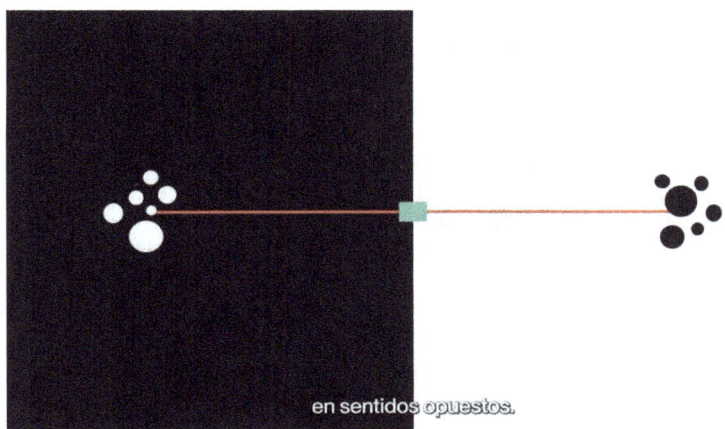

en sentidos opuestos.

Fig. 23: Politics as a tug of war. Source: Instagram page @ahorapodemos.

and more decent" way. That's why Podemos calls itself "the force that has changed politics in Spain" and claims to advance every day as "the engine of change in the coalition government", the one that allows for "serious dreaming".

The task Podemos assigns to its role in government is to "pull to the left" within the coalition's actions: a Council of Ministers without Podemos would not have enabled tangible progress, even if external support existed for a single-party PSOE government. The only real possibility for change, with all its resulting contradictions, is for Podemos to participate in the national government. This is the "mantra" that recurs throughout the interviews conducted for this analysis, where there was widespread appreciation for the decision to join the coalition with a "hostile" force like the PSOE. On this point, for example, Iglesias argues:

> The strengths [of participation in government] are to have achieved an unprecedented transformation in government practice with some of the most progressive laws. To have gained experience in government and somehow be an inescapable actor. I think this also explains the obsession of many sectors to make Podemos disappear and, let's say, to assume that there could be another kind of leftist more comfortable to manage for power than Podemos, which is simultaneously a very radical force in its ideological approaches and at the same time with a will to the state and to government. What they would like is a political force that is less radical ideologically and that, let's say, also assumes not to be involved in management. (Iglesias, 2022, Interview 1)

The only member of Podemos who responded differently was Prof. Juan Carlos Monedero. While he, as noted, holds no formal position within the organization, he remains an important theoretical reference. Despite this, his position regarding participation in the coalition government was not followed:

> J.C.M.: When we founded Podemos, we were aware that the transformative capacity of neo-liberal governments is poor. We already had the experience of SYRIZA. So, there were two main views. On one side was Iglesias and Errejón, who thought we would govern, and on the other side was me, who said we would not govern because they would not let us. There will be a grand coalition between left and right. The Socialist Party will dissolve. We have to create a Broad Front, and when people from the Socialist Party join our ranks, we will have a little more credibility. Because it is not true that there is a regime crisis like those in Latin America and, therefore, the transformation processes needed even more time. It was a wrong analysis, from my point of view, to think about going to govern.
>
> A.: Podemos, however, was born to govern.
>
> J.C.M.: It was born to govern, but accumulating strength to be able to do so. From the very beginning, for example, I was very clear, because of my Latin American experience, that it is not enough to take control of the government, because when you have the government, you don't have the power, you have the government." (Monedero, 2022, Interview 8)

This question of power is particularly interesting. For although, as mentioned, most responses about participation in government were positive, in all cases there is an acknowledgment of strong weaknesses in this process. That is, while everyone admits they would still choose to participate in the coalition government if they could go back, such participation brings contradictions that are hard to overcome and demand different governmental practices. In fact, everyone acknowledges what Monedero stated in the interview: being in government does not necessarily mean having power. For Iglesias, the presence of an "ideological and radical" force within the government creates many weaknesses that "have to do with the size of the enemy. In other words, Podemos has become an actor that serves to organize the whole reactionary movement against it, which is a reactionary power movement, where there are judges, the media, and sectors of the security forces" (Iglesias, 2022, Interview 1). The main weakness has been the challenge of implementing a government agenda as a junior partner, constantly negotiating with the PSOE. On this point, Rodríguez Martínez, former Vice Minister of the *Ministerio de Igualdad* (2021–2023), describes in the interview the intense tension that existed between the two forces in the Council of Ministers. This tension not only forced Podemos into constant negotiations regarding policies—even those within its ministries—but also projected an image of a weak and contentious government:

> The problem is that we have entered into a communicative framework that we call 'marriage'. We are like a marriage in which everyone understands everything that happens in the government as a matrimonial fight, in which the man, who is the PSOE because he is

the strong one, says 'this is what is going to happen'. Then the women come and protest and say, 'No, that's not what's going to happen', because what really has to happen is what the PSOE says multiplied by two. So, I think right now the only thing that people think Podemos can do is to say 'well, they are willing to make sure that the Socialist Party is able to go further'. But is that enough? No, it is not enough. And then there is the problem of daily internal management. In other words, my life, that of all of us in the government, ministers and secretaries of state, is a constant negotiation with the Socialist Party. Their constant answer is 'no, no, no'. This negotiation is hell, because it makes us ideologically opposed to the Socialist Party. And I think that's good, because it can put us back on the 'high-low' axis and take us off the 'left-right' axis. (Rodríguez Martínez, 2022, Interview 6)

The "marriage" relationship within the Sánchez II government was very visible from the outside, and of course, it was often exaggerated by the media debate, which emphasized all the lines of tension within the executive. During the first year, this element caused real management difficulties for Podemos, which was caught between the need to implement policies aligned with the will of its electorate and the impossibility of doing so to avoid splitting the majority and bringing down the government. As a result, this has become a veritable battleground where the *Morada* formation tries to gain media space, electoral consensus, and advances to implement its policies. In this way, Podemos does not want to appear as a mere responsible force accepting the majority's decisions. Instead, it has chosen to externalize its points of divergence with the institutional and strategic desires of the PSOE, making them a key element of its communicative narrative, with which it constantly updates the progress of the government's actions.

This change was able to take place because of two elements. First, the Covid-19 crisis ended in January, allowing government action to move beyond the emergency dimension that had focused solely on limiting the health, economic, and social damage of the pandemic. Second, as the former Vice Minister herself admits, Podemos entered the government with a political staff that had never held institutional positions at the national level, revealing a glaring lack of properly trained personnel after a few months of institutional practice:

We entered the government without having any government cadres, and the pandemic broke out immediately. In other words, we had been in government for three weeks when the state of alert was decreed. And as an anecdote, during the negotiations it was planned that Podemos would take the Ministry of Health, but in the end, we didn't get it. I'm not a believer, but I said it was God who wanted this, because if we had had the Ministry of Health…maybe not, or maybe it would have been great, but we didn't know how things were done, we didn't know how to handle it. We've learned that now, which makes me think it's extremely relevant for the next election cycle that we don't have a flight of cadres from government. Right now, it is extremely important to preserve these cadres. This is a very important idea for me. (Rodríguez Martínez, 2022, Interview 6)

Podemos, therefore, pursued the "second phase" with greater governmental experience, showing two clear characteristics: first, as already noted, it presents itself as a "challenging" force even from within the Council of Ministers, acting as the "left-wing goad" to the PSOE and not shying away from criticism or externalization in moments of disagreement and clashes within the majority. It uses these very moments as opportunities for media relevance and to mobilize its electoral base. Secondly, it implements a governing practice that addresses the specific needs and demands of certain social groups, which form its militant and electoral base.

As we have shown in Chapter 3, government activity has not resulted in a positive trend in national, local, or autonomous elections. Thus, the choice to focus on a specific area of government intervention, addressing the demands of precise social sectors, has not immediately translated into greater consensus or appreciation of its political power. On this point, which appears essential to understanding the effects of participation in a governing coalition, I questioned Pablo Iglesias:

> A: If Podemos is now in power, why for you do the polls show worse results than when you started? What are the causes?

> P.I.: Because there is no direct correlation between public policy and electoral support. This operates on the ideological terrain, and there the key thing is the ideological narratives that are imposed. And that basically has to do with the media. This, which seems obvious to me, is sometimes forgotten by the left. The left thinks that if it can make the working class live better with its policies, the working class will vote for it. That is a blushing naivety.

> A: So if you make strong public policies and radical changes for the people, doesn't that mean maintaining electoral consensus?

> P.I.: An ideological change is needed. The fundamental political struggle is always ideological. This is not to say that what is tangible does not influence, is not decisive and does not ultimately define political projects. But a system that somehow assumes that the selection of elites has something to do with the views that people have of those elites is a system dominated by ideological devices that are ultimately driven by the media. (Iglesias, 2022, Interview 1)

For Iglesias, the battle that Podemos has not yet been able to face—due to the overwhelming power of its enemies and the lack of material and economic resources—is the ideological one. That is why, once Iglesias left all political and institutional offices, he committed himself to building an alternative information network (*Canal Red*). The ideological battle, and therefore the media battle, is more significant than the battle to control the government. The inability to influence this area during his time as Vice-President of the Council is, according to Iglesias, one of his failures:

A: When you are in government, is it possible to implement ideological change?

P.I.: Well, the government should be able to change the balance of power in the media. Another question is whether it has the will to do so. One of my big failures was not to convince the government partner that things had to change in the media. It is true that the government has a communication capacity in itself, but often the government rots in the management thinking that the vote has the capacity for ideological transformation in it, and often it does not. (Iglesias, 2022, Interview 1)

6.2 A mutant "gene"

Podemos was born with the stated intention of winning and becoming the first Spanish party capable of leading a progressive government coalition in Spain. For this reason, especially in its early years, it structured itself as an "electoral war machine" using a transversal leftist populist rhetoric that allowed it to break, for the first time in history, the Spanish two-party system. Today, it finds itself outside the center-left government coalition at a moment of great uncertainty regarding its electoral space. Ten years after its founding, Podemos has evolved from its genetic form, changed its leadership and electoral alliance, gained experience in government at both local and national levels (which has now ended), and is relaunching its political action in a political and social context completely different from the one in which it was born.

Can Podemos, then, be considered in crisis?

There can be no single answer to this question. As already pointed out, a portion of the literature agrees in viewing Podemos as an example of the normalization and exhaustion of the propulsive energy of leftist populism, especially when it reaches government. In fact, Podemos has experienced two splits in the last three years: one from its more moderate wing, which pushed for maintaining the "populist moment" (Errejón and *Más País*), and one from its more radical faction, specifically because of the alliance with the PSOE (*Anticapitalistas*). According to this perspective, these internal quarrels—receiving an uncommon amount of attention from *mainstream* media—have reversed the party's initial ability to present a "fresh", new, popular, and attractive identity, instead restoring the image of a combative radical leftist force, self-absorbed in its internal differences. The difficulties shown in recent elections, both at the European and autonomous levels, symbolize this backward movement.

Moreover, the initially highly vertical and formal nature of Laclau's conception of politics—centered on the leader and his transversal electoral machine rhetoric—slowed down the organization's evolution by hindering its structural development and territorial connections. This issue is reflected in current leadership assessments, which identify this area, namely the strengthening of the party on the ground, as one of the primary goals for Podemos' organizational advancement.

The communication skills of a leader like Iglesias, with his significant rhetorical, media, and political abilities, were key elements in Podemos' sudden success and its effective discursive and media battle. However, strong dependence on charismatic figures can also become a liability, as it tends to polarize potential supporters around the leader rather than the political project itself. Iglesias, among other things, became the target of unparalleled media attacks, including reports and investigations often centered on personal issues with little relevance to political content, which were later judicially proven baseless. The so-called "mediafare" and "lawfare", against which Iglesias has waged a tough personal and political campaign in recent years, have undermined his image and, by extension, that of Podemos.

The difficulties, however, are not solely the result of subjective limitations within the *morada* formation. As demonstrated in Chapter 2, Podemos historically broke the two-party dominance of Spain's institutional and political system, opening a new season of greater political volatility at the national, local, and European levels. This volatility manifested through sudden and continuous changes in Spain's institutional balance, leading to prolonged political deadlocks and an inability to achieve stable and lasting majorities. While Podemos was an architect of this new political dynamic, it has also become one of its clearest victims, suffering sharp changes in polling results and electoral trends. This reflects the party's struggles to build the networks of mediation and representation necessary to secure the stable loyalty of a specific segment of the electorate.

The opening of new electoral spaces also saw the emergence of new political forces in Spain. First, *Ciudadanos* appeared on the national political scene as the "Podemos of the center-right", almost an antithesis designed to contest its discursive and mobilizing space. Second, the meteoric rise of *Vox* ended the absence of a far-right force, previously a "Spanish exception" in the European context (Ottaviano, 2019: 140). These developments eroded Podemos' exclusive role as a "transversal" force and populist challenger, gradually favoring a return to a left-right axis of political confrontation between opposing blocs. Third, *Sumar*, the "unexpected opponent": if Yolanda Díaz's appointment as the UP leadership successor had been made by Iglesias himself—something not well received by many in the party—the creation of a new personal political entity that overtook the coalition was seen by all, including Iglesias, as an act of "betrayal". As analyzed earlier, the *Sumar* option initially occupied the electoral space previously held by UP, incorporating IU, *Verdes Equo*, and *Más País*. Podemos joined only weeks before (June 10, 2023) the national elections, only to break definitively on December 5, 2023, leaving the parliamentary group due to Irene Montero's exclusion from the government team as a minister. Podemos consequently fell from its 23 seats in *Unidas Podemos* (which represented a coalition total of 35 deputies in the *Congreso de los Diputados*) to just 5 seats, forcing it to join the mixed group. On January 26, 2024, the party lost another seat when Lilith Verstrynge resigned, and her replacement, Candela López Tagliafico of *Catalunya en Comú*, assumed the position, leaving Podemos with only 4 seats. The 2024 European elections marked the first national elections since 2015 in which Podemos ran independently, outside a coalition, and still managed to elect two female deputies, Irene Montero and Isa Serra. Nonetheless, electoral volatility has not challenged the relative stability of the two traditional forces, PSOE and PP, which remain the primary competitors in the Spanish context, a strong contrast to the decline of traditional conservative and social-democratic parties elsewhere in Europe.

Additionally, other external factors have intensified Podemos' challenges: the Catalan crisis of 2017–2018, which completely overshadowed other political issues, placed Podemos in an initially unrewarding middle ground amid high polarization. Furthermore, as European social movements (particularly anti-austerity movements) and left-wing populism receded—except, notably, for *La France Insoumise*—populist rhetoric and practices became increasingly difficult to sustain during attempts to form and run a government. The government's planned actions had to adapt to two major external events that disrupted the European and global political and economic systems. As previously mentioned, just two months after the Sánchez II government was sworn in, the COVID-19 pandemic struck Europe, forcing governments to implement unprecedented policies to address an unforeseen health, social, and economic crisis. Then, in February 2022, the Russian-Ukrainian military conflict began, creating major instability for European governments due to international political positioning and the worsening energy crisis.

However, in an extremely challenging exogenous and endogenous context, Podemos has accomplished in a short period what very few other forces have managed to do in the European context: it has hegemonized the space of the Spanish left, freeing it from the bipartisan bloc to which it had been relegated; it has governed in Spain's major cities, demonstrating its pursuit of alternative—or at least discontinuous—governmental practices; and it has achieved, though not entirely in line with its initial expectations, a governmental alliance that was unthinkable only a few months prior. It secured positions of significant importance within the executive and succeeded in progressively shaping the government's program.

In light of these considerations and the analysis conducted in this book, the following section aims to outline the key changes observed by positioning the values of the indicators identified in Chapters 5 and 6 within the proposed theoretical framework.

6.2 The evolution of Podemos

	Podemos I (2014 – 2017)	Podemos II (2017 – 2020)	Podemos III (from 2020)
Participation	Horizontal participatory platform	Multi-speed membership	Militancy in concentric circles
Discourse	Left-wing transversal populist	Left-wing populist	Innovative Left
Organization	Electoral war machine + Movement party	Top-down movement party	Hybrid party

Tab. 6: Evolution of Podemos participation, discourse and organization. Source: author's elaboration.

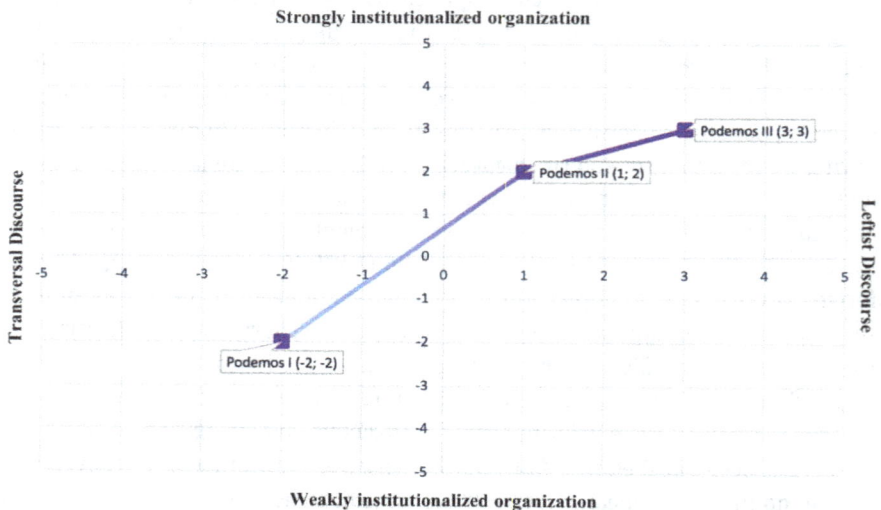

Fig. 24: The evolution of Podemos within the proposed theoretical paradigm. Source: author's elaboration.

Tab. 6 summarizes the organizational and discursive evolution of Podemos from its inception to its current form, with the simplifications that this summary implies. We have divided the evolution of Podemos into three phases: "Podemos I", which corresponds to the period from the organization's birth until the *Vistalegre II* Congress; "Podemos II", which begins at the turning point of *Vistalegre II* and runs until 2020, the year of its entry into government and the III Congress;

and "Podemos III", which corresponds to the current nature of the *Morada* forma-tion. Fig. 24 shows the evolution of the three phases of Podemos within the theo-retical paradigm proposed in the Introduction. The positioning of the points on the Cartesian axes is derived from the values of the indicators described and assigned in the previous Chapters. The progression on the x-axis thus represents the discur-sive evolution, from a completely transversal discourse (x=-5) to one completely embedded in the rhetoric of the radical left (x=+5). In contrast, the progression on the y-axis represents the organizational evolution, from weakly institutional-ized (y=-5) to rigidly institutionalized (y=+5). By crossing these characteristics, Quadrant I includes all those parties that configure themselves as "leftist parties" to varying degrees, thus political parties with strong institutionalization and a clearly left-wing discourse. Naturally, the more leftist the discourse, the more rad-ical the political force. Instead, political subjects that exhibit a very transversal discourse and public communication, but at the same time have a strong organi-zation with defined boundaries and a closed bureaucracy, will be placed in Quad-rant II. Political subjects of this kind can be called, to varying degrees, "catch-all parties" (Kirchheimer, 1966), or even "transversal populist parties" since transver-sal discourse is largely characteristic of populist political forces. On the other hand, Quadrant III includes, with varying nuances, "catch-all movement parties", which combine a light and permeable organizational structure with an open and transversal discourse. Finally, Quadrant IV includes forces we can define as "left-wing movement parties", which, depending on the value of the organizational var-iable, can resemble either a participatory platform like a social movement or a more institutionalized movement parties.

As argued in Chapter 3, the "transversal" discursive strategy at Podemos' ori-gins was extraordinarily effective: through clear positioning within the economic crisis and the mainstream political system, Podemos achieved an unprecedented result in the 2014 European elections for a political platform created only a few months earlier (7.98 %). This success was primarily due to four factors:

1. The decision to launch the project 'downstream' of a historic moment of social mobilization. At the time, 15M was still active but was entering a phase of weakening and decline after three years of activity. The push for institution-alizing the social movement—or rather, its social demands—led the 15M par-ticipants to immediately identify with a political option aiming to represent these demands and bring them to the national government. As noted earlier, Podemos is not the evolution of 15M, but without 15M, it would not have ex-isted;

2. The figure of Iglesias is the second cornerstone of Podemos' success. Iglesias was disruptive and symbolized populism in its essence: a young, new figure from a working-class neighborhood who emerged from the university to rep-

resent social movements and mock the powerful on television and in the media. Moreover, his use of personal information channels, such as *La Tuerka*—a podcast that was not "mass" but resonated with the content and sentiments expressed by 15M—turned Pablo Iglesias into a symbolic figure of anti-establishment politics. During the interview, Iglesias recounted that, in the early stages of his media presence, he made a strategic decision to appear on mass news channels, especially the right-wing ones, because they had a larger audience among segments of the population less embedded in the classical left (the so-called "popular classes") and because they allowed him to deliver an extremely aggressive and polarizing discourse. Without a central leader embodying the general will of the anti-austerity public, Podemos might have existed, but it would never have achieved the same level of success and media attention;

3. The populist discourse was the primary weapon with which Podemos constructed its image of reality. The "Troika" was identified as the first common enemy to fight against because it forced national elites to adopt policies of "tears and blood" that impoverished Spain's social majority while protecting the privileges of the "caste". This initial Manichean and mobilizing rhetoric entered Spain's moderate bipartisan debate with force. Through the use of digital populist tools and constant media presence, it emotionally captivated hundreds of thousands of people who, at that time, no longer felt represented by traditional political forces. While the populist discourse initially conveyed leftist themes, it used completely new language, symbols, and terms to break with the image of the traditional left. Without left-wing populism, Podemos would not have existed;

4. The hybrid and highly open organizational form enabled the early Podemos to mobilize those eager to contribute actively. The need for participation, discussion, and building visible territorial outposts was still a tangible legacy of 15M in Spain. Podemos could never simply be a vertical "cartel party" (Katz, Mair, 1995) that called on its supporters solely to vote, nor could it merely function as a "personal party" (Calise, 2000) centered around Iglesias. It necessarily had to provide tools for participation that, as in 15M, were both a decision-making mechanism and a visible representation of its political program and the vision of participatory democracy it sought to promote. Means and ends were united in the opportunity for territorial participation and decision-making at the national level. The genetic organizational form of Podemos was, from the outset, its first practical machine for maintaining consensus and its strategic program for the organization's future.

As we have described, the analysis shows that the evolution of Podemos from an organizational point of view has followed a clear process of institutionalization: from the First Congress, Podemos adopted a vertical structure while maintaining a permeable, horizontal type of grassroots organization. This approach would continue to characterize the party's entire evolution. For this reason, it was decided to assign "Podemos I" the indicator y=-2 (i.e., an electoral vertical war machine with a movement party organization on the ground) in terms of organization: although still influenced by its horizontal genetic nature, Podemos had already begun a phase of institutionalization at this stage. The victory of the "pablist" hypothesis at *Vistalegre II* clearly marked the beginning of the organizational structuring process. The organization then took on the form of a "top-down movement party", which is why the indicator y=+2 was assigned to highlight the process of progressive institutionalization. The III Congress further solidified the organizational structure of Podemos (refer to Chapter 4 for details). Thus, Podemos adopted a party structure with an internal bureaucracy and a clear division of tasks and powers at the national, autonomous, and local levels, without abandoning its innovative genetic roots. Today, however, Podemos is a full-fledged party, though with characteristics that are not entirely traditional due to its origins, which we define here as a "hybrid party" (y=+3).

Thus, in terms of discourse, the first Podemos discourse can be described as "left-wing transversal populist" (x=-2 according to the proposed theoretical paradigm), based on our analyses and interview results. *Vistalegre* II, as has been repeatedly emphasized, not only altered the organizational nature of Podemos but also changed its electoral positioning and discourse. This was the moment when Podemos' "left-wing populism" (x=1) was most pronounced, a shift further driven by the departure of Errejón, a theorist and proponent of the more transversal strategy. Especially after entering the government, Podemos has reduced, or in some cases eliminated, its use of populist Manichean discourse in favor of a leftist but innovative (x=+3) communication style. This represents a clear leftist discursive strategy that seeks to move beyond the communication and symbolism of the traditional radical left.

To summarize, examining the linear progression shown in Fig. 24, Podemos has, in its 10 years of existence, followed an evolutionary path that, on one hand, led to increasing institutionalization—shifting from a loosely organized movement to a form comparable to that of a political party. On the other hand, it has modified its discourse and external communication, positioning itself more firmly on the left-right axis. This shift is particularly evident in the phase we refer to as "Podemos III", which began when the party convened the III Congress to reorient itself following its entry into government.

But what kind of policy line has Podemos pursued in government?

This question warrants a separate discussion (allow me to refer you to Giardiello, 2023), but here I will highlight some important features relevant to the analysis of ideological positioning and discourse. During its time in government, Podemos has emerged as a force responsive to the main cleavages that characterize its discourse. However, more than focusing on issues inherent to its primary discourse—placed on the left-right axis (i.e., socioeconomic issues)—its governmental activity has been primarily positioned on the GAL-TAN axis (Green-Alternative-Libertarian and Traditional-Authoritarian-Nationalist; Hooghe, Marks, and Wilson, 2002). Most of its policies have addressed civil rights, gender equality, combating patriarchal violence, and the rights of LGBTQI+ communities—issues on which Minister Irene Montero has become a symbol both nationally and internationally. Similarly, the policies advanced by Ione Belarra's Ministry of Social Rights, particularly those addressing poverty and housing rights, fall within the GAL framework, although this ministry has also emphasized redistributive policies to support the most disadvantaged segments of the population. These considerations pave the way for further analysis to identify the causes of this phenomenon. On one hand, as Hooghe and Liebstet argue, in the Western European context "parties that are Left tend to be GAL; parties that are Right tend to be TAN" (2006). However, this claim would require a more in-depth comparative investigation of party forces currently present in the Spanish political context.

Another possibility stems from the fact that Podemos, as a junior coalition partner, has been unable to secure control of key ministries concerning economic and redistributive issues, which are traditionally dominated by socialist forces. Indeed, its relationship with the other coalition party, the PSOE, is tense and a source of frequent conflict within the Council of Ministers. On this front, Podemos has not always sought to appear as a responsible force willing to accept the decisions of the governing majority. Instead, it externalizes its disagreements with the institutional and strategic objectives of the PSOE, turning these conflicts into a political and ideological battleground. Podemos has thus been a "rebellious" force, even while holding government positions, but with two main characteristics: it has focused primarily on its ministries' issues, while incorporating the achievements of the other three *Unidas Podemos* ministries, particularly Yolanda Díaz's Ministry of Labor, which leans closer to the left-right axis. Secondly, Podemos, while often serving as the PSOE's "left-wing goad" within the government, has moderated its discursive style in recent years, especially following Pablo Iglesias' departure, in favor of a communication strategy more attuned to the needs of its core social base.

In conclusion, it is important to note certain limitations regarding the assumptions that shaped our research questions. First and foremost, Podemos' evolution materialized as a result of its entry into government but was already underway in earlier stages. The "government vs. opposition" variable is thus essential for understanding the dynamics of organizational institutionalization and discursive change, but it is not the sole factor. As previously noted, other endogenous and exogenous factors contributed to these changes. The willingness to institutionalize—to adopt a party-like structure—was already present in the first Podemos as a necessary phase following the end of the "blitzkrieg" period and the beginning of the "positional war" phase. The use of highly mobilizing populist rhetoric may yield short-term results, but it requires a subsequent phase of organizational stabilization to ensure a political force's long-term survival. Second, additional causes can be identified for the shift on the discourse axis. Participation in government is key: Podemos had to define itself as a more radical force and align itself with a specific ideological and social sector to which it could be accountable. Simultaneously, it could no longer rely on anti-caste rhetoric while in government and increasingly had to define its identity within "socioeconomic" boundaries. However, the changing political landscape had already shaped its discourse prior to this period. For instance, the rise of *Ciudadanos* and *Vox* forced Podemos to position itself as a leftist outsider to counter these parties, as the "right-left" axis regained prominence in the Spanish political system over the "high-low" or "new-old" axes, which had been particularly mobilizing earlier.

Moreover, the evolution of a political force—especially one with a recent history—necessarily coincides with the gradual stabilization of its constituency. This process should not be interpreted, as described in some analyses, as a return to an "old" or "traditional" stance, a "normalization", or the end of its initial energy. Instead, it is assumed here that participation in government inevitably leads to greater ideological definition unless it relies on fragile electoral majorities and a highly volatile consensus base. Inclusion within the "left-right" axis is an unavoidable step in the development of a political entity unless it chooses to remain a perpetual outsider protest movement. But, as Manu Levin argues, this approach undermines the very purpose of politics:

> Doing politics means contending for power to organize society. If you don't contest power, you don't do politics. You are a social movement protesting in the street to get power to do something, but what really makes a political movement, unlike social movements, is contesting power. So, the project of being the eternal opposition I don't share. (Manu Levin, 2022, Interview 4)

Finally, Podemos has undoubtedly undergone a paradigm shift from its initial populist "moment", evolving both organizationally and discursively. This evolution has led to an organizational and discursive form distinct from its origins, but not comparable to that of traditional political parties: while there is a clear tendency toward institutionalization, it surpasses classical patterns, successfully integrating top-down executive action with bottom-up participatory engagement. Simultaneously, Podemos identifies as a leftist force but strives to innovate the discourse, symbols, and lexicon of the traditional left while remaining anchored in its themes. At the same time, certain populist tools and structures—such as the *Asamblea Ciudadana*—remain central to the party's identity, highlighting the lasting value of its origins.

6.3 Podemos, present and future

"La fuerza para seguir transformando" ('The force to continue transforming') is the new slogan of the party. The reference to its predecessor is clear: if Podemos was the transformative force in government, now, even without government positions, Podemos must organize itself to continue the transformation process it began. This is the leitmotif and core of the new political document—a clear call to reactivate and reorganize the party's militancy.[2] "Podemos must strengthen itself as an autonomous political organization" (Ione Belarra, 2023). This statement encapsulates the new direction Podemos seeks to pursue. "Autonomous force" means "that we will only participate in pre-election alliances when it is useful and, above all, when there is respect for Podemos with primaries and no vetoes, no more disrespect for Podemos". The reference and pointed criticism are clearly directed at the *Sumar* coalition, which vetoed Irene Montero's candidacy and which, according to Podemos:

> It has imposed conditions on us that no other political force will ever be asked to meet. However, we have not achieved the objectives that we set ourselves in our IV *Asamblea Ciudadana*: to widen the political space and to be the majority force in the government, in order to promote with greater strength, the changes that our country needs. This was the reason that led us to propose Yolanda Díaz as our candidate, but in these years, she has led us through a hard and deeply unfair process of 'electoral unity' that has not lived up to expectations and has resulted in a loss of votes and seats. (Political Document, *La fuerza para seguir transformando*, 2023: 3)

Regarding the *"fortalecimiento"* ('strengthening'), the document explicitly mentions ideological and organizational strengthening. On the ideological front, Podemos aims to build a clear leftist program around key issues such as feminism, ecology, social justice, municipalism, and the republic. On the organizational

---

2 A small note: the militancy has always been called "you" and not "we", a symbol of the vertical setting of the party, as we have analyzed, and for which "leadership" is something separate.

side, the main goal is to improve relationships with militants, strengthen the party's presence on the ground, and deepen its connection with social movements.

Podemos is not a "normalized" subject but rather a "mutant gene" in constant evolution and experimentation. It is an organization that has leveraged the "populist moment" as an essential tool for its electoral and media success, but it no longer considers this tool indispensable for its strategic action. As the latest political document states, Podemos still sees itself as "a governmental force that seeks to transform all the institutional and social positions it occupies. We are here to govern and to profoundly change people's lives, with the strength to continue transforming through courageous proposals" (Political Document, *La fuerza para seguir transformando*, 2023: 37).

The analysis of the Podemos case thus provides significant insights into the development of left-populist parties. Left-populist forces face unique challenges due to their particular origins and characteristics. Their emergence, often tied to social movements or horizontal participation dynamics, results in a light, horizontal organizational structure with permeable boundaries and vertical national structures necessary to mobilize an electoral war machine to capitalize on the populist strategy. At the same time, their success has been driven by an effective polarizing populist discourse. The creation of the populist "we" occurred through a transversal discourse, which defined "the people" in socio-economic rather than nationalistic or ethnic terms, as seen in other types of populism. This populist strategy was implemented through the extensive use of social networks and centered around a recognizable, highly charismatic leader. The electoral success of such forces brings specific demands: first, the construction of an organizational apparatus capable of sustaining institutional or governmental challenges and, more importantly, the need for greater structuring to ensure long-term organizational stability. Participation in government coalitions represents a major push for institutionalization, often resulting in the adoption of a party-like structure while still reflecting their unique genetic nature. Entry into government further necessitates clearer ideological positioning and a shift to prioritizing the left-right axis over the high-low axis. Dynamics within the governing coalition also play a crucial role: if the political force is a junior partner, it must differentiate itself from the majority partner and radicalize its government actions.

Populism, therefore, is a highly effective tool in contexts where political polarization and crisis factors create opportunities for success. However, this success is not permanent, and populism does not yield the same effects across all political moments. Political forces face significant strategic challenges that require constant adaptation and evolution in response to changing contexts. To use a metaphor, *populism is like an efficient fuel, but it burns quickly:* it becomes essential to enhance and upgrade the machine's components to ensure a long journey.

The future of Podemos will depend not on the use of new "populist techniques" but on its ability to adapt to ongoing changes, particularly in strengthening territorial presence, increasing participation, and renewing its leadership. It will need to rebuild its political and electoral space in a scenario like Spain's, which has evolved and is once again marked by a strong bipolar dynamic. It will be crucial, therefore, to analyze Podemos' evolution beyond simplistic linear assessments of "failure" or "success" and instead observe its actual development trajectories:

> In the media there is often a tendency to see things in a linear way: a glorious beginning, an unexpected end.... But reality is much more complex. Many phenomena, including populism, have a recurring nature. They come in cycles. And this goes back to the root cause of populism: within modernity, we have regimes and political systems that are based on this promise of 'popular sovereignty', which is difficult to materialize, especially in systems that are very much influenced by a hierarchical structure and unequal distribution of resources. People suffer, there are inequalities and injustices, polarizations and cleavages are established, and someone will emerge from time to time to claim that he or she will be able to solve these problems. In the context of a crisis, for example, when these problems are exacerbated, this creates the potential for populist movements, leaders or parties to emerge and flourish. This is a recurring phenomenon because it is endemic to representative systems. It is therefore bound to return. (Stavrakakis, 2021)

References

Akkerman, T., & M. Rooduijn. (2015). Pariahs or Partners? Inclusion and Exclusion of Radical Right Parties and the Effects on Their Policy Positions. *Political Studies 63, no. 5*, 1140–1157.

Akkerman, T. (2016). Conclusion. In Akkerman T., De Lange S. L., & Rooduijn M. (Eds), *Radical Right-Wing Populist Parties in Western Europe: Into the Mainstream?*, 268–282. London: Routledge

Akkerman, T., De Lange, S. L., & Rooduijn, M. (2016). Inclusion and mainstreaming? Radical right-wing populist parties in the new millennium. In T. Akkerman, S. L. De Lange, & M. Rooduijn (Eds.), *Radical right-wing populist parties in Western Europe: Into the mainstream?* (pp. 1–28). London: Routledge.

Albertazzi, A., & D. McDonnell. (2015). *Populist in Power.* London: Routledge

Arditi, B. (2007). *Politics on the Edges of Liberalism: Difference, Populism, Revolution, Agitation.* Edinburgh: Edinburgh University Press

Belarra, I. (2021). *Speech at IV Asamblea Ciudadana.* YouTube video. https://www.youtube.com/watch?v=zPM5t5NEyqs (accessed January 2025)

Belarra, I. (2023). *Speech at Conferencia Política de Podemos – La Fuerza para Seguir Transformando.* [YouTube video]. https://www.youtube.com/watch?v=xw9akbvxDEc (accessed February 2025)

Bernhard, L. (2020). Revisiting the inclusion-moderation thesis on radical right populism: Does party leadership matter?. *Politics and Governance, 8*(1), 206–218. https://doi.org/10.17645/pag.v8i1.2515

Betz, H. G. (1994). *Radical Right-Wing Populism in Western Europe.* New York: St. Martin's Press

Bischof, D., & Wagner, M. (2019). Do voters polarize when radical parties enter Parliament? *American Journal of Political Science, 63*(4), 888–904

Böhmelt, T., Ezrow, L., & Lehrer, R. (2022). Populism and intra-party democracy. *European Journal of Political Research, 61*, 1143–1154. https://doi.org/10.1111/1475-6765.12509

Caiani, M. (2014). Le grandi contraddizioni della destra populista. *Il Mulino. Rivista Trimestrale di Cultura e di Politica, 3*, 450–458. https://doi.org/10.1402/76974

Caiani, M., & Graziano, P. (2019). Understanding varieties of populism in times of crises. *West European Politics, 42*(6), 1141–1158.

Calise, M., & Musella, F. (2019). *Il principe digitale.* Bari: Editori Laterza.

Campolongo, F., & Caruso, L. (2021). *Podemos e il populismo di sinistra. Dalla protesta al governo.* Milano: Meltemi Editore.

Campolongo, F., Raniolo, F., & Tarditi, V. (2021). La comunicazione online di Podemos ai tempi del governo. *Comunicazione politica. Quadrimestrale dell'Associazione Italiana di Comunicazione Politica, 2*, 169–198. https://doi.org/10.3270/101608

Canovan, M. (1999). Trust the people! Populism and the two faces of democracy. *Political Studies, 47*(1), 2–16.

Charalambous, G., & Ioannou, G. (2020). *Left radicalism and populism in Europe.* London: Routledge.

Chironi, D., & Fittipaldi, R. (2017). Social movements and new forms of political organization: Podemos as a hybrid party. *Partecipazione e Conflitto, 10*(1), 275–305. https://doi.org/10.1285/i20356609v10i1p275

Conti, N. (2018). National political elites, the EU, and the populist challenge. *Politics, 38*(3), 361–377. https://doi.org/10.1177/0263395718777363

Crouch, C. (2004). *Post-democracy.* Cambridge: Polity.

Dal Lago, A. (2017). *Populismo digitale.* Milano: Raffaello Cortina Editore.

https://doi.org/10.1515/9783111591537-011

Damiani, M. (2016). *La sinistra radicale in Europa. Italia, Spagna, Francia, Germania.* Roma: Donzelli Editore.

Damiani, M. (2020). *Populist radical left parties in Western Europe.* London: Routledge.

De Benetti, F. (2021). I populisti di destra rinnegano le loro battaglie anti euro. *Editoriale Domani.* https://www.editorialedomani.it/politica/europa/i-populisti-di-destra-rinnegano-le-loro-batta glie-anti-euro-r5vscpd6 (accessed February 2025)

Della Porta, D., Fernández, J., Kouki, H., & Mosca, L. (2017). *Movement parties against austerity.* Cambridge: Polity Press.

Dennison, S., Leonard, M., et al. (2019). *How to govern a fragmented EU: What Europeans said at the ballot box.* European Council on Foreign Relations.

Diamanti, I. (2014, April 22). Siamo tutti populisti. *La Repubblica.* https://www.repubblica.it/politica/2014/04/22/news/siamo_tutti_populisti84158852 (accessed February 2025).

Dieckhoff, A., Jaffrelot, C., & Massicard, E. (2022). *Contemporary populists in power.* Cham: Palgrave Macmillan.

Duverger, M. (1961). *I partiti politici.* Milano: Edizioni di Comunità.

Errejón, I. (2015). Pateando el tablero. El 15M como discurso contrahegemónico. *Encruzadas. Revista Crítica de Ciencias Sociales, 9*, 1–35.

European Parliament. (2007–2019). Socio-demographic trends in national public opinion – Edition 5. *Eurobarometer.*

Fittipaldi, R. (2021). *Podemos, un profilo organizzativo.* Milano: Meltemi.

Freeden, N. (2003). *Ideology: A very short introduction.* Oxford: Oxford University Press.

Gerbaudo, P. (2020). *I partiti digitali: L'organizzazione politica nell'era delle piattaforme.* Bologna: Il Mulino.

Giardiello, M. (2021). Populismi digitali al tempo del Covid-19. *Rivista di Digital Politics, 2*(2021), 341–362. https://doi.org/10.53227/101947

Giardiello, M. (2023). Politics of left populism in power: The institutional challenge of Podemos. *Perspective Politice*, 89–100. https://doi.org/10.25019/perspol/23.16.0.9

Gomez, R., & Ramiro, L. (2019). The limits of organizational innovation and multi-speed membership: Podemos and its new forms of party membership. *Party Politics, 25*(4), 534–546. https://doi.org/10.1177/1354068817742844

Gramsci, A. (1971). *Selections from the prison notebooks* (Q. Hoare & G. Nowell Smith, Trans. & Eds.). New York: International Publishers

Heinisch, R. (2003). Success in opposition, failure in government: Explaining the performance of right-wing populist parties in public office. *West European Politics, 26*(3), 91–130.

Heinisch, R., & Mazzoleni, O. (2016). *Understanding populist organization: The radical right-wing in Western Europe.* London: Palgrave Macmillan.

Hooghe, L., & Marks, G. (2018). Cleavage theory meets Europe's crises: Lipset, Rokkan, and the transnational cleavage. *Journal of European Public Policy, 25*(1), 109–135. https://doi.org/10.1080/13501763.2017.1310279

Hutter, S., & Grande, E. (2014). Politicizing Europe in the national electoral arena. *Journal of Common Market Studies, 52*, 1002–1018. https://doi.org/10.1111/jcms.12133

Iglesias, P. (2014). *Intervención Vistalegre I* [YouTube video]. https://www.youtube.com/watch?v=q8nvIuyzkGc (accessed February 2025).

Iglesias, P. (2014). *Intervención cierre de campaña Europeas 2014* [YouTube video]. https://www.youtube.com/watch?v=DipcspGXx7k (accessed February 2025).

Iglesias, P. (2015, May 17). El espacio de la socialdemocracia quedó vacío y lo hemos ocupado nosotros. *La Opinión de Málaga*.

Iglesias, P. (2015). Understanding Podemos. *New Left Review, 93*, 8–22.

Iglesias, P. (2017). *Intervención Vistalegre II* [YouTube video]. https://www.youtube.com/watch?v=a2RpjStPw7M (accessed February 2025).

Iglesias, P. (2021). Pablo Iglesias deja el Gobierno para enfrentarse a Ayuso en las elecciones de la Comunidad de Madrid. *El Mundo*. https://www.youtube.com/watch?v=xuKU8XQ0rjw (accessed February 2025).

Iglesias, P. (2021). *Cierre de campaña de Pablo Iglesias en Madrid* [YouTube video]. https://www.youtube.com/watch?v=dfG5N0v_x_4 (accessed February 2025).

Iglesias, P. (2021). ¿Y si gobernaran PP y Vox? Las fuerzas a la izquierda del PSOE deberían aumentar su colaboración en todo el Estado, compartir espacios de reflexión estratégica y explorar vías confederales. *CTXT*. https://ctxt.es/es/20210901/Firmas/37096/Pablo-Iglesias-tribuna-politica-izquierda-PSOE-gobierno-Vox-PP-ultraderecha.htm (accessed February 2025).

Ipsos. (2025). European elections 2024: Post-voting analysis. https://www.ipsos.com/it-it/elezioni-europee-2024-risultati-elettorali-analisi-post-voto-ipsos (accessed February 2025).

Jagers, J., & Walgrave, S. (2007). Populism as political communication style: An empirical study of political parties' discourse in Belgium. *European Journal of Political Research, 46*, 319–345.

Kaltwasser, C. R., & Taggart, P. (2016). Dealing with populists in government: A framework for analysis. *Democratization, 23*(2), 201–220. https://doi.org/10.1080/13510347.2015.1058785

Katsambekis, G., & Kioupkiolis, A. (2019). *The populist radical left in Europe* (1st ed.). London: Routledge.

Katz, R., & Mair, P. (1995). Changing models of party organization and party democracy. *Party Politics, 1*(5), 5–28.

Kirchheimer, O. (1966). The transformation of the West European party system. In J. La Palombara & M. Weiner (Eds.), *Political parties and political development* (pp. XX–XX). Princeton, NJ: Princeton University Press.

Kirk, R., & Schill, D. (2021). Sophisticated hate stratagems: Unpacking the era of distrust. *American Behavioral Scientist*. https://doi.org/10.1177/00027642211005002

Kitschelt, H. (2006). Movement parties. In R. Katz & W. Crotty (Eds.), *Handbook of party politics* (pp. XX–XX). London: SAGE Publications.

Kitschelt, H., & McGann, A. J. (1995). *The radical right in Western Europe: A comparative analysis*. Ann Arbor, MI: University of Michigan Press.

Knight, A. (1998). Populism and neo-populism in Latin America, especially Mexico. *Journal of Latin American Studies, 30*(2), 223–248.

Krause, W., & Wagner, A. (2019). Becoming part of the gang? Established and nonestablished populist parties and the role of external efficacy. *Party Politics*. https://doi.org/10.1177/1354068819839210

Laclau, E. (2005). *On populist reason*. London: Verso Books.

Levitsky, S., & Ziblatt, D. (2018). *How democracies die*. New York: Broadway Books.

Ley de Garantía Integral de Libertad Sexual. (2022).

Lipset, S. M., & Rokkan, S. (1967). Cleavage structures, party systems, and voter alignments: An introduction. In S. M. Lipset & S. Rokkan (Eds.), *Party systems and voter alignments* (pp. 1–64). New York: The Free Press.

Machuca, P. (2015). 2014: El año de Podemos. *Huffington Post*. https://www.huffingtonpost.es/2014/12/29/podemos-repaso-2014_n_6391270.html *(accessed February 2025)*.

Mair, P. (2009). Representative versus responsible government. *MPIfG Working Paper 09/8*. Cologne: Max-Planck-Institut für Gesellschaftsforschung.

Mackie, T. T., & Rose, R. (1983). General elections in Western nations during 1982. *European Journal of Political Research, 11*, 345–349. https://doi.org/10.1111/j.1475-6765.1983.tb00067.x

March, L., & Mudde, C. (2005). What's left of radical left? The European radical left after 1980: Decline and mutation. *Comparative European Politics, 3*(1), 23–49.

Martínez, M. A., & Wissink, B. (2021). Urban movements and municipalist governments in Spain: Alliances, tensions, and achievements. *Social Movement Studies, 21*(5), 659–676. https://doi.org/10.1080/14742837.2021.1967121

Marks, G., Hooghe, L., Nelson, M., & Edwards, E. (2006). Party competition and European integration in the East and West: Different structure, same causality. *Comparative Political Studies, 39*(2), 155–175. https://doi.org/10.1177/0010414005281932

Mazzolini, S., & Borriello, A. (2021). The normalization of left populism? The paradigmatic case of Podemos. *European Politics and Society, 23*(3), 285–300. https://doi.org/10.1080/23745118.2020.1868849

McDonnell, D., & Newell, J. L. (2011). Outsider parties in government in Western Europe. *Party Politics, 17*(4), 443–452.

Mény, Y., & Surel, Y. (2002). The constitutive ambiguity of populism. In Y. Mény & Y. Surel (Eds.), *Democracies and the populist challenge* (pp. XX–XX). Basingstoke: Palgrave Macmillan.

Meloni, M., & Lupato, F. G. (2023). Two steps forward, one step back: The evolution of democratic digital innovations in Podemos. *South European Society and Politics*. https://doi.org/10.1080/13608746.2022.2161973

Moffitt, B. (2015). How to perform crisis: A model for understanding the key role of crisis in contemporary populism. *Government and Opposition, 50*(2), 189–217. https://doi.org/10.1017/gov.2014.13

Monedero, J. C. (2018). *La izquierda que asaltó el algoritmo*. Madrid: Los Libros de la Catarata.

Mouffe, C. (2005). *On the political*. London: Routledge.

Mouffe, C. (2013). *Hegemony, radical democracy, and the political*. London: Routledge.

Mouffe, C. (2018). *For a left populism*. London: Verso Books.

Mudde, C. (2004). The populist zeitgeist. *Government and Opposition, 39*(3), 541–563.

Mudde, C., & Kaltwasser, C. R. (2007). *Populism: A very short introduction*. Oxford: Oxford University Press.

Mudde, C. (2007). *Populist radical right parties in Europe*. Cambridge: Cambridge University Press.

Mudde, C. (2013). Three decades of populist radical right parties in Western Europe: So what? *European Journal of Political Research, 52*(1), 1–19.

Narud, H. M., & Valen, H. (2008). Coalition membership and electoral performance. In K. Strøm, W. C. Müller, & T. Bergman (Eds.), *Cabinets and coalition bargaining: The democratic life cycle in Western Europe* (pp. 369–402). Oxford: Oxford University Press.

Nunziata, F. (2021). Il platform leader. *Rivista di Digital Politics, 1*(1), 127–146.

Norris, P. (2020). Measuring populism worldwide. *Party Politics, 26*(6), 697–717. https://doi.org/10.1177/1354068820927686

Ottaviano, G. (2019). *Geografia economica dell'Europa sovranista*. Bari: Laterza.

Padoan, E. (2021). *Anti-neoliberal populisms in comparative perspective: A Latinamericanisation of Southern Europe?* London: Routledge.

Palano, D. (2018). *Populismo*. Milano: Editrice Bibliografica.

Panebianco, A. (1982). *Modelli di partito: Organizzazione e potere nei partiti politici.* Bologna: Il Mulino.

Panebianco, A. (1988). *Political parties: Organization and power.* Cambridge: Cambridge University Press.

Pizzorno, A. (1966). Introduzione allo studio della partecipazione politica. *Quaderni di Sociologia, XV.*

Pérez Royo, J. (2014, December 29). El año de Podemos. *El País.* https://elpais.com/elpais/2014/12/29/opinion/1419838727_407577.html (accessed February 2025).

Podemos. (2014). *Claro que Podemos. Borrador de principios organizativos* (P. Iglesias, Í. Errejón, J. C. Monedero, C. Bescansa, & L. Alegre, Eds.).

Podemos. (2014). *Documento organizativo.*

Podemos. (2017a). *Documento político, Plan 2020: Ganar al PP y gobernar España* (P. Iglesias, Ed.).

Podemos. (2017b). *Documento político, Recuperar la ilusión desplegar las velas: Un Podemos para gobernar* (Í. Errejón, R. Maestre, P. Bustinduy, & C. Serra, Eds.).

Podemos. (2017). *Documento organizativo.*

Podemos. (2020). *Documento organizativo.*

Podemos. (2021). *Documento organizativo.*

Podemos. (2023). *Political document, La fuerza para seguir transformando.*

Ricolfi, L. (2017). *Sinistra e popolo: Il conflitto politico nell'era dei populismi.* Milano: Longanesi.

Riera, P., & Pastor, M. (2022). Cordons sanitaires or tainted coalitions? The electoral consequences of populist participation in government. *Party Politics, 28*(5), 889–902. https://doi.org/10.1177/13540688211026526

Roberts, K. M. (1995). Neoliberalism and the transformation of populism in Latin America: The Peruvian case. *World Politics, 48*(1), 82–116.

Roberts, K. M. (2012). Populism and democracy in Venezuela under Hugo Chavez. In C. Mudde & C. R. Kaltwasser (Eds.), *Populism in Europe and the Americas: Threat or corrective for democracy?* (pp. 136–159). New York: Cambridge University Press.

Rokkan, S. M. (Ed.). (1967). *Party systems and voter alignments.* New York: The Free Press.

Rosanvallon, P. (2020). *El siglo del populismo: Historia, teoría, crítica.* Barcelona: Galaxia Gutenberg.

Rose, R. (1991). Comparing forms of comparative analysis. *Political Studies, 39*(3), 446–462. https://doi.org/10.1111/j.1467-9248.1991.tb01622.x

Sassoon, D. (2020). *Morbid symptoms: An anatomy of a world in crisis.* London: Verso Books.

Scarrow, S. E. (2015). *Beyond party members: Changing approaches to partisan mobilization.* Oxford: Oxford University Press.

Schwörer, J. (2022). Less populist in power? Online communication of populist parties in coalition governments. *Government and Opposition, 57*(3), 467–489. https://doi.org/10.1017/gov.2021.2

Strøm, K., Müller, W. C., & Bergman, T. (Eds.). (2008). *Cabinets and coalition bargaining: The democratic life cycle in Western Europe.* Oxford: Oxford University Press.

Sumar. (2022). *Un nuevo proyecto ciudadano.* https://sumarfuturo.info/manifesto/ (accessed February 2025).

Taggart, P. (2000). *Populism.* Buckingham: Open University Press.

Taranu, A., & Pîrvulescu, C. (2012, July 8–12). The populist confusion: Populism, nationalism, extremism-Expressions of antipolitics in Europe. *Paper presented at IPSA World Congress,* Madrid, Spain.

Tarchi, M. (2002). Populism Italian style. In Y. Mény & Y. Surel (Eds.), *Democracies and the populist challenge* (pp. 84–99). New York: Palgrave.

Tarizzo, D. (2008). Introduzione. Populismo: Chi starà ad ascoltare? In E. Laclau (Ed.), *La ragione populista* (pp. VII–XXX). Bari: Laterza.

Tormey, S. (2015). *The end of representative politics.* Cambridge: Polity.

Treib, O. (2021). Euroscepticism is here to stay: What cleavage theory can teach us about the 2019 European Parliament elections. *Journal of European Public Policy, 28*(2), 174–189. https://doi.org/10.1080/13501763.2020.1737881

Verstrynge, J. (2017). *Populismo: El veto de los pueblos.* Barcelona: El Viejo Topo.

Zulianello, M. (2020). Varieties of populist parties and party systems in Europe: From state-of-the-art to the application of a novel classification scheme to 66 parties in 33 countries. *Government and Opposition, 55*(2), 327–347.

Index

https://doi.org/10.1515/9783111591537-012

www.ingramcontent.com/pod-product-compliance
Lightning Source LLC
Chambersburg PA
CBHW070342270326
41926CB00017B/3944